JOURNEYMEN

JOURNEYMEN

THE OTHER SIDE OF THE BOXING BUSINESS
A NEW PERSPECTIVE ON THE NOBLE ART

MARK TURLEY

First published by Pitch Publishing, 2014

Pitch Publishing
A2 Yeoman Gate
Yeoman Way
Durrington
BN13 3QZ
www.pitchpublishing.co.uk

A CIP catalogue record is available for this book from the
British Library.

ISBN 978-1-90962-653-9

Typesetting and origination by Pitch Publishing

Printed in Spain by Graphycems

Contents

'Bulls do not win bull fights.
People do.'

Norman Ralph Augustine

Dedication

MY wife Elisa showed martyr-like patience in helping me with the boxer interviews and accompanying me on long drives all over the country for many months. My daughters Lola and Libby often suffered the same fate and handled it with grace. None of them have seen me as much as they should have this year. Like most large undertakings completed within a family scenario, this book has happened both because and in spite of them all.

I couldn't publish a boxing book without mentioning my dad, Dennis, from the fighting village of Penmaen in South Wales. He taught me to throw a jab before I could ride a bike. A hefty chunk of my childhood was spent watching and talking about boxing with him. I don't imagine there were too many other primary school kids in 1980s south London who could reel off stories about Jimmy Wilde, Tommy Farr and Dick Richardson.

The fighters all gave me their time for nothing and many other people in and around the game answered my questions over the phone, provided views via the web or generally offered support in one way or another. It may be an unforgiving sport, but a lot of the people connected to it are the most down to earth and genuine you can find. As much as I'd like to thank all of them there are just too many to name.

Chin down, hands up.

Mark Turley

July 2014

Introduction

A different sort of boxing book

IN the same way that history is usually about kings, generals and events of great importance, boxing stories tend to focus on world title nights, champions and the characters around them, those perceived to be winners and those who live in the shadows of their glory.

But what if there were a history of foot-soldiers or anonymous infantrymen? Their struggles, spirit and humour? Of the guys who worked like donkeys, defended the rear and took bullets without receiving a second look? Is it possible that seeing battles through their eyes would make us view the whole war differently?

The stories here come from the wrong end of the fight game, where mad blokes with day jobs get clobbered by young whipper-snappers for a few weeks' worth of wages. Where rings are assembled on top of basketball courts or nightclub dancefloors and TV cameras are a rarity. If this was a *Rocky* film, it would be about Spider Rico.

For that reason these pages will not serve up the fantasy that many fans are used to – multi-million purses, rafts of quotes from Don King and whore-and-coke splattered after-parties on the Las Vegas strip. For large numbers of young men drawn towards the alpha-male glamour of the fight game, this pastiche of over-indulgences qualifies as 'living the dream', but if we're being honest, there are more than enough books like that already. I have a couple of shelves full of them at home, penned by some of boxing's great scribes and as much as I have enjoyed them all, they tend to fuse in my memory. If you've read any before, you'll know what I mean; deprived background – fighting as an escape route – sudden wealth/pressure of the spotlight – demons that can't be slayed – ultimate redemption in some form.

Tried and trusted. Not here, though.

The other major difference is me. By the time this book is published I will have been a boxing journalist for about two and a half years, mostly on the internet, on various sites, with a few bits in print. Unlike the guys who received awards for the books on my bedside cabinet, I can't claim to have particularly impressive credentials – neither decades of ringside experience nor a phonebook full of contacts – or at least I didn't before I started work on this. I do come from a boxing family and have been watching boxing for as long as I can remember, but before the last couple of years I wouldn't have considered myself any sort of insider. I was just a fan, like millions of others.

This perhaps puts me in a strong position, though. Unlike some of the best-known pundits, I have nothing to lose. I don't have a lifetime's worth of carefully maintained fight-game relationships or even a salary that will have to be sacrificed if I write things that certain people don't like. I have no vested interest in telling the story one way or the other and if this means doors closing in my face and the end of my stint as a boxing writer then so be it. I'll just go back to what I was before and watch on the TV or buy tickets.

If nothing else, this book will be honest.

As much as it tells the stories of ten men who fight to supplement their income in the small-hall scene in the UK, painting a picture of the workings of the sport at that level, to some extent it will chart my journey from naive fan to where I am now, having attended these kind of shows for the last couple of years. In that time I've gained a new perspective on a sport I've followed all my life. Imagine being besotted with an actress you've seen in movies, then meeting her in a nightclub and finding she has bruises and needle tracks on her arms. That's my relationship with boxing.

It still fascinates and attracts me, I still want to be around it, but parts of it make me uneasy.

Boxing holds an ambivalent place in the world today. The spectacle of two men (or women, lately) attempting to concuss each other with their fists is at odds with modern morality. Polite society has turned its back on it.

Foolish calls for a ban have been with us since the 1960s. They are less vociferous now but have had a creeping effect. It is no longer a sport taught in schools. It is rarely on free-to-air TV any more, Mick Hennessy's recent deal with Channel Five being the only exception, and is only superficially covered by the newspapers. As a result, world champions are not the household names they once were and the casual sports fan, replete with football trivia and everything else from rugby to golf, mostly has no idea who British or European titlists might be.

This means that within the boom industry of live sport, through which Premier League players have become a new class of aristocracy, boxing has been reduced to a sideshow. Small-hall boxing is barely even that. Paying £45 to watch a bunch of guys you've never heard of beat each other up at the York Hall is simply not on the radar of mainstream entertainment for most people. Attending such shows therefore has an illicit, retrogressive, almost guilty feeling, like going to a titty bar.

In spite of this, at the peak of the pyramid, where welterweight champ Floyd Mayweather Junior – the world's highest-paid sportsman – can be found, pay-per-view records continue to be broken and a handful of fighters receive sums unimaginable for the big stars of previous decades. Boxing clearly isn't dying, as some say, it is just carving an ever deeper, more isolated niche for itself. The wealth it generates is increasingly held in fewer and fewer pairs of hands.

At its core, for competitors, the modern, less-celebrated version of the noble art retains truths from its golden past. It remains a physical pursuit which demands unique inner strength. You can call it bravery, recklessness or even desperation – fighters all have their own motivations for doing what they do and not all of them are noble, but I am aware of no other sport where you can watch an athlete bleed himself dry in a career-long chase for glory that so rarely has a happy ending. Not many ex-tennis pros end up punchy and broke. In the words of Bud Schulberg, 'Fighters don't grow old, they just die slowly in front of your eyes.'

Like a ghost hovering behind every bout is the knowledge that competitors have been killed in that squared circle, while the spectre of *Dementia Pugilistica* with its Parkinson's-like symptoms lurks with equal menace. Muhammad Ali, the sport's most famous practitioner, embodies, in retirement, the affliction that will affect 20 per cent of those who fight professionally.

Yet the moral balance lies in the way it nurtures so much too. It channels and focuses those who need it desperately, gives an awkward boy self-belief, shows a weak man where his strengths lie and generally introduces an individual to himself. Many a wayward youth has been saved from a life behind bars or an early grave by morning runs, dieting and gym-time. They find solace in it, a form of spirituality. It demands devotion.

Boxing gives, then boxing takes away.

This is the yin-yang that all fight fans must balance. Do its pros outweigh its cons? Most of us are simply too far gone to care. The adrenaline and sweat are powerfully addictive and the nuances enough to keep you learning forever. We are hooked.

I started scribbling boxing articles in 2011. Through this work I attended shows that previously I would not have paid to go to, small-hall nights where the top of the card would be an area title or something similar. What's more, I would sit at the press table, at inner ringside, often right up against the ring apron, where you can see the fighters' eyes and hear what they say. I no longer felt like a spectator. I was involved.

My baptism came in my second ringside event when I was spattered with blood, which I believe came from the Irish heavyweight Declan Timlin – a rite of passage. And it was during these early shows, hunched over my notepad and pen, that my curiosity about fighters who lose habitually was aroused. They seemed to me the anti-heroes of the game, eschewing the usual trappings of success, even victory itself. I was intrigued, but lacked insight.

Then one summer evening in 2013, I watched from close quarters as Nuneaton's Kristian Laight, who at the time had completed 172 bouts, of which he had won just seven, lost every round at York Hall against Dean 'Bad News' Burrell. As I watched him walk back to the dressing room, head held high, something clicked into place.

This book will attempt to tell the story of Kristian Laight and others like him – the much maligned and misunderstood category of professional boxers known as Journeymen.

In doing so, boxing records and statistics will frequently be mentioned. For those who are unfamiliar with the shorthand, wins are always first, losses second and draws (if any) third. Thus a fighter with a record of 25-4-1 has 25 wins, four defeats and a draw.

All statistics are correct to 1 August 2014.

Journeyman

noun

(plural) –men

1. a craftsman, artisan, etc, who is qualified to work at his trade in the employment of another

2. a competent workman

3. (formerly) a worker hired on a daily wage

From the *Collins English Dictionary,* online version

1

Two Sides of the Same Sport

Bethnal Green, London, Friday 1 June 2012

T HE York Hall is going absolutely volcanic. Its halcyon days may have been back in the 1950s but on this 21st century evening it is transformed again into the bellicose, sweaty bear-pit that made it world famous. Clouds of evaporated testosterone and beer swirl under the lights.

'There's only one Buglioni!' the fans crammed into the upper tier scream in chorus. There are more than 500 of them up there, wearing matching blue t-shirts, with 'Team Buglioni' across the back and 'Pride' emblazoned across the chest. They have paid £40 each for a seat but none of them are sitting. 'One Buglioni! Walking along, singing a song, walking in a Frankie wonderland!'

The opening notes of their hero's theme music blast from the PA. His arrival is imminent. In deference to his Neapolitan heritage, the north London idol has chosen 'Seven Nation Army' by the White Stripes for his ring-walks. The countrymen of his grandfather sing it in football stadia before the Italian national team play their home games. He emerges from the dressing room, robeless, shadow-boxing vigorously, clenching then unclenching his jaw and the rabble roar like Spartans. He swings hooks at the air with both hands and begins a slow walk to the ring, matchmaker/cornerman Dean Powell behind him, trainer Mark Tibbs in front, a mini procession of London boxing nobility. Arms around each other's shoulders, the mob jump up and down, fists raised to the rafters, singing along to the riff. 'Boh, bo, bo, bo, boh, bohhh, boh!'

Frank 'Wise Guy' Buglioni is one of a new breed of professional pugilists. From Winchmore Hill, in the London borough of Enfield, an extremely affluent suburban area boasting family properties worth in excess of £5m, the ghetto-fighter stereotype could not be further from his reality. While generations of boxers have arrived in the public eye via the school of hard knocks, Frank emerged as a star pupil from an outstanding, over-subscribed secondary then took up a place at Westminster University to read Building Surveying. He found that once there, however, something set him apart from his fellow students.

A gifted athlete who excelled at most sports, he had ventured into a boxing club as a 14-year-old boy and fallen, like legions of lost souls before him, madly in love with it. Intoxicated, the lure of the ring proved too much. Frank quit life as an undergraduate to fight full-time.

His phalanx of fans hold smartphones and tablets aloft as Tibbs parts the ropes for him. Frank stands momentarily still by the ring apron, giving them all a good shot, spawning tomorrow's blog entries and YouTube videos. His career will be lived out in the age of the internet where every move is broadcast a thousand times. He touches gloves to the outstretched fists of a couple of die-hards in the front row and then he's in there, that 20-foot square, roped and raised platform where he has chosen to seek his fortune.

If not for the incessant demands of the boxing lifestyle, which if attended to properly are all-consuming, the kid could have been a model. He has a boy-next-door face, a toothpaste-advert smile and the clean physique of a classical statue. Girls go nuts for him, boys wish they were him. To complete the package, he is also a genuinely nice individual, with a word and time for everyone.

This appealing combination of attributes has made him one of British boxing's hottest young properties. Off the back of a successful amateur career, which saw him pick up 60 wins from 70 fights without quite scaling the peaks of Olympic or international glory, he signed to Frank Warren promotions, one of the UK's biggest outfits, at the age of 22. They have invested in him and expect a return. Buglioni carries this with him, on those broad shoulders, every time he climbs through the ropes. He is required to win, to be the shining star they all want him to be and he knows it.

This night, his fifth professional contest, is no different. He must live up to the hype. As the massed ranks of the Buglioni Bloc continue to sing his name he plants his feet on the canvas, looks up and salutes them, gladiator-style, with both fists. The hall quivers at the volume of their response.

While the young star limbers loosely and bounces around the ring, weaving between officials, anticipating the action, testing the ropes, someone waits for him. Across the way, from the other corner, Frank makes fleeting eye-contact with his opponent.

His adversary is egg-bald, staring, motionless with an expression that manages to be both malevolent and light-hearted. He has a rugged, rather than chiselled build and a pale, Nordic complexion. He wears the slightest of smiles. Put a horned helmet on his head and you could imagine him raiding Saxon villages, brandishing a battle-axe. He looks like a loon.

Jody Meikle grew up on the Riddings estate in Scunthorpe, north Lincolnshire. There are no million-pound houses there. By day he is a roofer and before the fight had been at work until 1pm, allowed to knock off early by an understanding boss. He travelled down the M1 in his manager Carl Greaves's car, eating lunch on the way, with his girlfriend tagging along for a night out in London. By 6pm, when he reached the venue, the morning's graft and four-hour journey had drained his enthusiasm.

On arrival he lay down wearily in the dressing room, closing his eyes, contemplating sleep. For a while he wished he could be somewhere else but the noise of the crowd revived him. When he heard Buglioni's crew take up their throaty chants, adrenaline kicked in. He sat bolt upright, grabbed Greaves by the shoulders and shouted, 'Come on!'

Back in his home town, Jody's reputation is unshakeable. The 'One Man Riot' will have it with anyone. End of. Even the bouncers are scared of him. He has fought regularly since childhood, just not usually with gloves and rules. He has had three spells in prison. If Buglioni dared take him on in the street, Meikle would eat him up and spit him out inside a minute. But this is different, Marquess of Queensberry, the sport of gentlemen, with a referee and an arena full of spectators.

The north London legion hiss and shout insults as the MC, a former child actor from *Grange Hill*, reads Meikle's name. Jody's girl, sitting at ringside, is reduced to tears by the hostility in the air. A lesser man, fighting hundreds of miles from home with barely a friend in the house might feel intimidated, but not the Riot. He nods eagerly, spreads his arms, embraces the boos and grins broadly, manically, like a Halloween pumpkin. He is absolutely loving it.

The fight follows the expected pattern with Frank taking centre ring from the start and hunting his foe down. He launches assault after assault in his upright, typically European style, working in straight lines – jab, right hand, jab, jab, right hand. Defying logic, Jody sometimes lowers his guard, almost seeming to invite the punches in.

Buglioni is known as a banger. Three of his first four wins have finished in less than a round but Meikle takes and takes his shots, to the extent that sometimes his smooth white head resembles a ping-pong ball attached to a bat on a short string, being swatted back and forth. After every volley of blows bouncing off his cranium, Jody grins his mad, pumpkin grin and walks forward again. Sometimes he catches Buglioni with his own fists, the youngster's defence is by no means impregnable, but Frank is too quick and sharp, too well trained for him to sustain any pressure.

While the Wise Guy has been training for this night since his last bout at the end of April, conditioning himself daily with the famous trainer of champions, Jimmy Tibbs, Meikle, by contrast, was only told about it ten days before. It is all his role requires. Frank works with a nutritionist, a fitness coach and uses a state of the art cryotherapy chamber to aid recovery after workouts. Free time is regulated. He 'lives the life', as boxers say. Jody fits training in around his job, running up and down Scammonden Dam by the side of the M62 and doing a couple of evenings in the gym when he can. He likes a curry and is partial to the odd drink. To ensure he made weight, he stopped boozing a few days before the bout.

The complexion of the contest changes in the third round when Meikle is caught by a scything right cross. It opens a gash over his left eye and Buglioni, who had begun to show signs of frustration, is reinvigorated. Boxers, like predators, sense weakness and target it, no matter how nice they may be when not fighting. The professional prize ring is no place for compassion.

Frank hits him with everything, going for the injury, trying to worsen it and force the stoppage, but Jody laps it all up, smiles and carries on. Every now and then, when the action lulls, or the fighters clinch, Meikle glances up at the Buglioni Bloc in the gods, grins, winks, pokes out his tongue and waves at them. Enraged, their coarse, vocal displeasure tumbles down from the balcony. The insults and jeers don't faze him. It is what he wants. 'You see! Your boy can't hurt me!' he shows, with each gesture.

John Rawling, commentating for the BoxNation digital TV channel, is incredulous, 'He's hit him with everything but the kitchen sink' he says, 'and the guy's just smiled at him.' Sidekick, Barry Jones, a former world champion at super-featherweight, agrees. 'Buglioni's fought at a decent pace, but he's just up against a super-durable guy.'

For six rounds, everyone gets their money's worth and at the final bell the fighters embrace. In a way both have won, Frank because he has taken a points victory and Jody because he got to the end. Meikle applauds his conqueror and raises Buglioni's arm before the referee can. The announcements are made and 'Seven Nation Army' is played again. The blue-clad fans dance and shout some more. Amid the torrent of plaudits for Frank's fifth professional victory, Rawling says, 'In the unlikely event that in the future I'm on a night out in Scunthorpe with Jody Meikle, I'm on his side. What a character!'

Both men leave the arena. They speak warmly backstage then get changed into their civvies in their respective dressing rooms. Frank has promotional obligations to fulfil. He does a few media interviews before going to greet the loyal punters who bought tickets, all smiles and handshakes, a real pro, accepting the back-slaps and congratulations like a politician who has won an election. This, he knows, is the fuel for his rocket-powered drive to stardom.

Later he will sit down with his promoter and discuss which carefully planned move he will make from here. In three months or so, he will fight again, against another well-chosen opponent, someone who can stretch him a little more, nudge him closer to a title and give those ticket-buying supporters their next happy night out. He will have a week off before starting his next training camp.

Meikle has no such concerns. His cut is stitched and he collects his fee, a higher one than usual, which is more than welcome, then jumps in the car and starts the journey home. He is pleased not to have been stopped, happy with the show he put on but annoyed about the injury. He will have to cancel the bouts he had lined up for the next couple of weeks, forced to wait at least 28 days until he can do it all again, Boxing Board rules.

On the way back they have to pull over by the side of the A1, near Peterborough, so his girlfriend can be sick. The proximity of the violence was too much for her, she is shaking and tearful. Its 1.30am and the cold, night air stings Jody's cut, contracting the skin around the wound.

He gets home at 3am, checks on his seven-year-old son, who is sound asleep, and falls into bed. On Monday he is back at work.

2

Writers write, fighters fight...

What is a journeyman?

AS much as boxing itself is an industry, so is commenting on it, both verbally and in print. There are many well-informed, perceptive and creative people who work in this field but also some who tend to rely on worn-out words and phrases, which can be tossed around amidst the excitement of the action or conjured up instantly in the face of an impending deadline.

It can be an instructive sight on press row at boxing events to witness how many of the mainstream media have written their fight reports before the fights actually happen, leaving a few gaps to be filled in as the action progresses. They can then be e-mailed, from a ringside laptop, as soon as the winner has his hand raised. It may not make for genuine or insightful reportage but this is how the world works now.

Body punches, as one example, will too frequently be described as 'sickening'. While spectators at a show at London's Camden Centre on 30 May 2014 did actually witness the Bulgarian super-bantamweight Stefan Slavchev spew his pre-fight meal all over the canvas, after a solid right to the guts from Cheshunt's Charlie Hoy, this is not a regular occurrence.

Similarly, a title-holder will often put on a 'master-class' or use a 'ram-rod jab'. A man who can absorb a lot of punishment is 'teak-tough' or 'granite-jawed', takes his opponent 'into the trenches' or even 'drags him into deep water, then drowns him'. The terms become tired and lose whatever impact they once had.

Sadly it would be easy to make a case that within the current boxing lexicon, 'champion' is the most overused word, being repeated far too often due to the madness of the ever-proliferating alphabet organisations, their lust for new titles and the sanctioning fees they bring.

It sometimes seems that almost every contest is for a belt of some sort these days and at the top level, this is an era in which any good fighter can hope to pick up a world title during his career rather than spending his professional life as a contender as he would have done until the 1970s. In each weight class there are four credible world champions (the WBA, WBC, IBF and WBO) and far too many others. New organisations come and go like the tide. There are guys holding versions of world titles who are not independently ranked in the top 50 in their division while with super titles, interim titles, silver titles, intercontinental titles and the rest, it seems that new strands of championship are invented almost monthly.

In a similar vein, the WBO and WBU now recognise their own champions of Europe, alongside the traditional EBU title, meaning that there are now three potential claimants to that honour in each weight class. Happily, the time-honoured British title with its famous Lonsdale belt is still a notable and worthy accolade, as to a lesser extent are the English, Scottish, Welsh, Irish and Celtic championships.

Below that exist the regional belts, such as the Southern Area and now the frequently contested, new clutch of Masters titles which are either British or International and awarded in Bronze, Silver and Gold.

These latter baubles, created by the promoter Bruce Baker, are not recognised by the British Boxing Board of Control but have proved popular with other promoters who like to put the words 'title fight' or 'championship' on their promotional materials. Often they are held by fighters who are little more than novices.

But of all the misunderstood words common in boxing-speak, the one for which there seems to be most varied usage is clear – journeyman. It is repeated frequently, by fans, pundits and journalists, usually in a negative context. 'Oh, he's nothing more than a journeyman.' 'He should beat that guy easily, he's only a journeyman.' 'I used to really rate him a few years ago, but he's a journeyman now.' Some fighters consider being referred to as a journeyman an insult. More than once, when speaking to boxers about aspects of this book, after telling them what it was about, I was given a cold look and reproached with the words, 'But I'm not a journeyman…' Even those who are authorities on the sport and write or talk about it publicly often confuse its meaning.

In a 6 November 2010 headline, Examiner.com described Jamaican veteran Glen Johnson as 'The Ultimate Journeyman'. At the time Johnson's record stood at 50-14 and he was a former world title holder at super-middleweight and light-heavyweight, with an outstanding knockout win over Hall of Famer and ring genius Roy Jones Junior on his CV. As this book was being written and at the age of 45, Johnson was still an active pro and had won three of his last four bouts.

Similarly, on 12 September 2013, Gareth A. Davies, esteemed broadcaster and boxing correspondent for *The Telegraph*, penned a piece in which British welterweight Ashley Theophane was described as a 'journeyman boxer at the heart of the biggest fight of the year in Las Vegas, with Floyd Mayweather as his sponsor.'

It may be true that Theophane's career received a massive shot in the arm when Money May signed him up to fight on his undercards, but with a career record of 35-6-1 and having previously been British light-welterweight champion between 2011 and 2012, the man they call 'The Treasure' could more accurately be described as a high-level domestic fighter trying his luck on the world stage.

The Boxing Tribune, an independent boxing website and news service, published a retrospective in August 2013 in which Dennis Andries (49-14-2), who won a clutch of professional championships throughout his career in the 1980s and 90s, including the WBC light-heavyweight world title three times, was described as 'the journeyman who became a three-time world champion'.

Top-level success was indeed a while coming for the strong but crude Andries, who turned pro late for the time, at the age of 25, but even in the early stages of his career he had a solid winning record. He won the Southern Area light-heavyweight title in his 13th bout, at which point he stood at 10-2-1.

These sorts of uses of the word are very common. Yet to describe a stellar performer like Johnson or the other examples above as journeymen, promotes quite a major misunderstanding of who journeymen boxers are and what they do.

For readers without much knowledge of the fight game to be able to access this book and appreciate the issues the journeymen discuss, it is going to be necessary to explain some things first. To this end, over the next few pages I will lay down some truths about how UK boxing functions. My experience is only related to the UK circuit. I have never attended a show abroad and what comes next is concerned mainly with the lower end of the business in Britain, although some of it is equally applicable to the bigger promotions.

As far as I know this has never been explicitly explained in a book or publication before. I am not sure why, perhaps it is just that within limited coverage that focuses mainly on stars, this stuff isn't relevant. People to whom all this is new will probably find some of it surprising while for those who already have some inside understanding, this background will be all too familiar.

Fighters can often be heard saying that 'boxing is all about levels'. This is unreservedly true. For obvious reasons media attention tends to focus on prestigious championship bouts and the layers just below them. Competitors in the early stages of their career, unless they were outstanding Olympic-medal-winning amateurs, will receive little attention and perhaps go unnoticed until they compile a record of 8-0 or something similar. At this point casual fans will begin to pick up their interest in a boxer as he starts to compete on bigger shows, garners press attention and enters the second phase of his professional path, looking towards local and national titles. But what happened to him before? Where did he come from? Do young boxers with impressive-looking records appear out of nowhere?

To answer these questions we have to delve into the workings of the game and as Danny Connor (11-8-1), the 27-year-old former Southern Area light-welterweight champion, explained, 'That's what you have to understand, this isn't a sport. It's a business.'

National treasure Frank Bruno, who reigned for six months as the WBC heavyweight champion of the world in 1995, also famously described the fight game as 'showbusiness with blood'. Most people don't realise how true that is.

Having taken the decision to turn pro and paying upwards of £1,000 for all the medicals and certification involved, the harsh reality is that a young prospect will be expected to provide his own audience. In the vast majority of cases, if he cannot then his career is over before it starts. Friends and relatives will be harangued via word of mouth and social media to turn out to see him, usually paying, in the present market, about £30–£50 per head to do so. A fighter who is unable to sell at least 80 tickets in this way is unlikely to be allowed to fight. Either that, or if he's lucky, he may be offered the chance to fight for nothing.

After participating in his 20th pro bout, Danny Connor confirmed, 'Apart from the fights on Sky TV I've never earned from a fight. Sometimes I've even had to pay so I can fight.' Connor funds his training expenses through employment as a youth worker and sponsorship deals with various local companies.

Recent British boxing history is littered with untold stories of talented fighters whose careers didn't even get off the ground because for one reason or another – perhaps they were introverted characters, rather than gregarious, popular types – they couldn't sell enough tickets.

Like Connor, at this stage most prospects will depend on the generosity of friends and family, often still living at home with parents, while holding down a part-time job of some sort to pay their way. Their costs far outweigh whatever they earn. They will begin boxing in small halls on cards full of other, similar prospects, where they will climb through the ropes before audiences measured in hundreds rather than thousands, hoping to attract the attention of the bigger promoters.

If they can create a buzz and pick up a few wins they will dream of signing a deal with Matchroom Sport, run by the Hearn family, or with Frank Warren or Mick Hennessy. The opportunity to box on televised shows, where the money is bigger, can then arise. Without this kind of backing they may still be plying their trade at the Town Hall in Dudley, the Coronet in Elephant and Castle or a leisure centre somewhere in the provinces, hoping for a minor-title fight after 12 or 15 contests. There are many young hopefuls who get to this sort of stage, lose a couple and quit, slinking off to get fat and learn a trade, disillusioned with the business, realising that real opportunity is not going to come their way.

Tyler 'Tornado' Goodjohn, an honest, ballsy competitor, who at 23 years old with a record of 10-3 and as a former holder of a British Masters Silver light-welterweight belt is representative of many early-career fighters, spoke about some of this after being outpointed by Tyrone Nurse for the English title in that same weight class.

It was a gruelling bout, on the undercard of a fairly big show at Manchester's Phones4U Arena that was televised live on Sky in April 2014 (the Goodjohn v Nurse fight was not part of the live broadcast). Goodjohn worked like a demon throughout the ten rounds but was unable to impose himself on the longer-limbed Nurse, who won by a wide, unanimous decision. Speaking several weeks later he said, 'Boxing is tough as fuck. I put my life on the line in my last fight. I properly went to war and after I lost, all I got was shown the exit out of the venue. I even had to call and pay for my own taxi to take me to hospital. Glamour? No way! We are just money makers unfortunately, it's all about ticket sales, but I came to terms with that a long time ago. The pro game isn't what you dream it is growing up as a kid. It's ruthless and if I didn't love the sport so much I would have turned it in a while ago.'

When a young boxer with ten or so wins turns up on TV and commentators describe him as being a 'promoter's dream' it is actually all of this that they are referring to, not his pugilistic prowess. Twenty-four-year-old Frank Buglioni, mentioned at the beginning of this book, the former WBO Europe super-middleweight champion who lost his unbeaten record in April 2014 to go to 11-1, is an excellent example. His stablemate 'Gorgeous' Georgie Kean (3-1), a welterweight who suffered his first defeat on the same night, is another. Somehow they each sell upwards of 500 tickets per show and have done since their debuts.

Beyond any other qualities they may possess, popularity has been by far their biggest asset. They may be good looking, they may have charisma, they may even, as a side issue, be able to fight a bit, but rather than any of this, it is their ability to punt out £20,000 of tickets for each contest that gets the businessmen excited.

Such fighters will be very carefully matched throughout their early career. Their promoter will nurse them up to real title level, probably picking up some of the new, meaningless belts on the way, in the knowledge that a few defeats could pop the bubble and ruin their profitability. Once they get to genuine British, European or world level, the mollycoddling stops and most will be unable to cope. Meanwhile, more talented fighters who sell fewer tickets may never get an opportunity. There is no other professional sport that organises itself like this.

For a moment, transpose to football and imagine a scenario in 2002 in which Wayne Rooney, as a 16-year-old youth team prodigy at Everton was approached by his manager David Moyes and told, 'You're making good progress, Wayne, I'm considering putting you in the first team in a couple of weeks, but you'll have to sell a few hundred tickets to your pals if you want to play. If you can't do that I'm going to pick another lad instead. He isn't half as good as you, but he can bring a crowd of four hundred, no problem.'

In such a situation, English football would potentially have lost one of its premier talents and filled its place with a mediocre one. This is how boxing operates.

It is very similar to the lower levels of the music business, where bands will get booked for small venues based not on how good or bad they may be, but on how many mates they bring. Some venues or music promoters specifically state a minimum of 20 ticket-buying 'fans' for a weekday gig, or 50 for a Saturday. Bands who bring less don't get paid and won't be rebooked. Frank Bruno was spot on.

Typically, a novice pro – lets call him Jack – will sign with a manager who also promotes shows. If Jack has signed a contract with promoter Mr Smith, who is putting on a night at which Jack is fighting, he will box in the 'home' – or usually blue – corner. Most, if not all the fighters in the home corner on the show will also be managed and promoted by Mr Smith, although there may be some guesting there via other promoters or managers with whom he has struck a deal. The opponents brought in to fight them in the red corner are 'away'.

This is a very important point which is totally misunderstood by casual fans. The terms 'home' and 'away' in boxing do not necessarily have anything to do with the proximity of the venue to the boxer's home town. They refer to who manages and promotes them, whether or not they are the ticket sellers and which corner they are fighting from. If the show promoted by Mr Smith takes place at the York Hall and contains a fight between Jack, who grew up in Luton and an opponent from Bethnal Green, Jack is still the home fighter, while the east Londoner is away despite being able to walk home after the fight. Jack will sell tickets and will therefore hope to have a large contingent of supporters in the building while the man from Bethnal Green receives a wage just for turning up and so is unlikely to have more than a handful of family or friends there.

Once armed with this knowledge, it is an interesting experiment to go to boxing shows and count how many times home fighters win, particularly on points, compared to those fighting away.

Jon Pegg, a manager from the Birmingham area who is known affectionately as the 'Fight Wizard' by his stable of boxers for his outstanding matchmaking ability, explained a little bit about this. 'People have to understand that in boxing there is no league table with fixtures or anything like that and matches are made in the interests of everyone involved. The home fighter, his promoter and the rest of his team are looking for a win, to boost his record and push him towards bigger things; the away fighter is generally looking for a payday. So fights are matched to meet everyone's needs.'

Having signed his contract with Mr Smith and with his heart set on glory, young Jack then has to set about the difficult task of making his name. In order to build the impressive-looking CV that he needs to be marketable and push towards the bigger money of TV and title fights, he first has to beat a bunch of guys. And this is where journeymen, in the true sense of the word, enter the scene.

A journeyman is a fighter who spends a lot of time on the road, usually going in with early-career boxers on their home shows. He will fight maybe two, three or four times a month (the British Boxing Board of Control does not allow professional fighters to compete more than once a week) and he will have a losing record, often quite a dramatic one that to the untrained eye may look fairly shocking. Kristian Laight, who provided the inspiration for this book, stood at 7-166-7 when it was started. The last of his wins came 36 fights previously[1].

---

1 Since interviewing Kristian Laight he has won twice, beating Craig Whyatt by a point at a Mayfair Sporting Club event in January 2014 and Aaron Flinn by the same result at Bedworth Civic Hall in March.

Johnny Greaves, who also gives his insights within these pages, retired in 2013 with a record of 4-96. Bheki Moyo, the South African fighting out of Wallington in south London, another contributor here, turned pro in 2005 and since then has amassed statistics of 0-67-2. Just to confirm, that is not a typo. In 69 professional contests, Moyo has never won.

How is it possible, fans ask, that fighters with such poor stats are allowed to continue to compete? The answer is that they provide a service that young prospects and their promoters need. The hopefuls need someone to fight, someone who is happy to box them within a system that is heavily stacked in their favour. The prospects are prepared to pay for this person to get in the ring with them, in fact, in the inverted economics of small-hall boxing, the reality is that the journeyman will receive a larger purse than the home fighter and this money will come from the ticket sales the prospect has generated himself.

Many young fighters dislike this system, but feel they have no choice but to participate in it. Freddie Turner, 24, the current Southern Area light-middleweight champion, 11-0 at the time of writing, had to wait until his ninth contest before his first real, competitive fight, against the former champ Nathan Graham, from Aylesbury, which he won by a very narrow points decision. Speaking of his career up to that point, he said, 'I never wanted to fight journeymen. Those guys are hard to look good against. They come in, keep it tight and don't give you anything to work with. I'm a natural counter-puncher so my style doesn't mesh well with someone who just wants to stay on the back foot and survive.'

Danny Connor had similar feelings. 'I never saw the point in fighting journeymen. All they want to do is hang in there and not get hurt so they can fight again in a couple of weeks. I always resented this idea of having to pay for my opponent.'

Still, journeymen fill this necessary gap in the boxing marketplace. Someone has to be prepared to help the prospects pad their fledgling records and in the current set-up, prospects do not fight each other.

Many journeymen rely on their ring earnings to feed their families and pay their bills. Earning, on a standard show, £1,000–£1,500 a time, keeping busy and avoiding injury are the keys.

Johnny Greaves explains it like this, 'For me, being a paid opponent was the obvious choice to make. I knew I was never going to be a world champion so going down the journeyman route gave me a way to make a living. The thing is, I didn't go in there to lose, not exactly, but if you upset the ticket sellers then the promoters won't use you. They'll see you as a risk. So if you want to get rebooked you have to do enough to make the fight interesting without causing a problem. That's how it is in the away corner.'

Johnny's instinctive honesty exposes an accepted but generally unspoken truth. People within the fight game take it as read. Those outside are basically unaware of it. It is the elephant in the room of professional pugilism.

Most fights at this level have a predetermined outcome.

That is not to say they are 'fixed', not always, anyway. Fixed is a big and litigious word in professional sport. Officially, there is nothing stopping a journeyman going all out for a win and knocking out the home fighter in front of their friends and family. This does happen, rarely. But as Johnny pointed out, a journeyman who makes a habit of beating the ticket sellers will soon find that the phone stops ringing. If he wants regular work and the pay cheque that comes with it, he needs to play the game.

Jon Pegg puts it like this, 'The role of the journeyman is to be always ready to fight and always fit. Their job is to go in there to test the prospects and further their education. About 80 to 90 per cent of the time, they're not in there to win. If you want to fight again next week you're not going to take too many risks, are you? The last thing you want is to get stuck in and end up needing stitches because then you're going to get a 28-day suspension. Obviously, sometimes they might go in with someone who can't hurt them and then they might have a go, but mostly they're there to give the kid something to think about and stay safe.'

Mickey Helliet, a London-based promoter/manager who has had dealings with most of the fighters featured here, provided his interpretation. 'There are different kinds of journeymen, some you can use as opponents for top-level fighters, but for the most part, they are there to help prospects build records. If you want to make big money and get on TV you need a solid, unbeaten record. Boxers want to make money, first and foremost, so of course they'll do what they need to do to get that winning record. If that means having some less competitive fights, against opponents who are doing a job, so be it. People might not want to hear that, but that's what it is.'

Steve Goodwin, another London-based manager and promoter, agrees. 'Journeymen are there to provide stiff opposition and educate a developing fighter. I would generally pay a UK journeyman £1,100 for a fight and I'd expect him to be worth that money. What you don't want is someone who's going to come in and fall over at the first punch. There's an art to matchmaking that a lot of people don't appreciate. At the same time you don't want to ruin a young lad's confidence by putting him in with someone who'll smash him all over the place, so journeymen have to tread a line between the two.'

Effectively this means that to an extent, professional boxing, as witnessed on the undercards of many small-hall shows, is something of a pretence. Not to the same level as pro wrestling, with its choreographed moves, scripts and silly stories, but if you know of a young fighter who started boxing a couple of years ago and has racked up seven or eight consecutive wins, the truth is that in the majority of cases, his opponents haven't been trying to beat him. In that way, he probably hasn't had a real fight yet. And when he does, he may well come unstuck.

3

Hearts of gold, bodies of steel

The eerie tragedy of Ernie and Billy Smith

TYLORSTOWN, South Wales, a name written large in fighting folklore for giving the world its most famous son, Jimmy Wilde, the phenomenal flyweight who conquered the world in the early 20th century. Ever since those antiquated days of milk carts, liniment and coal-tar soap, the story told by proud Taffies to their kids has remained the same; that the diminutive Wilde's freakish strength – as a booth fighter he reportedly often knocked out men weighing in as heavyweights – developed as a teenager working in the Ferndale colliery near the village. In this way his wondrous achievements became mythically bound up with local community and culture.

A century on from the era of the 'Mighty Atom' there is little to commemorate his former glory. The pits he worked in closed in the 1980s, triggering decades of decline. Unemployment is high. Population has dwindled to around 4,000. Nestling in its picturesque valley, whose steep sides still provide an ideal landscape for training runs, the village has become just another provincial outpost, a monument to Thatcherism, linked only to its great fistic legacy by occasionally hosting cheap and cheerful shows at its modest Rhondda Fach leisure centre.

On 4 May 2013 Warrior Promotions staged a small night there, showcasing a Welsh welterweight title as the main event with a few neighbourhood boys building their records on the undercard. As usual the ring had been constructed on the indoor five-a-side pitch and folding chairs were arranged in neat lines for friends and relatives of competitors. In addition to the dinner tables of inner ringside, where family groups sat with pints of local bitter, just seven rows of seating separated the ropes from the sides of the room.

Near the bottom of the bill that night, Stuart Brewer, a 23-year-old welterweight from Penygraig, made his debut against the familiar figure of Billy Smith (13-138-2), a short, solid, rough-hewn journeyman and a busy and popular figure on the circuit. By that time, Smith had spent 13 years earning a reputation as immovable, impervious to everything, as if body and head had been lasered out of the same lump of steel. That evening it was two and a half years since his last win. He was on a 31-fight losing streak, all of which had come via decision.

Headstrong and hungry, desperate to make an impression, Brewer piled into Smith from the start, running across the canvas to meet him then driving hooks into his midriff with both hands. Smith tucked up, absorbing the onslaught on his elbows and gloves, allowing the younger fighter to dictate the action and push him around. The lad was clearly excited, but there was no cause for alarm.

During that madcap first session, Brewer's boxing was unruly and immature, basics forgotten. He telegraphed everything, throwing so much bodyweight into his shots that sometimes both feet were off the ground when they connected. It was almost Hollywood stuff. While the kid bounced around, hands down, swinging from his boots, Smith stayed on the back foot and waited. 'Go on Stuey, smash him up!' called a croaky old boy from the back of the hall, as another wave of combinations broke on the cliffs of Billy's defence.

Two minutes and 15 seconds into the round, with the whirling youngster still pouring it on with both fists, Smith peeked through his guard and threw a sudden left around the shoulder. It didn't appear to be the most vicious of hooks but the novice, high on his own adrenaline, had neither expected it nor seen it coming. It landed straight down the pipe and Brewer collapsed in a jumble of limbs against the ropes. The meagre crowd murmured in shocked unison.

Up at five, with the startled look of someone who had been out jogging and tripped over the kerb, Brewer dusted himself down, had an unusually long conversation with referee Martin Williams and was allowed to continue.

For the rest of the round he held, moved and boxed without the recklessness he began with. He remained the busier man as the fight progressed but kept his right glove by his chin, sometimes showing a feint in his movement on the way in. He stopped loading up, trying to score a KO with every punch and began to pick his shots. The results of the knockdown were clear to see. Brewer had been given his first pro lesson.

Smith grinned at him at last bell and hugged the lad like a nephew, acknowledging what had passed between them. He had done his job and taught the boy some manners. Stuart Brewer scraped a 38-37 decision that night. Three months later, Billy Smith was dead.

Originally from Worcestershire in the Midlands, identical twins Ernie and Billy Smith both fought under the nickname 'Gypsy Boy' due to their traveller background, emerging from the unlicensed circuit to take on the role of paid opponent from the beginning of their pro careers.

Billy, a landscape gardener by trade, lost his first 24 fights before managing a slightly suspect draw with his good friend Baz Carey in 2005. Despite this he was a useful fighter, game and tough, with a decent knowledge of his craft. Unusually for a journeyman, he later won the Midlands Area light-middleweight title twice.

Ernie, blond-haired, slightly broader and according to many, the harder of the two, in the same way that diamond is harder than tungsten, had an early career that was more mixed. He started boxing professionally in 1999 and initially took the attitude that he was coming to fight no matter what, even having a winning record until his 11th fight, but after a year or so as a professional he realised that playing the game was the path of least resistance and the wins dried up. He worked as a tree surgeon by day and used the money from boxing to make extra money for his young family.

The twins became fixtures on small-hall events nationwide, sharing a reputation as sturdy yet amiable men. Current journeyman Jason Nesbitt recalled, 'Billy always made me laugh. Whatever mood I was in and whatever nonsense was going on with the promoter or whatever, Billy would walk in the dressing room and before long I'd be in stitches. He was one of those people who made it his business to speak to everyone and make everyone else feel good.'

In some ways they epitomised the British ideal of the small-hall boxer – hearts of gold, bodies of steel. It has also been suggested that in common with many fighters, both suffered with occasional bouts of depression, yet any emotional fragility they possessed was not apparent inside the ropes where their resilience has become the stuff of legend.

It is said that Ernie took a punch so well that more than 30 of his opponents broke their hands on his head. Billy too was like hitting concrete according to several men who shared a ring with him. It was as if genetics had somehow predisposed the Smiths to be able to absorb punishment, which they often did with a smile, joking with their opponents and the crowd.

Ernie's presence on the scene was typified by his performance against Davy Jones at the Winter Gardens in Cleethorpes on 23 May 2005. Jones had originally been slated to fight Grimsby's Luke Teague, but Teague had broken both hands in his last fight, (against Ernie), meaning he had to withdraw.

Smith was brought in to replace Teague, and Luke's brother Matt recalls the contest clearly, 'I spoke to Ernie before and told him he could beat Jones. Jones was one of these lads that started off as a prospect but found his level and wasn't going anywhere. So I suggested to Ernie that he go on the front foot and put some pressure on him and Jones might crumble. He thanked me and followed my advice. He really took it to him, which was nice to see, you know a journeyman having a real go for a change.

'Anyway, end of the last round, you know how it is, the referee, Dean Bramhald, raised Davey Jones's hand, classic home decision and all that. Ernie went crazy, shouting at the ref and no word of a lie, Bramhald automatically turned around and raised Ernie's hand too! It was hilarious. I don't think he liked the look of Ernie in that sort of mood. Anyway, it ended up being a draw and Ernie left the ring, got changed and in a couple of minutes he was in the bar having a beer and a smoke. That's what he was like.'

It was a similar story when Ernie took on Graham Delehedy in Huddersfield in May 2004. Delehedy's friend and former light-middleweight pro Shaun Farmer recalled watching the bout, which the heavy handed Delehedy won on a third round stoppage. 'Ernie went mad when Graham stopped him, he wasn't happy at all. He didn't get stopped very often but Graham could really bang and the ref probably did the right thing. Graham always said he learned a lot from Ernie. He'd been blowing everyone away with his power, but Ernie kept coming and firing back. He was so tough, Ernie Smith, but a top guy as well.'

Ernie's career motored on for ten years and would doubtlessly have stretched for several more if he hadn't failed an MRI scan late in 2009. If anomalies appear on a fighter's brain image it is standard practice for the British Boxing Board of Control to withdraw licences, to protect against serious injury. But after ten years as a pro Ernie had become used to the buzz of boxing in front of an audience and the additional income it brought.

No one fully knows the financial pressures he was under or what demons he faced but on the morning of Wednesday 27

January 2010 he was found hanging from a tree at a beauty spot in Llanelli, South Wales, through which he often went running with Billy. He was 31. At the time of his death he had contested 161 fights, winning 13.

Billy was distraught and as perhaps is natural when faced with such a close, personal tragedy, in some ways he blamed himself. In an interview with Michael J. Jones, published on the Worldwide Boxing Predictions League website in December 2012, he spoke of Ernie's death.

'It was a total shock that day [finding out]. I never had the first clue anything was wrong with him. To say we were close is an understatement. We were very close and helped each other out all the time with money and favours. He was fanatical about boxing and was the one that got me into it. I think when he got told he'd failed an MRI scan and lost his licence it was hard for him to take. He seemed OK after that though and wanted to open a gym. The day it happened I went for my run and somebody said not to go that way. I took a different route and when I returned I got told. I still think if I'd gone the normal way I might have been able to stop him doing what he did.'

In an interview with Matt Christie of *Boxing News* months after Ernie's death, Billy was still clearly struggling to come to terms with it, 'People say as time goes by it will get better…but it doesn't get better because it does not leave your head. There was not a day that passed where I did not see him…It wouldn't have been so bad if he had been killed by somebody else because you would have more peace of mind. But when somebody kills themselves, you are always thinking, "What could I have done to help him?" But I didn't know what was bothering him. Not on that day. Not on his last day.'

Still, Billy fought on for three further years, going in with all-comers from welterweight to middleweight. Those who knew him within boxing felt he had put his grief behind him. He frequently mentioned his brother and talked of him with fondness but maintained his chirpy manner, remaining a very popular figure in dressing rooms and arenas until the summer of 2013. By late June and early July of that year, he seemed different to some, reflective, detached, often sitting by himself, not communicating much. Poignantly one fighter described that Billy looked 'haunted'.

On 23 July he also took his own life. Friends or associates largely expressed shock. Only those who knew him very well felt they had seen any warning signs.

The whole tale is given a macabre twist by the fact that Billy died in the same place and by the same method as his brother. Not only that, but at the time of his passing his record was identical to Ernie's. He had won 13 of 161.

Jon Pegg worked in Billy's corner throughout much of his career. 'I spoke to Billy's family after his death,' he said, 'and they told me that in the last couple of weeks they kept finding him at Ernie's grave. He was sleeping up there and everything. He'd lost it a bit. His head had gone.'

The boxing community struggled to make sense of the double tragedy and the media soon picked up on it. In the November 2013 edition of *The Ring* magazine, legendary fight-writer and Muhammad Ali biographer Thomas Hauser gave his interpretation in a feature article entitled, 'Billy Smith and the Case Against Boxing'.

'A professional boxing match,' Hauser opined, some might say naively, 'is supposed to be a competitive athletic event. Based on Smith's record, it's fair to say that, when he came to fight, he was expected to lose...No other professional sport would tolerate a failure rate like that.

'Fighters who lose again and again are different from perennial losers in other sports. Athletes "play" sports like baseball, basketball, tennis and golf. No one plays boxing. Fighters are punched in the head hard by men trained in the art of hurting... Smith's ring record tarnishes boxing.

'Every time you get in the ring you lose a part of yourself that you can never get back...Fighters know when they shouldn't fight any more. They might not admit it, but they know.'

Hauser concludes, 'There came a time when Billy Smith knew.' Wallop.

It was a powerful piece, with the implication that journeymen like Billy and Ernie Smith aren't much good at boxing. By repeatedly entering the fray with limited skills, they are putting themselves at risk. They need rescuing rather than being used by others to make money.

Natural conclusions could be that a fighter whose wins-to-losses record is as unbalanced as the Smiths should have his licence revoked. Perhaps a promoter who continues to use fighters with these kinds of records should be fined or have his activities suspended? Perhaps psychologists with expertise in boxing injuries and mental frailty should rigorously examine those with heavy losing records for signs of depression or emotional distress?

Another possibility is that to be a journeyman you have to be a strange or damaged character to begin with, that it is only those with low self-esteem that would want such a life. All the hours spent on the motorway, arriving at venues where virtually everyone expects and wants to see you get beaten up, to sometimes fight your heart out, just to be on the wrong end of home decisions from referees and judges. All those nights risking your health, enduring physical pain, rolling with and taking the blows of those who see you as nothing more than a stepping stone, while being regarded as a loser by the wider world. If nothing else, it's a highly unusual way to live.

Who are these unheralded grafters and what drives them to do what they do? To find out, we must let them speak for themselves.

4

'Boxing saved my life'

Johnny Greaves

Light-welterweight/welterweight
Born: Forest Gate, London, 4 March 1979
Active: 2009–2013
Record: 4-96

'I'M not going to lie,' the man opposite me says, stirring his coffee. 'I always liked a scrap.'

We have spoken on the phone a number of times, I interviewed him for an article when he retired, but this is our first face-to-face meeting. We are sitting in the reception of the Peacock gym, Canning Town, his home turf. Photos of famous fighters cover the wall behind his head.

As I had sped around the North Circular, the roaring ribbon of concrete that loops over the river, heading east to meet him, I recalled the image of him crying after his last bout.

'I miss it like crazy,' he had told me on the phone. 'It's hard to put into words. I've definitely retired, but at the same time I'd give my right bollock for another 50 fights. I've been trying to get fat,

41

I always thought that's what I'd do, but it's fucking hard work. It must take a while for your metabolism to slow down or something.

'I'm still in the gym most days and I do a little bit because I enjoy it. It's something I've always done. It's who I am. I've got quite an active job, too, but honest to god, I am trying my best to get some flab on. It's just not happening. I'm about a stone above my old fighting weight, which is nothing major, but you know I could still be in shape to fight again in a couple of weeks' time, if need be. But nah, look, don't get any funny ideas. A comeback? Behave! Never say never, but I don't think so. It would take something pretty special to get me back in there.'

Travelling in that direction across the capital is like watching a real-time documentary about gentrification. It is not really possible to talk about east London as one place any more. There is east London and then there is *east London.* You can drink and dance in Dalston's trendy dives, alongside white men with dreadlocks and girls who design their own hats, or wander the chic streets of Shoreditch, but if you keep going, through Bethnal Green's Brick Lane where the air smells of balti and the York Hall where so many journeymen have done their thing, you start to notice a difference.

As soon as the whiff of the Thames hits your nose like a stiff jab, the landscape's become heavily geometric. Skyscrapers make shapes against the sun. Great, angular roads criss-cross the vista and carve it up. East India Dock Road, Victoria Dock Road, Silvertown Way– the names provide memories of an old, disappeared London, Jack the Ripper territory, a bawdy, Cockney tableau of dockers and thieves.

The towers of HSBC, Citi Financial and JP Morgan condescend to look down from Canary Wharf, gazing on the housing and industrial estates that dwell in their shadows. Around the gym is a sugar refinery, a doner kebab warehouse, a scrap metal merchant and an animal rendering plant. The buildings are squat and secretive, almost sinister. Closed-faced men stand outside them smoking. On the pavements the fashionable 20-somethings of Hackney have disappeared, replaced by folks squeezed out of the trendy zones by high rent. People with worry carved on their features and guarded eyes.

It is this, latter east London that the man recently called 'Britain's most famous journeyman' calls home. It suits him. This is a guy, after all, who would get changed on fight night, then pop out the back to smoke a quick roll-up before walking to the ring. Unlike many of those he faced, he was always a fighter, not an athlete. There is a big difference.

Greaves grew up an Ali shuffle from Upton Park, home of West Ham United Football Club, an area which is almost universally Bengali now. Being tough was important to him from the beginning and he learnt to fight the old-fashioned way. Like many of the truly great boxers, his first gym was the street.

'I think toughness is like punch power. It's something you're born with,' he says. 'As a kid I had two older brothers and we used to scrap. I was always fighting out in the area with other boys. I was well known for it around East Ham/Upton Park/Canning Town. Like my dad always says, if you grow up around the inner city, like I did and you can't fight, you're going to get taken advantage of. So there was no choice, really.

'But yeah, I'm not going to lie, I liked a scrap. In school, in the street, wherever. As a boy I was always testing myself, fighting against older lads and bigger lads, I was never the sort that would pick on someone smaller than myself. You know, if you had some older kids and one or two of them were mouthing off a little bit, I'd be the one to turn around and say, "Fuck you then, let's have a go." It was a way of challenging myself, I suppose.

'It's not that I was aggressive, but I just wouldn't back down. I couldn't suffer bullies or people that go around looking for fights. Even now, you get the young lads cutting about, giving it all this gangster bollocks and it fucking winds me up. Sometimes I'll go to a local pub and I'm trying to have a beer on the quiet and some little plank is sitting there staring at me and it just annoys me.'

Falling into boxing was virtually inevitable for an east London kid who liked a punch-up and Johnny started young. His first visits to the famous Peacock gym were at just ten years of age. His father, John Sr, frequently went there for weight training and the younger Greaves found that he enjoyed the ambience and camaraderie. He would watch the professional fighters and copy their moves, listening intently to the instructions given by their coaches, before mimicking what he had seen in front of a mirror.

Boxing became a part of home life too and he would engage in makeshift bouts in the living room with his older brothers, using one glove each if two pairs couldn't be found. Even there the youngest Greaves left no one in any doubt about his toughness. He more than held his own.

By 14 Johnny had been permanently excluded from secondary school for 'being a little git' and had started boxing at the East Ham and Boleyn Amateur Club. He was a decent enough competitor, contesting 40 bouts and winning more than half, but admits that even at this stage, his levels of dedication were low and he was 'fighting in spurts'.

The truth is that from ten years old he was already succumbing to the dark lure of the city and the night-time demons that have corrupted so many young men. He was staying out all hours, keeping bad company, on the booze and smoking weed. These would become spectres he would struggle to banish, even later, as a professional.

'You know,' he says, 'you start getting girlfriends and going to parties and boxing was always a big part of my life but never the be all and end all for me.'

John Sr was a big lump, a black cab driver and worked nights. He had split up with Johnny's mother when Johnny was nine. Shadows of alcoholism and domestic abuse hung over the house. To his dismay, the baby of the family and self-confessed mummy's boy watched helpless as his mum moved out and rented a bedsit. John Sr had always been the main breadwinner so all four children initially stayed with him. After a year or so Johnny's sister went to live with mum but she just simply wasn't earning enough money to support all the kids.

'My dad's a good man,' Johnny explains, 'albeit if you took liberties he'd give you a hiding, but that's OK. It never did me any harm. I still saw or spoke to my mum every day, which was important because we were always really close.

'But obviously when dad was out, working nights, I'd slip out. He didn't usually get in much before 1am and I'd be getting in shortly beforehand. I'd hear him come in and pretend to be asleep. I have three older siblings and I always knocked about with older boys and of course there was more dodgy business with them than there was with lads my age. So from very young I was smoking and involved in this and that around the area.'

It was a part of town that had a great many attractions for a directionless youth. Local lads were drawn to criminality like coins to a magnet, but Johnny wasn't enamoured with all of it. Growing up so near to the base of West Ham United, whose support carried a fearsome reputation back then, impacted upon him too though not in the way many might expect.

'I went to West Ham occasionally but the whole football thug mentality turns me off. There's not even that much real fighting that goes on, it's just a lot of running around and shouting. I knew some guys who were involved and they used to say it to me, "Oh it was mental, we had it with Tottenham" and it turns out they've stood outside a pub, thrown stuff through the windows and then legged it when the Old Bill turned up.

'I always thought how is that "having it?" It's not even a fight, is it? It's just a load of pathetic people trying to look hard. I often used to see about ten West Ham laying into two guys who supported another team, getting stuck right in, putting the boot in. Never appealed to me at all. To be honest, the average guy who goes to games every week and swears and shouts at the other lot and gives it all that, he's a plank as far as I'm concerned. Seeing that stuff happening helped me to understand my own attitude to fighting, because it's the opposite to theirs.'

The original ethos of boxing – the noble art, the sport of gentlemen as defined by the Marquess of Queensberry in 1867

– was in an honest and fair test of strength with another man, a violent code of honour. It may be a point that is lost on those who subscribe to the modern ideal that all aggression is wrong, but some fighting men have their morals too.

Finally, at 24 and after ten years of sporadic boxing in the amateur ranks, he was enticed to fight for money by Alan Mortlock, an almost mythical, gangsterish figure turned born-again Christian, who ran the unlicensed circuit now known as the IBA (Independent Boxing Association).

Johnny began on shows at the York Hall, the Circus Tavern in Purfleet and other local venues, quickly amassing a string of wins. Audiences enjoyed his resilience, aggression and in-ring character. It gave him an opportunity to play himself, his street self, before a crowd. The cheeky hard-case who wouldn't back down was suddenly in demand. Instead of being a nuisance he was an attraction. He would play with his opponents, dancing and joking while he fought. He entertained. Before long he was British champion in his weight class.

It was in one of these unlicensed contests that he had his first meeting with Colchester's Lee 'Lights Out' Purdy, a future world and European title challenger who he would also fight twice in the pros. Purdy won by narrow points decision, but the contest was a back and forth, ding-dong battle, so good that the audience was spiritually transported back to the 19th century and threw nobbins[2] in the ring at the end.

During these years, fighting for Mortlock, Johnny also got his first taste of the boxing business. He would sell tickets for his shows, receiving a 50-50 split with the promoter, meaning he often cleared £800 or so per contest. As the IBA grew in size and popularity however, it started putting on nights around the country, even as far away as Wales. Greaves clearly remembers the time when Mortlock made him the offer that got him thinking.

2 Nobbins is an old slang word, dating back to the bare-knuckle origins of boxing, referring to money thrown into the ring by the audience in appreciation of a good contest.

'"I'd like you to go up to Nottingham," Alan said. "Fight a boy up there. But listen, I want you to go in there, bounce around, make it look good, but don't win... And I'll pay you double."'

Financially, it was too attractive to refuse and Johnny did what he was asked to do, paving the way for how he would later make his name. After fighting Mansfield's Roger Brotherhood on one such away day, Johnny met Carl Greaves, the former Midlands Area super-featherweight champion, by then a professional manager.

'I first met Carl after fighting Roger,' Johnny remembers. 'Carl was in the crowd and having always been a big boxing fan I remembered him from when he boxed Alex Arthur on the telly, so I kept my eyes out for him. I was being paid double to lose that night and being me, I was pulling all the tricks out of the bag. It was my attitude even back then, I thought if I can't entertain people by winning I'll entertain them by acting a plank and messing about!

'So after the fight I got talking to Carl and he told me about turning pro and having to sell tickets for my debut and all that. The thing was, although in unlicensed I did OK with tickets, it was such an unbelievable pain in the arse. Even the day of the fight you're driving around collecting money, some people let you down and you get so stressed out that in the end, fighting is the last thing on your mind. It wouldn't be until you're on your way to the ring that you suddenly think, "I've got to have a fight here."

'Obviously the other thing, in the pros, it's not a 50-50 split. If you sell 80 tickets at £40 each, that's a face value of more than three grand, but there's so many overheads. Carl told me I'd probably get £600 for my debut. Well, I wasn't very impressed with that, so I said I'd think about it, but the truth was, I wasn't keen. It was going to cost about a grand for my medicals and I wanted a bit more money to make it worth my while. So anyway, Carl phoned me back ten minutes later and said he'd just had a request looking for someone to fight Rob Hunt in Doncaster. The offer was £1,200 all in. No ticket sales, £1,200, just turn up and fight, lovely! I accepted straight away.'

From that starting point under the guidance of Carl, Johnny went on to rack up 100 fights in six years. Every single one of them, apart from his final bout in September 2013, was taken in the same spirit as his first. He was on the road from beginning to end.

At 35 and five months into his retirement, Greaves still looks every inch the journeyman boxer. Small in stature and lively in movement, with a light-hearted manner but eyes that penetrate, he is an open and engaging talker. He describes himself as 'having a face like a robber's dog' but this isn't really fair. He does carry marks of his years in the ring, though. There is scar tissue over both eyes and his nose could be used to teach a maths lesson about obtuse angles. His ears look like they have taken a beating, too, but Johnny says he's always 'had big lug-holes'.

By far the most striking evidence of his career is seen on his hands. When he holds them up in front of his body and bunches his fists, lumps the size of golf balls pop up below his wrists, over his finger-bones. 'Kept breaking them,' he says. 'Bane of my life – when Lee Purdy stopped me in 2008 I was fighting one-handed, if that. My head wasn't right either, but that's another story.'

In a professional journey spanning six years and 96 defeats, he lost 12 inside the distance but was never counted out. 'Look, I'm proud of that,' he says. 'I've been in with all sorts, future world champions, real bangers, guys fighting in a weight division or two above me and I've never finished a fight on my pants. That tells you something. People might call me a bum or say I just did it for the money but I was never one of these guys – and there's a few about – that would bounce around for a while, take one good shot and fall over. I wasn't going over for anyone.'

The end finally came on 29 September 2013 after a specially arranged match with another journeyman, Dan Carr, from Wiltshire. It took place at the York Hall, his local venue and for the first time in his professional career he boxed in the home corner and was expected to sell tickets. The memory makes him smile.

'It was a tough one in some ways. I hadn't sold tickets since the unlicensed days. Shifted 140 though, which was nice. I really felt the pressure. I was nervous, genuinely nervous. I hadn't been nervous before a fight for years. My kids were there to see me for the first time. I didn't want to lose in front of them. Imagine if I had been knocked out in my last fight? Plus it was me against another journeyman. There's pride at stake – it's one thing losing to a prospect in his backyard, but a fight at the York Hall against another journeyman? I couldn't lose that.'

Johnny got the happy ending he was looking for. Referee Richie Davies awarded him a 39-37 decision and promoter Miranda Carter came up into the ring to present him with a bottle of bubbly and a commemorative photograph. He was visibly moved and interestingly, considering the pride with which he discusses his journeyman status, he ranks the whole experience as being the highlight of his professional career.

'All of it, the audience, the result, my kids being there, everyone coming down the pub after to say "well done" – it couldn't have gone any better. It meant a lot to me.'

As that last fight faded into memory, Johnny was still frequently spotted working out at the Peacock gym, his second home and where brother and erstwhile manager, Frank, works as a trainer. Boxing is littered with stories, often very sad ones, of fighters who just couldn't walk away from the game when they needed to. Old habits can be hard to break.

'There's times when I'm struggling mentally and I miss it all so much and I do think I could go back in and have a few more. My family don't want me to, but some days I wake up and my mood's so bleak I just feel like I need it.'

Early in June, five months after our interview, Johnny announced on social media that he was re-applying for his licence. He had been through a bad period psychologically and thought competing again could help him to re-balance. 'Stopping boxing has left a big hole in my life. It's hard to fill. But I went down the gym for sparring and just didn't feel like I have it in me anymore. Maybe its motivation, I dunno. My heart's writing cheques my body can't cash.'

The next day he posted another message confirming he would stay retired. He told me that the only thing that could tempt him back is a journeyman Prizefighter[3] tournament, an idea he had promoted himself several years ago, starting a campaign on the internet which gathered considerable public interest.

'Even Matchroom were quite interested in the idea,' he says. 'But the TV people put the mockers on it. I reckon it would be one of the best possible shows they could do. There's more than enough good journeymen out there and I tell you something now, most of the Prizefighter events, there's only one or two likely winners and the other guys are just there to make up the numbers.

'If you put eight journeymen in together, we'd all have a go – it'd be the most money any one of us would have earned in one night and it'd give the guys a little bit of glory, a little bit of publicity. They could do a back story to all of us, about our lives, all the fighters we've been in with and I reckon people would absolutely love it. In and around my weight class there's me, Kristian Laight, Sid Razak, there's loads of them and they all deserve it. They really should get more attention.

'I've always campaigned for more publicity for the journeymen fighters because I genuinely think they deserve it, not me because I'm retired now and I've been through it all for years, but the boys that are out there. The bottom line is a lot of people, nearly everyone, doesn't understand our job or how it all works. With the internet now, everyone can have their say and most of them don't have a clue. If I had a pound for everyone who said to me, "What was your record"? And I tell them four wins and 96 losses and they turn around and say, "You must be crap!" or something like that, I'd be a millionaire. People just assume that you can't box, I even read articles in newspapers where they've written things like that

---

3 Prizefighter is a boxing event run by the Matchroom promotional company and televised on Sky Sports, in which eight contestants fight over three three-minute rounds through quarter-finals, semis and a final, all in the same evening. The winner receives somewhere in the region of £32,000.

about me. They're trying to be nice but then say that I had no skill, but that's not the way it is at all.'

He leans forward and his expression becomes more serious.

'I tell you something right now, a rubbish fighter could never be a journeyman, there's plenty of winning fighters that couldn't do our job. We sometimes take fights at an hour's notice. I've been on the sofa having a couple of beers and a cigarette and the phone's gone and it someone asking me to be down the York Hall that same evening for a contest. How many of these prospects, or even champions, who, let's get this straight, are a little bit pampered, do you reckon could do that and go out there and put on a show?'

His personal record is that he once took a fight an hour and a quarter before it was due to start. He was at the York Hall as cornerman for his friend Jody Meikle and was approached by a panic-stricken promoter. 'Johnny,' he said. 'What weight are you right now?' 'About ten stone three,' came the reply. The promoter smiled, 'That'll do, wanna fight tonight?'

Of course, he knew what answer he would get. There had been a very late withdrawal, leaving a young prospect with no opponent and the possibility of going home without a contest, despite having sold a few hundred tickets. Johnny called his wife, asked her to put his shorts and boots in a bag and jumped on the train from Bethnal Green to East Ham. He was back in the venue, with his kit, 15 minutes before fight time. The show was saved.

'The thing that people should really appreciate,' Johnny says, 'on my night, when everything held together, I could always fight a bit. The other thing of course with a record like mine is that there's been plenty of times when I should have got decisions that I didn't. Sometimes it was blatant.

'For example, I fought a kid in Dublin and I was in a funny mood that night. I didn't want to play the game so I bashed him up. Really took it to him. He was hanging on. But the ref gave it to him anyway. You've got to laugh, literally. It was such a comical decision and I was laughing on my way out of the ring. Anyway it turned out later, the ref was related to the geezer's cornerman. You know, it's difficult enough fighting as the away fighter and some people don't even understand that, but once you throw things like that against you, you've got no chance.

'Of course, you know what really happened and so do they. I always made a point after every fight to go into the opponent's dressing room, shake their hand and say "well done, thanks a lot", maybe give them a couple of words of encouragement or advice. Sometimes I would walk in and it was a loser's dressing room. They know they've lost, I know I've won, the referee might have given it to them, but they know full well they haven't beaten me. And I can take satisfaction from that. I look back at my record now and I know the fights I've really won and the fights I've lost and it's not the same as what it says on paper.

'Now some lads have a few fights, struggle to sell tickets or whatever and turn around and say, "OK, I'll be a journeyman" but that double bugs me. Do you know what, most of them can't be journeymen because they're not good enough. There's an art to being a good journeyman. You learn a lot of tricks, how to ride a shot, how to waste a few seconds if you need to, turn your man, don't get hit with the big swings. There's a way to do it and I learned it through experience, but a lot of these youngsters haven't got a clue about any of it.

'People think it's just about tucking up, but it's so much more, knowing when to hold, if my opponent tried to get tricky on the inside I'd blindside the ref and hit him in the bollocks. I'll get in his ear and say, "Have you brushed your teeth today, your breath doesn't half stink. Is that your bird at ringside? She can't take her eyes off me. Look at the face on her though, do you need a licence to take her out in public?" And all this sort of thing.

'Sometimes in a clinch I'll give him a little kiss, grab his arse, anything I can think of to make him angry. If I can get him swinging at me and he's raging, we could do a hundred rounds and he's never going to stop me, I see everything he's throwing before he's done it. He'll be trying to hurt me with everything he throws and it's an easy night's work. I want him to be wild. Basically there's a lot of ways of doing it, of getting through a fight.'

Johnny's defence of his own record is spirited, anger bubbles behind it, his eyes flash. There is a part of him, no doubt, that would like the world to know how good he really is, how good he could have been, to look beyond the numbers, while another part acknowledges that he hardly ever fought with the result in mind. He attributes this to a lesson he learnt early in his career.

'In my 11th pro fight they put me in with this kid who had a losing record as well and I went after him and knocked him out in the first round. Now after that I had a couple of fights booked already, but beyond them the phone stopped ringing for a while. That's the way the game is. I couldn't afford to go without the work so generally after that I would toe the line. It's a balancing act between letting the home fighter get the decision but at the same time making the fight interesting.

'That's what a lot of the new, Eastern European boys don't understand. They bring some kid over from Latvia or wherever, the promoter pays him less than us and the boy thinks all he's got to do is follow the prospect around and take punches. It was never as simple as that for me.

'If the average Joe in the street thinks I'm rubbish, I don't care because it's fed my kids for the last few years. It's a tough game, you're going in there with these young pros, they're fit, strong lads, even the ones who aren't so talented. They train twice a day and they're up against me, I work long hours decorating and I smoke twenty a day. It's not always easy, but at the same time, I took pride in doing it the right way, standing up, not just caving in. You get the average pisshead in a pub sitting around saying "I could do that" but they've got no idea. Not a Scooby. Boxing's one of the easiest things to watch and think you can do, until you get in there and try it yourself.'

While he's speaking Johnny gives the impression that he's holding back. His arms, which are wiry and lean, rather than heavily muscled, are folded across his chest, hugging himself. His fingers twitch. Then suddenly he leans forward, his body opens up and so do his words.

'But let's also be completely honest here and maybe I shouldn't say this, but I'm retired now so I can speak the truth. People need to understand what they're looking at when they watch small-hall boxing. I have had fights, as a pro, where the promoter has said to me, "Look Johnny, for this one, here's a bit of extra money, you need to make sure. Go in there, have a move about."

'That means I have to guarantee the other lad gets the result. A lot of people have no idea about this side of it. Mostly journeymen are free to do what they want and if they start winning all they do is hurt their own livelihood, but there have been times, as a professional, when I have been paid to lose. The individual doing the paying wouldn't use those words, but that's what it is. I might ruffle a few feathers saying it, but there it is.

'The thing is, most of these kids, these prospects, they're not world-beaters and their management and promoters all know it. They don't tell the kid that, of course, they blow a load of smoke up their arse to make them believe in themselves. For those sort of jobs they'll only give you a day or two's notice. They do it on purpose. It's like playing cards with a stacked deck. They're doing everything they can to make sure their boy gets the "W" on his record. If they could get away with making you fight with a blindfold, they'd do that as well.

'That's what I mean when I say they're pampered. Everything's organised to be in their favour. From our point of view, it's an easy night's work. You know most of these kids can't hurt you so you go in, take it easy, bounce around, pick up the money and go home.'

The scenario seems straightforward enough: walk the opponent around, allow him to have a little workout, let him take it on points, but Johnny found that even this could sometimes present its problems. Young, naive, over-eager ticket sellers would not understand the reality of the game and put in performances so inept that his job was made difficult. In 2010 he fought a debutant called Floyd Moore, who went on to become Southern Area lightweight champion in December 2013.

'That night', Johnny says, 'I was given a little bit of extra money to look after Floyd. They said to me, "He's a massive ticket seller, we can be quids-in on him for years, so do your thing and give him a move about." When they say that and there's extra money on the table there's a reason for it. So obviously I went in there expecting a certain kind of fight, but I couldn't believe how it went. By the end of the third round I was literally holding Floyd up, over my shoulder!

'When they made the offer before the fight, I told them straight, same as always, "Look, I'm nobody's punchbag." So I said, "You tell your boy to take it nice and easy, box around, don't try anything silly and you'll have a points win no problem. I couldn't give a monkey's." But I don't know what happened, breakdown in communication somewhere, but Floyd has come out, straight from first bell, swinging away, trying to knock me out! And I weren't having it.

'There's a hell of a lot better fighters than Floyd Moore tried to knock me out and none of them could do it. So by the start of the second, Floyd had shot his bolt, he'd blown his beans and he was there, ready for the knockout at any time. All I needed to do was tap him. He could hardly lift his arms. It was an absolute nightmare! I could see the promoter watching from ringside and I'm trying to follow instructions – I tell you I couldn't have done any more to lose that fight!

'At the end of the third round I had him propped up on my shoulder and I'm saying in his ear, "Just stand up and move a bit, try and land a few, I'm not going to go after you." But he had nothing left. It was hard. And I remember straight after the final bell, trying to walk away from the referee, it was Mark Green I think and I saw him start heading towards me and I thought "oh no!" and turned my back. He was walking my way and I'm thinking, "Please don't!" and he's trying to lift my arm up and I'm trying to keep it down. So yeah, it was a bit of a problem that one because they gave me the win and I wasn't supposed to win.'

After the fight against Greaves, Floyd Moore went on to win ten contests, stopping seven of his victims inside the distance, including Johnny's friend Ryan Taylor for the Southern Area title. Greaves was genuinely shocked at the power Moore displayed in his other fights. 'I didn't think he could punch,' he says. 'I was talking about it with my brother, Frank, because he was in Ryan Taylor's corner when Floyd stopped him. Frank told me that he dropped Ryan heavily in the first and everyone in the game says Moore can bang, so I guess that's just me being a bit of a freak.'

After the decision over Moore was announced, Johnny had to be escorted from the ring by security due to the hostility provoked among Moore's large contingent of supporters. This was not an uncommon thing for him. Away fighters often contend with the vitriol of a crowd who are frequently related or connected in some way to the prospects they go in with.

'The thing is with it, there's stick and then there's abuse. To give you an example I was boxing a lad one time and someone at ringside shouted to him, "Go for his ears, you can't miss!" and I thought, fair play! I even stopped in the middle of the round and gave the geezer a clap. Now I don't mind that sort of stuff but when it gets too personal or people shouting things about your family, I used to think, well hang on, I'm here to do a job and that stuff did upset me. So if I felt they were crossing the line I'd give the crowd some stick back. Make faces at them and stuff. A few times I've had to get security walk me out of the ring.

'When I beat Floyd Moore it's just that his mob weren't happy. I think they wanted to give me the beating he couldn't, but you do have to be careful. There was a period when the Board were receiving letters complaining about my behaviour, saying I was inciting the crowd. I had to tone things down a bit because I didn't want to run the risk of losing my licence. But that was always out of order to me. You know, there's 500 people there giving me dog's abuse and I give a bit back, in a jokey way and the Board say I'm inciting violence!'

Despite the defensive nous and durability he displayed throughout his career, or maybe because of them, the 12 stoppage defeats still rankle with Johnny. Anthony Crolla, the former British lightweight champion and current WBO intercontinental champion, was the first man to stop him, in his sixth pro contest, followed by Darren Hamilton, the former British light-welterweight champ, in his eighth.

Altogether he lost inside the distance six times in his first 25 contests and then six times in his next 75. Of all those occasions, five were through cuts, meaning that only seven were as a result of the referee deciding he was taking too much punishment. Yet that part of his record is still something he is eager to address – although he took losing as a fact of life, being stopped troubled his journeyman pride.

'In all the stoppages I had, a lot of them were silly refereeing decisions, you know the ref being a bit of a jobsworth, looking out for the home fighter and jumping in when he landed two good punches, or on cuts. I always had a tendency to get cuts around my eyes which is a big problem for a journeyman. I would have got to a hundred fights much quicker if I hadn't got cut so much.'

Johnny states defiantly that he was only genuinely stopped three times: against WBA intercontinental welterweight champion Bradley Skeete, who at 6ft 1in is extremely tall for the weight; world and European welterweight challenger Lee Purdy – and Greaves says 'even that one was a bit iffy, really' – and former WBA world champion Gavin Rees.

'Skeete was just far too big for me. I swear to God, Skeete's arms must be about ten feet long. I remember the first round started and I was having a bounce about and having a look and he was miles away, so I had my hands down, all relaxed, waiting for him to get in range.

He threw a jab and it hit me right on the end of the nose and I was like, "Fuck! How'd you hit me from there?" My eyes were watering and I thought to myself, "Tonight's going to be a long old night." That one, I'm not going to lie, he hurt me a couple of times and when the ref stepped in, it was probably just about the right time.

'The other side to the Skeete fight is that I wasn't right mentally. I've always been a moody bastard and I was having a bit of an episode then. I remember having a blazing row with my corner in the middle of a round. My cousin Jason was working for me that night and he shouted at me, "Try to stay out the way!" just after I'd got done with a four punch combination, which pissed me right off. Stupidest bit of advice I've ever been given! I screamed at him, "What the fuck do you think I'm trying to do?" As if I hadn't thought of that! To be honest, boxing Skeete at the best I've been, I think I would have got through it, but not that night.

'To compare, when I look back on the fight with Johan Perez [the current WBA interim world champion at light-welterweight who boxed Johnny in November 2010] he was 9-0 and he'd knocked out seven. Now, he was a real heavy hitter. He hit me like a lorry. Seriously, the lad punches as hard as a heavyweight. He just had natural power, but I went the distance with him.

'The first jab that landed on my arms, I could tell he was so heavy-handed. I was lucky because the fight was scheduled for six rounds, but it was a floater on the bill and they ended up squeezing us in just before the main event, so it was reduced to four. I didn't want to lose my record of never getting knocked out, so I used every journeyman trick in the book that night – roughed him up on the inside, threw a few elbows. I even kicked him in the shin at one point!

'What was nice, after the fight he came into my dressing room to shake my hand. He didn't really speak English, but he tapped his head and said "loco" [crazy]. I took that as a compliment. Anyway, he was definitely the biggest puncher I went in with and I lasted the distance with him. That shows on my night I could hang in there with anyone.

'When I fought Gavin Rees, I took the fight at 16 hours' notice which was probably a bit silly against someone like that, but they offered me four grand so I took it. He's such a solid, stocky little lump of a bloke. He'd just lost his world title to Kotelnik when I boxed him and I thought you know, he's been world champion and I probably won't last two minutes, so what the hell, I might as well have a go here and I let my hands go.

'To be honest I was doing well for a while, but the thing with Gavin, he doesn't hit that hard but he's just so busy and he's constantly throwing shots at you. The sheer volume of work he produced made it difficult for me. He's a very good fighter, Gavin Rees.

'With Purdy, obviously there was history there. The first pro fight he came out all guns blazing, but it wasn't a problem. There was still a bit of needle from the scrap we had in the unlicensed days and Lee was desperate to knock me out. Things were getting a bit heated so to make a point, I sat on the ropes and gave him a few free shots, he must have hit me about six shots on the bounce and I laughed at him and carried on. Now maybe that's because I'm a bit of a freak, but also I don't think Lee's a banger, he's physically very strong and he'll bully you and push you about but he's not a banger.

'The second fight in the pros, when he did manage to stop me, I've come in there with two broken hands, virtually. I threw a punch, it hit the top of his head and it was so painful I just couldn't continue. The ref pulled me out and that was that. There's no needle there any more, I see him sometimes, down at Tony Sims's gym and I think once he got that stoppage in our third fight, that was his little bit of release and he's happy to see me now. The thing is with Lee he stopped almost all of his amateur opponents, virtually all of his unlicensed opponents, but when he got me it wasn't a genuine stoppage, really, it was on injuries. Still, we can let him have it if it makes him happy!'

Perhaps it is possible that in an alternative reality, in which Johnny had come into boxing with a different mentality, he could have left a mark at the other end of the business. His antics in the ring won him as many admirers as his toughness. Given a different set of circumstances, it is not inconceivable that his natural showmanship could have made him a ticket-selling title fighter.

'When you go in there and you're clowning it draws people in. Even with the unlicensed fighting I used to like to put on a bit of a show, I'd do the old windmill with the arms and make faces, the crowd always loved it. People enjoyed the way I performed. There were times on big shows with good fighters top of the bill and at the end people were talking about my fight. I'd do an Ali shuffle, although I don't think Ali had anything to worry about!

'I was a pale imitation, but people loved it. I'd have a bit of banter with the crowd before and during the fight. People hadn't really seen that sort of thing before. Some of the other boys do it now, especially Jody Meikle, but they'll tell you I taught them everything they know! It was really my thing that I started from the unlicensed days and I kept it going.

'I do know journeymen who have said, "Right I'm going to try going down the other road now and go for titles," but it's difficult. Once you've picked your path in boxing, that's that. You've got to start a training camp, eight weeks, ten weeks, whatever it might be, but then the phone's ringing and offering you this fight next week and that fight after that and if they're throwing one, one-and-a-half grand a time at you, it's difficult to turn down and before you know it, you're back to fighting three or four times a month.

'Even with my record, I was offered a couple of times to go for a Masters, but I never saw the point. It's a mickey-mouse title. No one who knows anything about boxing cares about it and what a lot of people don't realise is, if you win you have to pay for the belt out of your own purse. So if they're paying me a grand to be there, I might lose £350 just to take home one of those. You know I've been around professional fighters all my life and if I went down the gym all happy saying I'd won a title and they asked me which one and I said "a British Masters Bronze" or something, they'd all piss themselves laughing. It's meaningless.

'Now British title, if I'd turned pro ten years earlier, been looked after and lived the right life, got off the fags, gave up the booze, I reckon I could have got to that level. A lot of lads think it's all about the training, you just need to be fit and dedicated but I'll tell you that only gets you halfway. You need a bit of natural talent and I had that. Everything I did was self-taught, I went through all my unlicensed fights and I never had a trainer. I was just training in the Peacock gym and watching the pros. But yeah, turning pro at 29 and after having that first fight as an opponent, that was it, that was the way I went. I never had a time when I was picking and choosing my fights and having training camps.'

After saying that, Greaves' face drops, becomes melancholy. He pauses and sighs.

'Look Mark,' he says. 'There's more to it than that. Could I have done this? Could I have done that? The questions are always in my mind. I do feel, with my ability, I underachieved, but since I was a kid, I've had problems. Drink and drugs were huge things throughout my career. I was on the piss every day basically, three or four cans in the evening would be normal, but often I was bingeing as well, drinking all night, as well as using recreational drugs.

'On three occasions I was still pissed the morning I was fighting and then straight back on it after. The night before I boxed Oisin Fagan [at the National Stadium in Dublin, October 2009] I was holed up in my room with a couple of grams of coke and as much beer as I could chuck down my throat. They do a morning medical in Ireland and I was still out of it when they were checking me over. He was a decent fighter as well, Irish champion. Fuck knows how I got through that one.

'Another time I was travelling up to Sheffield to fight a lad, I was alone on the train, in a bit of a mood and got totally rat-arsed on the way. I took him the distance as well and the boy went on to win titles. Even when I fought Perez, the biggest puncher I faced, Frank barged into my room the morning of the fight, only to pull back the curtain and see endless empty wine and pint glasses. He's a world champion now and even after all that caper I took him to the final bell. I look back on my career and the things I did and in one sense you could say, a hundred fights? Not too shabby for a functioning alcoholic. But I'm not bigging myself up at all, quite the opposite. Really I should be dead.

'I think the truth is I was doing these things, knowing it was silly, but half hoping that I would go in the ring and something bad would happen. It was like I wanted to hurt myself, I suppose. I look back on it now and when I was fighting I sort of led a double life. Even from my close family. It just left me a fucking depressed wreck. If it wasn't for the support of my wife, my brother and my good mate Adam Darke I don't think I would have got through it.

'I've always let things get me down. I struggled with it even before I turned pro, even as a youngster. But if anything, boxing has given me something to concentrate on. When I was having a bad time, I'd get down the gym, get a sweat on, have a bit of banter with the lads and it would perk me up.

'I have actually thought about suicide. I have periods like that. Still do now. I knew Billy and Ernie Smith and what they did hit me quite hard, especially Billy, but boxing always pulled me around and now that I've finished and I look back, I do appreciate my career that I've had and the people that have nice things to say about me, it lifts me up. If anything, boxing was my saviour. It was never the cause of my depression.

'I think when mum and dad split up I took it very badly. I was the baby of the family, a young lad and that was the time I started to get into the smoking, drinking and fighting in the street and it's because nothing bothered me too much really, I didn't give a shit if I was in trouble or not. I didn't give a shit about anything and I didn't care about myself or any about consequences. It wasn't an easy time in my life and I guess I didn't cope too well.

'I think I'll always struggle with it. I can have a good couple of months, but all of a sudden I'll wake up and not want to talk to anyone. On the worst days I feel like I'd rather not be here. It's been the bane of my life for quite a few years now. When it crops up I see it coming and just have to deal with it. It is what it is. I wish I could put my finger on the reason why, but it definitely ain't boxing. Life for me is just hard work at times.'

Johnny speaks with obvious regret. Most people enter a sport for love and for the ten-year-old Greaves, who first went to the Peacock gym and admired the professional fighters he saw, there was something that captivated and excited him. Yet over time he turned boxing into something else, a way to act upon his self-destructive urges. Fortunately, he was streetwise enough to understand how the business functioned from the beginning. How he could turn it to his advantage and make it work for him.

'Hand on heart, no matter what anyone says, I don't regret my decision to be a journeyman. I never have. It was the best thing I ever did. Boxing saved my life. It gave me something to identify with, someone to be. And look, there's plenty of winning fighters who've had shorter careers than me, haven't boxed on the sort of shows I've boxed on and haven't been in with the sort of guys I have.

'I fought two world champions, more than ten British champions and I lasted the distance with these boys and that, to me, with all the odds stacked up against me was like a moral victory. I came away from that feeling like a winner, which I know some people might think is a funny way of looking at it, but it got me through it.

'Within the boxing scene I was known wherever I went. I remember fighting up in Sunderland against a boy up there and I came out and a load of young, local kids were all chanting my name. It was brilliant, gave me a lump in the throat and made me feel appreciated. Everyone likes that.

'Obviously the other side of it is when you come in against a lad and you think, well I could go and do a bit here, if I give it a go, I'm going to win this, but then again I could open up, bash him about, maybe catch a couple myself and I'm still not going to get the decision. So what's the point? I might as well make things easy.'

The decision to end his career was not an impulsive one. Since turning pro, the target of 100 fights had been set and stubbornly adhered to. As the number loomed towards him in 2013, doubt set in and he discussed with his family the possibility of continuing. The potential health risks of fighting on concerned his loved ones and his wife, brother and father dissuaded him.

'Every fight for me was another number closer to the hundred, which I said from the beginning was what I wanted to do. When I was thinking about going pro, I was already 29 years old and I told everyone I was going to have a hundred fights and they all said, "Nah, you won't do that." That's why I can't box again, because if I do, it'd have to be 150. But I can't pretend it was an easy decision.

'For the last few years, if I wanted to go on holiday, I've gone. If I wanted to go and buy something, I bought it. But now, I've gotta think twice. But then again, you're always going to miss it, I could have another 200 fights but I'll still have to retire one day. You can always tell yourself you're going to need the money, so you could carry on until you're 50 years old, I don't want to be fighting in my forties. I'm not Bernard Hopkins. That's a good way to end up in trouble.

'What I miss, more than the money, is the time with my brother and the other boys. Me and Frank have always been close and all the training and the day trips to here and there, it was such a big part of my life for so long and I do miss it. I miss turning up at the shows and seeing Kristian and Jody and some of the other lads, having a bit of a craic in the changing rooms. It's hard to fill that hole when you stop boxing.'

For the time being, the future for Johnny lies with his wife, Vicky, his young family and his job. He has little real interest in climbing back between the ropes, unless an irresistible offer comes his way, but he's already involved as a trainer, working with some youngsters at the Peacock, in particular Sonny Whiting, a super-middleweight who debuted in July by stopping a young journeyman called James Child.

Greaves has a wealth of wisdom to pass on, wisdom gained inside and outside the ropes. More than anything else he feels that through his boxing journey he has evolved as a person and is beginning to understand and appreciate himself. He is not quite there yet, but his days of recklessness and street violence are behind him.

'I have learnt to be careful now,' he says. 'The last time I had a problem, I was arrested for violence five years back. I was at a wedding and some fella was digging me out a bit. He was drunk and being a div and I'd told him to pack it in and he didn't, so unfortunately it all got a little bit out of hand. I had to do about 300 hours of community service for that. I was quite close to being banged up and that made me think a bit. Since then I try to keep a lid on it all. You know I've got a family now, so I've had to grow up. Boxing has been a big part of that too.'

So the country's most famous journeyman is not a journeyman anymore. His 15 minutes of fame seem to be over. The man who took the punches of some of the best fighters around for six years is just a regular guy now. Johnny Greaves – father, husband, painter and decorator. You can call him up if you need some wallpapering done, or some holes patched in your drywall. He could tell you a story or two while he's working. Yet those 100 fights have left their mark, forever, on him and on those who saw them.

'It'd be nice if people remembered how I performed, that I was an entertainer, that whatever they offered me, wherever it was, whoever it was against, I took it. If the money was right I would have fought in Timbuctoo or taken on Mike Tyson in his own backyard. I wouldn't ever say, "I don't want to go there, it's too rough." I'm not that sort of lad. Johnny Greaves fought anyone, anywhere, any time.'

5

The sins of the father, visited on the son

James Child

Super-middleweight
Born: Shoreham-by-Sea, Sussex, 3 May 1987
Active: 2012-present
Record: 1-12

IT is early September 1999 and the first day of a new school year. In Worthing, on the Sussex coast, in the kitchen of a terraced house full of the aroma of freshly-made toast, local fisherman and hard-case Greg Child imparts some well-intentioned words of advice to his boy.

At 6ft 4in, 266lbs and with a fearsome reputation, Greg towers over the lad, who is edgy and bites his lip. He has negotiated primary and middle school without too much fuss but is understandably nervous about joining the seniors.

'What you do,' Greg says, looking straight in his son's eyes, 'as soon as you get in there, look at the older boys, have a good look, all right? Now listen. I want you to single out the biggest, toughest one, the one who thinks he's the ringleader, the school bully, pick the right moment and go and beat the shit out of him. If you do that, you'll never have a problem.'

Young James, fair-haired and innocent, idolised his dad, not yet of the age where he might question his parent's wisdom. He nodded, absorbed the words stoically and put them into action, point-by-point. In doing so he set into motion a chain of events that would affect the rest of his life.

I drove to meet James Child, a 26-year-old southpaw still in the early stages of his professional journey, as I was curious to find out what would motivate a young boxer to choose the journeyman path. It can't be an easy decision to reach, I thought, as I followed him up the steps to his flat in windblown Goring-by-Sea, to abandon dreams of wealth and fame in exchange for a life on the road. Child is clearly in great shape, with weight distributed where he needs it, around the shoulders and upper back. On paper he presents a curious case.

In his early 20s, as a big punching amateur, James looked promising, winning 20 of 26 fights, with 19 victories coming by KO or TKO. He collected a silver medal in the Haringey Box Cup and a few other trophies along the way. There are many fighters with worse amateur records who have gone on to lift British titles or more, so to go from that starting point, to losing fights for a living did not seem an obvious transition. Once we had met and I started following his career, while keeping in touch, I learnt that this choice really was a source of inner conflict for him.

James spoke calmly and articulately, explaining that before that first day of secondary school, as a younger boy, he had steered well clear of trouble, even finding himself the victim of occasional bullying. It was never serious stuff, just the name-calling and jostling of infants but after one such occasion at the age of six, which he found upsetting, he went home and told his father, a prominent figure in nearly everything he speaks about, who had a suitably old-school solution.

'Dad got an old mattress,' James recalls, 'wrapped it around a pole in the garage and told me to hit it. That was my first punchbag. I practised that evening, just punching and punching. The next day I found the boy who caused me trouble and smacked him in the face. He never bothered me again. So there it was, toddler justice, after my first lesson!'

As a youngster he quickly developed into a promising sportsman and found that among his peers he excelled at everything from football to long distance running. He started attending judo club where he reached international class and developed impressive strength for his tender years, but he found when he made the move from primary to middle school, with older children around, social interactions became more challenging. Kids became cheekier. Some began to take liberties. Unlike at primary, there were those at his new school who wanted to try their luck against a boy who gave the appearance of being able to handle himself.

'I started to get in a few scuffles,' he says. 'I guess I just stopped taking people's nonsense, really, and I learnt that letting your hands go wasn't so difficult, that knowing how to fight wasn't a bad thing. People respected it a lot. So I didn't get bothered much.'

From there, James moved on to St Andrew's High School where his path was set by following his dad's advice and setting about the school bully on the first day of his first year. As a 12-year-old, being able to go in and physically dominate the toughest 16-year-old on campus automatically marked him out as top boy among his peers and a serious troublemaker among staff. Very often moments like this determine futures and James feels that his actions that day have had serious repercussions.

'That was when I started to become the aggressor,' he says. 'Up to that point I had only defended myself against kids starting on me. There were a couple of lads at secondary that were school bullies and my dad was right. I learnt if you gave them a good hiding, no one would try anything with you. So from that day on I had a reputation and when you have a reputation it's hard not to live up to it. That probably didn't set me off on the best path through school. I've only ever got in trouble for violence, never anything else. But when I was young and hot-headed, I thought I could beat everyone up and nothing else mattered.'

Even teachers sometimes felt his physical strength. 'I never went so far as to hit a teacher,' he says, 'but sometimes they would come to break up a fight up and I would grab hold of them, throw them out of the way and carry on. It would take two or three of them to restrain me.'

On one occasion, at the end of the school day, an angry father came to remonstrate with him about beating up his son. Rather than engage the man in discussion, the 15-year-old James took exception to his confrontational manner and simply battered him as well.

'I was a strong lad,' he recalls. 'In the gym I could outlift my PE teachers at 14. I guess I just didn't have the maturity to handle my strength.'

Child rapidly became known as the toughest kid at St Andrew's, a reputation he retained until leaving, which remarkably was at the end of year 12. The school's policy was that four suspensions would result in permanent exclusion but despite exceeding that fairly early on, his mother managed to keep him on the roll by pleading his case. This practice would soon come in handy as before long his infamy would spread beyond the school gates and mum would be defending him in court. James became a known face in the area, a boy at war with the world, but truly at war with himself. Leaning forward, he reflects gently, stroking his gingery stubble. There is a hint of sorrow in his voice.

'I was a big lad for my age, not necessarily huge in terms of frame, but I was always training. I started lifting weights when I was 12. And my dad was such a dominant figure. I love him, but having him around made me toughen up a lot quicker. He wasn't always the easiest man to live with. I think all the fighting side of me, it comes from him.

'I learnt from my dad that by being a tough guy you could earn everyone's respect and make your life a lot easier. So although I sometimes clash with my father, I've grown up to emulate him, maybe not in the best ways. I can have a bad temper. I try not to be as unreasonable as him at times, but I don't always succeed.

'My old man never boxed but he was a tough, brawling character and as a young boy I often saw him sorting out disagreements with his fists. I sometimes went to sea with him and I guess I enjoyed witnessing the respect he had from other fishermen. You know, disputes would break out and my dad had no qualms about settling them using force in front of me.'

James describes the memories, shiny eyed, half smiling. It is clear his father's actions left an indelible mark on his psyche. The boy was impressionable and learnt, as we all do, by example.

Predictably, before long, the belligerent attitude imbued in him led to trouble with the law. 'Unlike a lot of my friends and schoolmates, I wasn't interested in drink or drugs. I was just super fit, I preferred that high. When we were old enough to go for nights out, everyone would be getting smashed and I'd be on juice. I'm still like that now. But I still always got into fights.'

His willingness to engage in physical confrontation at a moment's notice began to lead to arrests and cautions. The first time he came to the attention of local police was after a conflict with a neighbourhood troublemaker who lived next door to his parents. The boy fancied himself as a hard-case, but attended a different school and was unaware of James's reputation. One morning he decided to try to knock James off his bike by swinging a length of chain at him.

As if that wasn't bad enough, he followed this up by launching fireworks at Child and a group of friends in a local park, before shouting abuse and walking off. Already riled from their first encounter, James flipped, chased the lad through the streets and caught him on a corner where he 'beat him until he stopped moving'. It was a savage attack, although many might say justified. The victim was hospitalised and James was arrested on a charge of actual bodily harm.

From there, the incidents continued to rack up. His mother was understandably mortified that her son should keep getting himself into trouble.

'She was in and out of courtrooms with me all the time,' he says. 'She was always dragging me there and back, making me deal with what I'd done and she'd be the one to have some harsh words with me. My dad would be very matter-of-fact. He'd always say that if you're going to do something naughty, you're going to get the punishment, so deal with it. He'd laugh about it most of the time. To give you an example, there was a time I beat up a kid in the town and got arrested. My dad came down to the police station to pick me up and he bought me a curry. "Did you win?" That was all he wanted to know.'

Child now has a fairly extensive criminal record with six convictions for violent offences, resulting in tagging orders, fines and community service, narrowly escaping prison on the last couple of occasions. On his most recent sentence he was sent to work in an animal shelter where he picked up a rottweiler, called Benson, who was about to be destroyed. The huge dog lolled around in his living room while we talked, showing admirable patience to put up with my one-year-old daughter who pestered it fearlessly. 'I've always had a soft spot for animals,' James explained. 'I couldn't bear the thought of letting him die.

'During that time when I was always in trouble I made a couple of visits to Shoreham boxing gym. My parents suggested it as a way to learn some discipline. I enjoyed it and trained really hard, but returned to my first love of football. I was a decent player. I got sent on a scholarship scheme to Newcastle United and had trials at several professional clubs but in the end I got frustrated with the game. I was always being let down by my team-mates.

'I was playing at county level and was always fit and ready. I trained so hard but guys were turning up pissed to play, like drinking before games and I used to get really annoyed about it. When it came to sport I always had a professional attitude, even then. It's funny that I've ended up becoming a journeyman because I've always wanted to win, had to win, in everything I've done.'

By the age of 18, James had been hampered by continuous niggling injuries and realised the opportunity for professional football had probably passed him by. Other options were limited. He had left school with a few GCSEs, an AS Level and some NVQs but there was nothing he wanted to go for. He toyed with the idea of training to be a diver in the Navy, but was prevented from applying because of his criminal record.

'That's when I started to go to Cheetahs boxing gym in Brighton, just for something to do, really. Pretty soon I was sparring with far more experienced fighters. From the beginning I was heavy handed. I always had that. I loved training, but at the same time I was still going out and getting into trouble around the town. Pretty much every time I went for a night out I'd end up in a fight. I was a bit young, mentally and I thought the boxing was just making me tougher. I hadn't learnt the discipline that goes with it.'

Before long he was on the cusp of being carded for his first amateur contest, but got himself into an altercation on the street and broke his right hand. He had several operations over a period of months before it healed and by then the chance for his debut had gone. Once the pins and plates had been removed, James started again at the Hove Boxing Club, recommended by his mother, where former British and Commonwealth heavyweight champion Scott Welch worked as a trainer.

'I was a little intimidated the first time I walked in,' James remembers. 'There were some big guys in there and it had a serious atmosphere. It was a proper boxing gym.'

For six months he knuckled down to his new craft, often being the first to arrive and the last to leave. 'I fell into myself,' he says. 'It just seemed so natural. I would start hitting the bags and it wouldn't just be a few rounds, I would be in there for hours and hours, just hitting and hitting. Being surrounded by those guys, who had won professional titles, it was inspiring. I wanted to be like them. I guess one of the things I love about boxing is that we are like the last living gladiators. It's not a usual thing to do and people respect that. On that level, it suited me down to the ground. At the time, there was nothing else I wanted.'

Eventually he caught Scott's interest and after one particularly long session Welch offered James a lift to the station. The two spoke properly for the first time in the car and from then James found he started to receive more attention in the gym. Before long he was training regularly with the big man.

'Scott has been a massive influence on me, a huge part of my life. He sorted me out and steered me on to the right path. He stopped me being such a bad lad. He had been a rough kid himself and he was able to relate to me. He knows how to talk to me, to make me see sense. It's exactly what I needed back then.'

Child's amateur career began at 19. His fitness levels and natural power, particularly with his southpaw left, gave him a great platform to build on. He blitzed his way through most contests and the majority of his amateur opponents simply crumbled under his assault. 'I thought I was indestructible,' he grins. 'I just used to run out of the blocks and try to get them out of there. Usually I could.' As boxing careers go, it was a strong start.

His continuing problems with the law continued to have knock-on effects however. At one time he had to apply to court to have a tag removed so that he could go to a venue and box. Curfews and community service orders often interrupted his training. His life still seemed to lack any sort of clear direction.

At 24, Welch felt James had more dues to serve in the amateurs but the young buck was eager to start making something of his life and earning money. Gym-mates Lloyd Ellet and Chris Eubank Jr had turned pro and he felt it seemed like the right thing to do. Eubank's trainer Ronnie Davies actually got the professional registration forms for James and he sent a message to west London's Mickey Helliet requesting his managerial services.

Looking forward to a successful paid career, he spoke to a local paper, the *Littlehampton Gazette*, which ran a story in May 2012 with the headline, 'Boxer Child turns pro and eyes British title'.

In the interview, James made the accurate observation that all-action, pressure fighters such as himself often fare better in the pros than the amateurs. Towards the end of the piece he is even quoted discussing world championships.

By the middle of 2014 however, Child had fought 13 contests in Norwich, Walsall, Milton Keynes, Birmingham and other venues far from home, of which he had only won one. Reality had bit on his debut.

'It was just the paper hyping it up,' he says. 'They were trying to build it into something massive when it wasn't. It was just another lad turning over really, but yes, I was thinking of titles back then.'

His first professional contest, in November 2012, was scheduled for the Coronet Theatre in Elephant and Castle, south London, against 25-year-old Lithuanian Arnold Lydekaitis, another Helliet-managed boxer. It should, in theory, have been a cakewalk for Child. Unfortunately, James found ticket selling tougher than expected. Large crowds had turned out to see him in the amateurs but for his local fanbase, a Friday afternoon trip from the south coast to the capital was a major inconvenience. For many people it involved organising time off work. They were reluctant to commit themselves.

'It was tough because I was determined to be a home fighter. I wanted to get looked after and do as well as I could,' James says. 'I can't blame people because it was a difficult situation, but it made things tricky for me.'

He only managed to sell 68 tickets. It was enough to pay for the opponent, the house, his manager's cut and the officials, but James was left out of pocket. Rather than cancel his debut, he agreed to fight for nothing.

'By the time of the fight I was so full of nerves. But it was more to do with the ticket sales than the actual fight. The guy wasn't as good as me, it's as simple as that. I should have wiped the floor with him. But I'd built so much pressure on myself and I didn't deal with it well. It was strange, I was never hurt at all, but when I hurt him, I backed off. I was tentative. Because of all the ticket problems, I was questioning myself and whether I should be doing it, before I even got in the ring. It just all felt wrong.'

The mental side of his game had gone and at the final bell, he was forced to face a harsh truth. Referee Jeff Hinds scored 40-37 for Lydekaitis. The reality was almost too much to bear. 'I felt terrible,' he says. 'I cried in the changing room afterwards. It took me a long while to get over it.'

He returned home to girlfriend Kayleigh, licking his wounds and promising that if he was going to fight professionally again it would have to involve a guaranteed payday. Back in the gym he got talking to trainer Paul Newman, who first floated the idea of going in as the away fighter. 'The idea scared the hell out of me at the time,' James says. 'It was never the direction I imagined my pro career going.

'The more Paul talked about it though, the more sense it made. He spoke about the money that could be earned, how regularly the fights can come up, how you don't need to worry about ticket selling, so I thought it over and decided to swallow my pride and do it. I phoned up Mickey and told him I'd like to book my next fight as the away fighter. Mickey just said OK and that was that. It went from there.'

James's second contest was against debutant Jake Gosling in Southampton. He was more relaxed this time and bombarded his opponent with an arsenal of heavy shots, wobbling him on several occasions. But Gosling was a strong boy himself and fought back.

'I have to be honest, in that the pro game is tougher than the amateurs. There's more to it than just the home and away corner thing. That's important, of course it is, but it's not just that. For the guys you're fighting, it's their livelihood and they're not just going to fall over when you bash them a couple of times.'

It turned into a 50-50 tear-up. 'For my part,' James says, 'I hadn't got it in my head yet, because it was only my second fight, that I was there to lose.' Nonetheless, he did lose and despite the closeness of the contest was surprised that referee Grant Wallis scored every round for Gosling.

Even by his sixth pro bout, in September 2013, old habits were hard to break for Child. He fought east Londoner Kevin Greenwood at York Hall and started every round aggressively, pushing his man back to the ropes before seeming to tire, stepping off and allowing him to take over. He won only one session of six that night.

James would go on to lose his first seven fights by decision. In all of those contests, amounting to 28 rounds of boxing, the round against Greenwood was the only one he won. He tied two rounds and lost the rest. Life in the red corner was making its mark.

'I still struggle now with the idea that I'm not supposed to win. Sometimes I hit the guy with a good shot and I can see he's buzzed and I think, "Why don't I just jump on him?" But slowly I can feel my mind slipping into the journeyman train of thought – it becomes a habit after a while. Once my mindset started changing, I went off the boil a bit with the training. I did feel a bit demotivated. Sometimes I'd just turn up to fight half-fit and tough it out.

'So I know what it's like to go in the ring and feel unprepared. You know you're just there to survive then. It's a lonely place. Even my last fight as an amateur was at cruiserweight, I'd been on holiday for two weeks, I'd come back and basically went straight in there. My only chance was to knock him out in the first, which I didn't manage to do so I knew I was going to lose. Sometimes as a pro it's been a bit like that too.'

In his ninth fight, in November 2013, he suffered a TKO defeat, for the first time, to Lennox Clarke in Walsall. The memory still annoys him.

'It was never a stoppage,' he says. 'It was the trademark scenario that the guy that was there to lose was getting the better of the home fighter and I was going to stop him. And the first opportunity they got, they jumped in and gave it to the big ticket seller. I mean he put me down in the first round with a genuine shot, but I came back at him strongly and was taking the fight to him. I put him down and he was down for quite a while, then he got up and the ref ruled it a slip! I hit him with a big hook and he was all over the place, holding on, trying to tangle me up for a good minute. As we came out of the clinch he caught me with one shot, but I was fine and the referee's waved it off. Even his own fans were booing!

'But that's the fight game at this level for you. It's all about money and the money side of boxing corrupts a lot of elements of the game. Lennox Clarke is a big ticket seller and they had him out again a month later, which he wouldn't have been able to do if he'd been stopped himself. Obviously if that had happened, they'd be losing out on a lot of ticket sales. So it couldn't be allowed to happen. For me as well, it was just before Christmas and it stopped me working.

'I definitely wouldn't say that officials are all corrupt but the promoters do seem to have a sway on the fight and the decision. I've experienced this a bit from my side. A couple of times I've been told before a fight that it's my job to look after the opponent and stay on the back foot.'

Through his experience of turning professional and realising, perhaps for the first time, that he is unable to just bludgeon his way through anyone and anything, James has started to re-evaluate his life. He has been out of trouble with the law for two years, basically since turning pro. Some of this he puts down to girlfriend Kayleigh, who would 'tell me off' if he repeated his old habits. He also accepts that ever since school he has had a problem with authority and that this led to a massive chip on his shoulder in later life.

'It got to the stage where I was such a known figure, the police even used to stop me when I was out for a run. Of course, being me I would just carry on running. They'd put the lights on and everything and I'd just ignore them until I'd finished. Then I'd stop and say, "Sorry, I had my headphones on." That was the sort of attitude I had. And I realise now, it didn't do me any favours. Kayleigh has really helped me to evaluate things and I feel like I've calmed down a lot. I look at it now and think I don't want to end up in prison. I don't want to limit my opportunities like that. There's too much to live for to go down that road.'

He hopes to train as a diving instructor and is using the money from boxing, along with help from his father, to fund the course, which costs upwards of £15,000.

He also has plans to marry Kayleigh and possibly start a family. Being a journeyman, he recognises, can help achieve these things, even if it means keeping his natural instincts, to win and dominate, in check.

'The way I look at it is that I'm losing, but I'm not, because the money I'm earning is more than your average person and it's helping me get to my goals, so I'm winning in my own way, on my own journey, just maybe not in the eyes of the public.'

It does mean that through this process, boxing for him has ceased to be about enjoyment and 'falling into himself' as it once was and is now largely about pound notes. This could be seen as sad, but James has chosen his path. And in doing so, he has grown up. Deep within him though, the sporting fire still burns.

'I would still love to pick up a title of some sort before I get out of it, just as an accolade to have. Even for my family and the people who have backed me, it would be nice to do it, just an area title or something like that.'

He remains convinced that if boxing was structured differently and ticket sales and business were not such issues, he could have gone to title level, certainly domestically. Perhaps, for some, there is poetic justice in a one-time bully and tearaway now losing fights for a living. But he says he has made his peace with the choices he has made and the path he has taken.

Coming to terms with his ever lengthening loss column was made easier when after a year-and-a-half as a pro he finally picked up his first win, a 39-37 points decision over Didier Blanch, another journeyman, in Brighton in October 2013.

'I was so happy to get it. My dad had been taunting me, calling me a loser and once I'd got that win, it was a weight lifted off my shoulders. The old man congratulated me and said, "I can't call you a loser any more." That meant a lot to me. It might sound silly, but it did.'

He is now looking forward to a busy future and hoping to be as active as possible, to maximise earnings. For the first time in his career he had two fights in a month, in March 2014, both defeats. He was unlucky in the second of them, against big ticket seller Carl Dickens at Villa Park on the 14th. Child worked well off the jab for three rounds, then opened up in the fourth, cutting his opponent and having him hanging on by the end. True to form, however, referee Shaun Messer awarded a 40-37 decision to Dickens. James shrugged off the disappointment philosophically.

'From now on I just want to keep the fights coming. I'd like to have 20-odd fights a year. I've matured in my head, so if I rack up the losses it doesn't bother me. If I take nothing else from boxing, it set me up and got me back on track. I think a lot of kids can learn from that. Boxing really straightened me out. It's taught me to be humble.

'No matter how big you are or how strong you think you are, in the pro game there will always be someone who can knock you around and put you in your place. Until I boxed professionally I didn't understand that. The work ethic that boxing's given me will stay with me forever too. I can see a bright future now, whereas maybe I couldn't a few years ago.

'In terms of being a journeyman, you know, I could have hung on, trying to sell tickets. I'd probably only have had two or three fights by now. What would be the point in that? The main thing, through it all, the training, the defeats, the lessons that it's taught me, I've learned to respect myself.

'I look forward a few years to the time when I have hung up my gloves and the main thing is to have set myself up, financially. Obviously I also want to make sure that I retire from boxing and not that it retires me.'

He has mixed with many current and former fighters and met fellow journeymen in the away changing room, which in contrast to the nervous tension of the home side, is usually a place of banter, laughter and camaraderie. He sees plenty to admire but also things he is not so keen to emulate.

'I have tremendous respect for all these guys,' he says. 'They're absolute warriors and they've fought so many times in tough, hard contests and they always put on a good show. As much as these winners that do great things and win world titles, these guys are real heroes, very, very tough men. They deserve the respect of everyone and it's a shame they don't get it. But some of them and it's not nice to say it, but it's true, they've damaged themselves. They should have called it a day a long time ago.'

He is a keen student of boxing history and has seen the Benn v McClennan and Eubank v Watson fights with their associated tragedies. He has met and spoken to Michael Watson in person. As a result James is very aware of the dangers that fighters can face, especially in and around his weight division. At super-middleweight and light-heavyweight it is generally acknowledged that the risks are the highest. The combination of speed and power that lends sharpness to the punching, combined with smaller skeletons compared to the giant heavyweights means the risk of brain injury is increased, especially for those who take a lot of punishment.

'I would hate to end up like that,' he says. 'I don't want my girlfriend to be baby-sitting a vegetable at the end of it all. Boxing, for me is an opportunity, a chance to take something big out of it and earn myself a decent future.

'It does worry me sometimes, because around my weight there are some very dangerous guys and there isn't that much distance between me and them. At one point I was ranked 32 in the UK and I was thinking, "I'm only 31 behind Carl Froch!" That's a daunting thing!'

Looking back on his story, from start to finish, he nods gently. He speaks almost in a whisper.

'As a tough kid you attract the wrong kind of crowd. A lot of the kids who were up to no good, hung around with me because of my reputation. My ways of dealing with confrontational situations were always with my hands instead of with my head. So I learnt to handle myself from a very young age, but it's never like it is in the ring, when you're in a street scuffle. It's not as technical. You just go in there windmilling and get the job done. The thing about it all, I never questioned what I was doing until recently. Learning to box made me think, made me realise some things.

'Sometimes I wish I'd been brought up to be a bit cleverer with my mouth rather than my hands. It would have saved me a lot of trouble. But then I'm happy with where I am now and I couldn't have got to here without being there first. I will never regret having got into boxing, ever. It's the best thing I ever did.

'So they can call me a journeyman and that's alright. It's what I am. I've been on a journey and all journeys start somewhere. There can be problems along the way. But now I like where my journey is going.'

Six months after I interviewed James Child, things were not going quite as well as he had hoped. In the first half of 2014 he had fought only five bouts. This was partly due to the fact that he had been stopped in the first round in two consecutive fights, serving 28-day suspensions for each, followed up by being put down and stopped in the fourth in July by Johnny Greaves's protégé Sonny Whiting.

'He was game,' Johnny told me. 'Child had a real go and he's strong, but you can't walk straight at someone who's sharper than you. We've been working very hard with Sonny and he was just better on the day.'

'I've been working,' James explained. 'I wasn't earning enough in the ring so I've been working and not concentrating on my training. The last three results are just a show of that, I think. It's going to be different from now on. I've got a nutritionist and I'm training properly again. I'm hoping to move down to middleweight, eventually even light-middle, get back to making money and winning respect.'

James knew that if he continued suffering stoppage losses, especially early ones, it would mean the end of his career, journeyman or not. Even if the Board let him keep his licence, eventually promoters would stop using him. Durability is the number one requirement in the away corner.

It also seemed that despite everything, he still hadn't fully settled into the journeyman thought process. Losing habitually hadn't yet become something he could happily accept. Perhaps it would take him years. Perhaps he would never manage it. Ambition still lurked within. Part of him cherished ideas of starting again, taking the other path.

'Who knows?' he wondered, with the possibility in his mind that if he could take his punching power down to middleweight, he could yet be a force to be reckoned with. 'I might be the journeyman who came back and turned it all around.'

Even in the lop-sided world of professional boxing, I guess anything is possible.

6

The Enigma

Bheki Moyo

Light-welterweight
Born: Ladysmith, South Africa, 10 June 1974
Active: 2005–present
Record: 0-67-2

O N 17 November 2005, unbeaten Welshman Gary Buckland climbed into a ring assembled in a conference hall inside Ashton Gate, the home of Bristol City Football Club. It was the fourth fight of his professional career. Large windows edging the room afforded spectators a view of the pitch below and the crowd, already well-oiled from several hours of bar use, hummed with anticipation. Buckland was considered a fairly hot prospect, having won seven Welsh amateur titles as a youth and competed at world level, while his opponent, in a light-welterweight contest over four three-minute rounds, was a little-known South African, fighting out of west London, whose record at the time stood at 0-2.

At first bell, Buckland, craggy and square-bodied, an in-your-face pressure fighter, bore down on his opponent but found him an elusive target. The Welshman pursued from corner to corner, punches carving arcs in the air or landing on arms and gloves. Occasionally the away boxer would fire back jabs, not stiff, hurtful ones but little pokes off the back foot, just enough to give Buckland something to think about. The odd one sneaked through the Welshman's guard. It was a difficult round to score.

Unhappy with how things had gone in the opening session, Buckland upped his workrate in the second and applied yet more momentum. He was clearly the busier of the two fighters but still struggled to land anything of real note. The African used the ring nicely, moving with fluidity and boxing behind a tight defence. The effects of his sporadic offensive work were shown on Buckland's slightly reddened forehead. As a contest it was still waiting for a spark to bring it to life.

Both fighters clinched as the bell went to signal the end of the second session and the referee, Mike Heatherwick, said something that neither man heard as he separated them.

Bheki Moyo went back to the red corner with positivity. It was three years since his arrival in the UK, only four months since he had turned professional. This could be the night when things finally started to go his way. Buckland was tipped for big things but despite working hard, he had done nothing that Bheki couldn't handle.

Bheki felt he was frustrating the Welshman and suspected he would tire. As he sat on his stool, trainer Gary Innis offered some words of advice for the approaching third. With home advantage it was likely that Buckland was ahead on points but the fight was still very much within reach. Moyo heeded the message, breathed deeply through his nose, stood and tensed his arms, ready to return to battle. He would wait for the right moment, for the time when Buckland had expended just a bit too much energy and begin to turn the screw.

With only moments remaining before the bell, he bit down on his gumshield and looked across the ring. The Welshman had remained seated. Which Buckland would he be facing now? The one who had seemed a little off the pace in the opener or the more confident, second round version? He tried to read the Welshman's eyes.

Before he had a chance to find out, Moyo felt an arm across his chest. It was the referee. 'It's over,' he said. Without his knowledge, the fight had been stopped at the end of the second round. Incensed, he pushed away the ref's arm. 'What the fuck are you talking about?' he cried. Chaos ensued.

Cornermen from both sides jumped in the ring. A scuffle started. The arena reverberated with the boos and catcalls of the crowd. Even the Board officials seemed confused.

Moyo had grown up fighting. As a black South African born in the apartheid era, injustice was as familiar to him as breathing. Perhaps this is how he came to terms with what had transpired so quickly. While those around him lost their heads, Bheki's composure returned.

Soon he was acting as the peacemaker, breaking up the jostling cutsmen and spit-bucket carriers, asking others to calm down. He knew. It was done. It didn't matter that the stoppage was unjustified and bizarre. All that mattered was that he now had another 'L' on his record.

Since that night in Bristol, Gary Buckland has gone on to become British super-featherweight champion, win a Prizefighter tournament and go 1-1 in a high profile brace of fights against former world title holder Gavin Rees. At the time of writing he was independently ranked 46th in the world and was about to challenge for the Commonwealth lightweight title.

Moyo, on the other hand, has gone a different way and built one of the most intriguing records in professional boxing history. Even by journeyman standards, to have not won a single bout from 69 is unusual.

'People don't understand it,' Bheki says, 'because they are looking at it from the way they've been led to believe it's supposed to be. You're supposed to win your fights. All that really matters is whether or not there is a "W" on your record. They don't see what goes on in there, the home fighter/away fighter principle and the injustices that can happen. Decisions are not always based on the rules of the sport, but on other factors. I strongly believe that in a different business and if my fights were judged completely fairly I would have won more than I have lost.'

Bheki Moyo was born in a black township near Ladysmith in the Kwa-Zulu Natal province of South Africa, home of Thulani 'Sugarboy' Malinga, the two-time WBC super-middleweight champion of the world. He was one of eight children and their home was a rural idyll. His near-permanent grin gets slightly broader as he describes his early childhood environment as 'beautiful'. But life as a black South African in the 1970s and 80s was not always easy and his early years were tough by modern, British standards. Under the apartheid system, still in operation at the time, little race mingling went on other than in cities. The black majority were restricted to townships. It was a time of hope and eventual change, but for most of the black population also struggle and oppression. From these beginnings, Bheki the fighter was created.

'I was not a bully as a boy,' he recalls. 'I would not bother other kids, but from a young age, if a fight started, I would not hesitate to get in there. It was a stupid bravery of some sort. I really didn't care how big the other boy was, even if he was two or three years older I would just get stuck in! I found out quickly that I could hold my own. I could take on these much bigger guys and beat them. At the time, it gave me a sense of pride.'

At the age of nine he moved to Johannesburg and regularly saw faces of other colours around him for the first time, but it was still 11 long years before apartheid fell and most of the old institutions remained in place. Citizens had to carry an identity card demarcating their ethnic group, blacks and whites did not live in the same areas or share leisure facilities. Even parks and beaches were assigned to one race or the other and infringement of these laws could lead to arrest. Still, on the streets, at work and in some shops and businesses, races would intermingle. But for the citizens of the emerging Rainbow Nation, this was not always a happy experience. Bheki's genial manner becomes serious and his smile fades as he provides an example from his memory.

'On one occasion, I went into a shop to buy some bread and in South Africa in those days, when you bought bread there was a machine that you could use to slice it yourself. So I was slicing my bread and suddenly this guy jumps on me and says I'm making too much noise. I was like, "Come on, man, just relax," but he was losing his temper, pushing me and calling me names.'

There was one insult that Bheki was not prepared to put up with.

'He called me a Kaffir[4] and its one of those things, even now if someone called me that, I would get very angry. It got to the point that I didn't care about the consequences. He had crossed the line. I beat him and beat him. Luckily someone who knew me had entered the shop and they came and dragged me away. If they hadn't, maybe I would have killed him.'

There are many other such scenes in Moyo's memory, but he tenses up as they pass through his mind. Storm clouds gather behind his eyes. Suddenly he looks ready to go. Bheki is a man with ghosts in his past, a man whose childhood was blighted by one of the darker parts of 20th century history. 'I can feel my anger building,' he says as images come flooding back. 'There are too many things. I have tried to block them off. It's a part of my identity but I have to push it to the background. I cannot be angry forever.' In a moment he is himself again. 'This is how I deal with it.'

It is also how he dealt with the loss to Gary Buckland.

Just before apartheid's fall, in 1994, Bheki moved again, to Pretoria, to live with his uncle, who happened to be a huge boxing fan. His uncle saw potential in his indomitable nephew and introduced him to a local man called Shadrack. Shadrack had been a decent amateur boxer and took on the teenage Moyo to train. Facilities were non-existent and sessions would take place wherever they could, in an alleyway or on a patch of grassland, sparring, practising footwork and defence.

---

4 Kaffir originates from Arabic and means 'infidel' or 'non-believer' but was used in South Africa as an extremely offensive racist slur, due to its connotations with the slave trade.

'I didn't know anything at the time,' Bheki says, smiling. 'All I remember, every time we sparred, was his gloves bouncing off my head!'

The young Moyo was strong for his age and wasn't put off by this tough fistic baptism. He continued training and soon outgrew Shadrack's rudimentary approach.

'It all seemed natural to me,' he says. 'I really thought I could do something. I thought I could be a champion.'

In 1994, he began working at the United Bank in Pretoria, becoming friends with a white colleague by the name of Coen van Dyk. Van Dyk had connections in the fight game and offered to introduce Moyo to someone who could help him with his boxing aspirations. As a result, one day after work, the young Bheki was taken to a neighbouring part of town, where he met none other than Pierre Coetzer, the former South African heavyweight champion.

Coetzer had fought George Foreman, Frank Bruno and Riddick Bowe and at the time was a massive name in South African sport. In retirement, the big man owned a shop where he sold Biltong, the sun-cured beef snack popular in the region. 'He was always drunk!' Bheki remembers. 'Such a funny man!'

The two struck up a rapport and Coetzer in turn introduced Bheki to the proprietor of a local gym where Charles Beckhouse was chief coach, a man who would go on to make a huge name for himself and work with South African Olympians. Moyo found him initially non-committal. 'I asked if he would train me and he said "we can give it a go,"' Bheki recalls. 'That was all the encouragement I needed. From that point on, boxing became my life.

'I was working at the bank. Finishing at four and going straight to the gym. Every evening I would be there for three or four hours. At the time I was very into the game. I wanted to learn as much as I could, be as good as I could. I found it glamorous, as well, the idea of being a champion boxer. It was very exciting for me. I would watch boxing on TV and I felt I could be one of the big names.

'The truth is, as well, at that time I really enjoyed hitting another person. I enjoyed violence. I enjoyed the confrontation.

There is nothing quite like it, the feeling it gives you when you put someone's lights out. I would be sparring and dig one in, see my opponent go down. My spirits would soar. It is not something you can do too often in normal life.'

He showed enough dedication to be carded within three years of first lacing on a pair of gloves. Altogether, Moyo went on to contest 85 amateur bouts, winning 57 of them and stopping a large number of his opponents. He won provisional titles in South Africa and by the time he moved to London to further his boxing and see the world, in 2002, the scene appeared set for a promising professional career. He began training under Isola Akay at the All Stars Gym in West Kilburn. Akay had a lot of faith in his new African lightweight and encouraged him to enter the ABAs. Bheki was sparring regularly with pros like middleweight Hussein Osman and possessed superb natural strength for his weight class.

'The decision to turn pro wasn't about money for me. It was about glamour. I thought I would be a champion but of course, I didn't know how the game worked. Perhaps if I understood I would have taken another year and tried to go as far as I could in the ABAs. I could have built a reputation for myself and developed a fan-base here. I thought I could just fight and be recognised for my ability and drive. I thought I would make it like that.'

Bheki turned over under the guidance of Akay but for his first professional fight, in July 2005, was effectively managed and promoted by Jonathon Feld. He is reluctant to apportion blame to any particular party, but his debut was not a happy experience and was marred by confusion and contradictory information. The suspicion is that somebody was dishonest and sought to take advantage of the African debutant.

He fought Judex Meemea at the Equinox nightclub in Leicester Square. Meemea had the unusual record of 2-2-3 and ended up retiring two years later after only 17 fights. Bheki remembers going in, intending to win. 'But it just didn't happen,' he says.

The situation surrounding Bheki's debut became confused because he ended up boxing in the away corner, even though he had been led to believe beforehand he would be the home fighter.

'I was naive and I didn't know what was happening,' he says. 'I was told from the beginning I would be in the home corner and I sold something like 60 tickets for the show, which is what I said I would try to do. It's harder for me, not being from this country or having grown up here. I didn't have as many acquaintances as local people do.

'I told them I would sell more if I could but they said 60 was a fair number, so I was happy with that. It was literally on the night itself, just before I got into the ring, Jon Feld told me that things had changed and I was the away fighter. I didn't understand the significance at the time, so I didn't make a fuss. I still don't really know what happened behind the scenes, but obviously, looking back, it was disappointing.'

Bheki felt the fight was close and that although his opponent had more experience, he landed the more telling blows. The outcome surprised him a little, in that referee Seamus Dunne scored every round for Meemea.

Over the course of the next 15 months he fought five more times, always in the away corner, and was not awarded a round in any of them, until referee Lee Cook scored his contest with Martin Gordon a draw in October 2006. During these initial bouts, Moyo learnt the hard way how the lower levels of the professional game work in the UK.

'Several times I thought I clearly won, was even hurting the other guy, but not getting the decision.'

Despite this he refused to accept the notion of being a 'journeyman'. He still had aspirations and a fierce belief in his own ability. He also sees the word as something negative.

'It's not an identity I wanted to adopt,' he says. 'I still don't. I cannot define myself by this word. But it was really after the Buckland fight that I began to think something was going on. I employed the strategy of really moving and making myself an elusive target and I couldn't remember a meaningful punch that he landed on me. It was so bad that even the Board representative, the inspector, was asking the referee to explain what he had done. But what can you do? I just had to accept it and move on.

'I don't like the label journeyman and most of the people who apply these labels are the people who don't know shit about boxing. When most people say "journeyman" they mean this guy who thinks he's a boxer but he's not. It's a way of contrasting him with a real boxer, because he isn't one of those, he's something else. That's why I don't like it. It has a negative identity attached to it. I wouldn't wear it and say I'm proud of it. I am not just a boxer, but I am a boxer. There is no need to call me something else.'

After that fight, Bheki believes that subconsciously he began to accept his role and his fighting style changed.

'I see myself as being more effective when I take an aggressive, rather than passive approach,' he says. 'But it depends on the fight. I don't always know why I fight the way I do. It just happens when I get in there. Some of it might be to do with the opponent. I think as the away fighter you don't want to end up putting yourself at the mercy of somebody else. Of course there is the realisation that you need to preserve yourself too. If you are not going to get the decision anyway, you don't want to get hurt. It's one of those things.'

He discusses this with a tone of resignation, almost weariness. He sighs and shrugs his shoulders. It was noticeable that the pride, passion and humour with which he discussed his early training in Africa had disappeared. His voice became softer, more relaxed and his language almost academic.

'Officials favour home fighters, I believe, because it has become part of the culture within the establishment. I don't think there is anyone going around behind the scenes telling referees and judges who to give wins to, but I think it's got to the stage that those who are officiating know what they have to do to be part of the game. If you are a part of the establishment and you want to remain so, you are going to play by the rules and do what is expected of you. People within boxing expect these kinds of decisions to happen on every show really and if it doesn't happen, it's an exception. Instead of being an exception when something dodgy happens, it's an exception when it doesn't.'

In his last contest of 2013, in November, he was stopped in the second round by 20-year-old Joe Pigford in Southampton. Again, Bheki felt that referee Gino Piccinino jumped in prematurely, but as a result, in March 2014, he had to appear before the Board. When interviewed for this book, he was suspended from boxing and did not know if he would be allowed to fight on. This didn't seem to unduly trouble him and he told me he was prepared to accept whatever fate they threw his way. Having fought as a journeyman for so many years, he understood that the stoppage would trigger a general review of his career and that a possible outcome was the withdrawal of his licence, but was pleasantly surprised when he was, in fact, allowed to continue, subject to conditions.

In his first bout after the meeting, he fought Stewart Maclean of Tamworth on 22 March. *Boxing News* reported that although he fell short 'with a decent percentage of what he threw, which truth be told, wasn't much' he 'certainly enjoys his boxing and once again smiled his way through another 12 minutes'. The idea that Bheki could fiddle his way to yet another loss while at the same time exuding happiness just to be there, conjures a sweet, Forrest Gump-like image of a simpleton loser. Nothing could be further from the truth. Whatever really caused that smile, it certainly was not enjoyment.

Moyo is now 39. He accepts that the reality is that very few competitors fighting around light-welterweight continue beyond that age. It is partly for this reason that he is now contemplating retirement, but as he has got older, he has also developed interests outside of boxing. He is studying law and sociology and has keen political interests. Global, social and economic inequalities concern him deeply. Through all this, he has begun to question boxing's morality, a very unusual position for someone who is still an active competitor. Fighting in the away corner for so long has also made him wonder about damage to his body and brain.

Speaking to Bheki is very unlike speaking to any other boxer I have met, not only because his heavy South African accent lends a musical quality to his speech but because what he has to say is genuinely unique for a professional pugilist. Something has changed in him. Bheki the fighter no longer feels like a fighter.

'Even if I get my licence back, I see this as my last year anyway. It's been a gradual thing, it has grown in me with time, but the basic fact is that I don't love boxing anymore. I don't enjoy hitting people. That may sound crazy for a professional fighter, but I don't. I have become introduced to some other principles in life, concepts that I hadn't considered when I was young and so I started really questioning the whole thing as a sport.

'It will seem strange to anyone who reads it but I actually feel quite negatively about boxing now. Being exposed to the body of knowledge that I have been exposed to has turned me against it and given me a new way of thinking. It's not necessarily the business that I am talking about, although there are issues there too, but the sport itself. And it is not because of the way my career has gone – I know some people will think that. I could have been a many time world champion and I would take the same view. I have come to look at the sport with an objective approach and the evidence leads me to my present position.

'Here we are, as a species, humankind, *Homo sapiens*. We have evolved to have an organ that makes us unique. It makes us the most intelligent species, our brains. And what do we do? We participate in a sport that involves punching the hell out of each other. What is the aim? To become dumb again? Is that what we want? Maybe, you can say, it's a way to make a living, it doesn't matter what happens, but I see this as a paradox that doesn't really make sense. I don't see why we get so much pride from beating the hell out of each other. I think society made me believe that this was acceptable, but really, when you examine it, it is not.

'I thought it was a glamorous thing, that there was glory in it, but all it ever was, was beating the shit out of someone. Of course there is technique and skill, but underneath, that is what it is. And now, for me, I don't see any glamour in it at all. It was a shallow way to look at it.

'I have made many good friends in boxing and met so many people I respect, but beneath it all, it is a sport in which the purpose is to hurt the other person. If you want to be given the recognition of being "the man", that's what you have to do. You know, even people who go to watch boxing must accept this. Listen to the crowd at a boxing event. You can have a bout taking place and if it becomes technical, some clever shots, lots of good defence, nice footwork, elusive movement, people don't like it! It's only a very few people appreciate that.

'Those two fighters, they are hitting each other, hurting each other, for the amusement of others. And most of the crowd, they just want blood. They want to see someone get injured. Because that's what a knockout is, it is one fighter damaging the other's brain. But you know the silly thing? If it's gone a little bit too far and someone gets badly hurt and the paramedics rush in and the boxer is hospitalised or brain damaged or something like that, then everybody says, "Oh, it's a tragedy!" And you know, it is a tragedy of course, but what do you expect? The aim of the sport is to hurt each other.

'I don't even like this idea that it is a way out of hardship for young people with tough childhoods from the ghetto. To me, that is like exploitation. Surely we should desire a social system whereby poor youth have other options. They shouldn't feel that they have to fight. If they are forced in there by their circumstances, then as a society we must ask ourselves some searching questions. But regardless of anybody's background, poor or not, at the core is the idea that it is somehow glamorous to be able to beat up another person. I used to believe this myself and it is not the correct way to approach life.'

Bheki says that he tries not to let his principles affect the way he fights, but in some ways it is inevitable. As his professional career developed and he started to question his chosen profession, he settled into a mindset prior to contests that he was not going in to try to hurt his opponent. He just wanted to outbox them without causing them damage. His focus now is on completing one last year and passing his law degree. Despite that, when he looks back over his 20 years as a boxer, there is still a sense of loss, he smiles and sighs.

'I like to think, if boxing was set up differently and was not about ticket sales, that I could have gone far. In fact, ticket sales are only the tip of the iceberg. It's really about how boxing is administered at all levels and all these things feed off each other. I think I always had ability and obviously this is just speculation, but I think I could have won Area and maybe even National titles. But now? I will never know!'

7

'I love getting hit'

Robin Deakin

Super-featherweight/lightweight
Born: Crawley, Sussex, 19 April 1986
Active: 2006–present
Record: 1-51

'LET'S hear it for the world's worst boxer, Rockin Robin Deakin. He floats like a fridge and stings like a bowl of butterscotch angel delight. Rockin has lost his 51st consecutive fight and won only once in his professional career. That was a chap called Shaun Walton who I assume is entirely limbless and blind. But Rockin won't give in, even if he has been stripped of his license in the UK for his own health and safety. These days he fights under a German license but the result is always the same. Rockin puts it down to nerves and says that he's stuck in a rut – not to mention flattened on the canvas, but he won't give up, bless him. That's perseverance for you – or stupidity. I guess they are sometimes hard to tell apart.'

Rod Liddell, *The Sun*, Thursday 6 March 2014

I drove to Robin Deakin's house, near Brentwood in Essex, three weeks before the above piece of 'journalism' was published and spent an afternoon chatting with him in his lounge. He answered the door hollow-cheeked, stick-thin and smothered in fake tan (he has a sponsorship deal with a tanning company). It was a fortnight before his 52nd professional contest and he was heavily mired in the dieting process to make weight. At this stage of training boxers can often be crabby, but Deakin was hospitable, friendly and talkative. We spoke for several hours.

The week before our meeting, Robin's story had first broken in the national media. It had all begun with the *Brentwood Gazette* interviewing him about his comeback and running a piece headlined 'Is this Britain's Worst Boxer?' From there, the story snowballed its way to the nationals and the *Daily Mail*, *The Mirror* and *Metro* all printed their own versions. It was telling that the first thing he said, as soon as I had shaken his hand on the doorstep was, 'What did you think of that fucking press coverage then?' He returned to this topic again and again, throughout our conversation. It clearly played heavily on his mind, though I couldn't determine whether it bothered him or excited him. Perhaps a little of both is true.

The truth, from my side, is that before ever contacting him, I had to debate with myself whether to approach Robin about being involved in this book. He is a gutsy, battle-hardened trier, a very tough guy and although he has a journeyman's record, he neither fights nor talks like one. He hypes up potential contests between himself and boxing's hottest young things on social media, swapping jibes and trash-talk, just like contenders do when trying to goad a champion into taking them on. Anyone who has seen him compete will know he is at his happiest when standing and brawling, frequently leaving himself open. Knockdowns and stoppages are common and 12 of his 51 defeats have come inside the distance, although like most of the rest of the boxers featured in these pages and contrary to the impression given by Rod Liddle and other tabloid writers, he has never been knocked out.

After his 49th defeat, which came in June 2012 when he retired hurt at the end of the third round against Andrejs Pudosovs in Glasgow, he was called before the Board and had his licence withdrawn. Determined to set the record straight, Robin went abroad and got himself licensed in Germany. His first fight on this foreign licence, on a show at York Hall sanctioned by the boxing board of Malta, saw him lose on a third-round stoppage to the talented debutant Antonio Counihan, a former junior ABA champion and Team GB international amateur who turned pro on a Spanish licence after being refused by the BBB of C on medical grounds.

If nothing else the Counihan bout proved Robin had lost none of his old spirit. He entered the arena to catcalls and boos and despite a large group of home fans shouting that he was crap, was going to get knocked out and calling him a 'wanker' he took an eternity over his ring-walk, milking every drop of the belligerent atmosphere. He climbed into the ring, danced around a little, smiled at the baying mob and mimed the throat-cutting gesture made famous by Bernard Hopkins. This sent the Counihan crew into an even greater frenzy, which Robin clearly enjoyed. After the bout was finished, he made his way over to his adversary's supporters for a chat. With the battle now over and their boy victorious, Deakin was greeted like an old friend.

He then made a huge effort to reverse his fortunes with his most recent bout, which took place on 1 March 2014. Again he fought on a Maltese-sanctioned show, to circumnavigate his British ban, but this time he was in the home corner, made a great deal of effort to sell tickets and boxed a Pole with a record of 0-11. Despite all these advantages he still lost. Boxing is a hugely mental and emotional sport and Deakin had heaped pressure on himself by publicly going to war with the press and declaring that victory would see him vindicated. He certainly has strengths as a fighter, but that night he could not have beaten anyone.

Predictably, the tabloid vultures then redoubled their efforts to drive him to despair, with Alex Richards of *The Mirror* publishing a piece headlined 'Britain's Worst Boxer, Rockin Robin Deakin says he will not quit – despite 51st successive loss'. The same story, with misleading pictures of Robin on the floor even though he was not knocked down in the fight, combined with jokes at his expense and open sarcasm, appeared in the *Daily Mail* and *Metro*. Eventually *The Sun* got in on the act too, with the piece quoted at the start of this chapter.

Opinion within the boxing world was divided. Some of those close to Deakin encouraged him to persevere. Fellow pro Ben Day, who debuted against Robin in 2011, beating him on points despite being cut over the left eye by a clash of heads in round two, urged him to 'never give up'. Others weren't so sure. Jon Pegg was saddened, saying, 'This really has got to be the end for him.' Even Johnny Greaves, who knows him well, said, 'I want him to pack it in now.'

'I'd love to be able to say the media coverage doesn't bother me,' Robin said. 'But to be honest I cried when it first came out. I cried to my dad. The journalist who interviewed me is a freelancer and was very clever about it. He took out what he wanted from what I said and ignored the rest. I guess he got the story he needed and mugged me off. But it backfired on him. I phoned him up and said, "Where's your fucking office? I'm going to come to your office now." I said to him, "What the fuck have you put in this paper? Human punchbag? I'll punch you round the fucking office you prick."

'He told me to talk to his boss, so I did. I phoned his boss up, I said, "Dickhead, what's this in your paper?" He said, "Whom am I speaking to?" I said, "Robin Deakin" and he said, "Hello punchbag!" I couldn't believe it. He was trying to mug me off on the phone as well! Anyway, I found his office and went down there. So when I got there, I phoned him again and said, "I'm downstairs, now come and speak to me." But obviously he didn't want any of that and he called security.

'The whole point was I never said I am a human punchbag. I said I've been treated like a human punchbag by people in the business. There's a big difference, really, but the *Daily Mail* and all that lot don't care about telling the truth. You know they keep writing about me getting battered, but Stephen Smith [British super-featherweight champ] and Anthony Crolla [former British lightweight champion and current WBO intercontinental champion] were the only ones ever to hurt me. And after all the press rubbish recently, Stephen Smith even phoned me up and said, "Don't worry what the press say, people who've been in with you know how tough you are." That was really important to me.'

My gut feeling was that if he wanted to fight on, it was his decision and when I spoke to him by phone a few days after his 51st straight defeat, he was adamant he would continue. He joined up with a new trainer in Matt Marsh and seemed full of positivity. A truly feisty character, I got the impression that his battles with the media had emboldened him, that although the jibes hurt his feelings, he also enjoyed the attention. Robin even enlisted the help of ex-boxer, turned journalist, Ben Doughty and went to *The Sun*'s offices in an effort to track down and confront Rod Liddle on camera. As far as I know, they were not successful.

A couple of weeks later, when the furore had died down, Deakin contacted me and asked if I would write a tabloid piece about him trawling London nightclubs, accompanied by paparazzi-style photographs, which I declined. 'I feel like I should keep the publicity going,' he told me. In April he posted a picture of himself on social media, at a party, schmoozing with the actor, Danny Dyer. During our interview I discovered that he had appeared on a cable TV dating show called *Girlfriends* and was good friends with Micky Norcross from *The Only Way Is Essex*. It certainly seemed that he enjoyed and tried to cultivate fame, maybe even as much as his self-proclaimed love of 'having a row'. He even began using the tag 'Britain's Worst Boxer' as a nickname online, with a line of merchandise being made bearing the slogan. The impression I gathered through speaking and meeting with him is that Deakin is a one-off, maybe even deserving of a book of his own.

My doubts over his inclusion here were centred around the fact that he did not begin his career as a journeyman and by the time this book was being written he was trying to relaunch himself by fighting in the home corner again, selling tickets, winning back his BBB of C licence and competing for titles. I am not convinced, even now, that Robin was ever a career journeyman in the same way that Johnny Greaves, Kris Laight, or Jason Nesbitt are. He almost fell into the role by accident. Despite that, he has spent the majority of his professional life on the road, taking bouts at short notice and fighting in the away corner and it is for those reasons I decided to go to see him.

From the off, an awkward fact should not be avoided. At 28 years old, and having battled fiercely with many of the country's top young fighters around his weight class, Robin is already exhibiting some of the tell-tale signs of neurological damage. He is happy to talk and full of anecdotes but his speech is a little slurred. It is something he stated openly himself, before we even started the interview. 'I know my speech is a bit fucked,' he told me, while he made me a cup of tea, 'but I'm a fighter. That's how it is. You can't go swimming without getting wet.'

Any avid boxing fan will know it is very, very common for fighters to have hard-luck stories about their childhoods. Many of the greatest ever grew up in poverty, in broken homes and among families with all kinds of problems, from drug addiction, to domestic violence, to gang-related deaths. The rags to riches and then often, back to rags again motif has been repeated so many times it is now a cliché of boxing autobiographies, but if tough starts to life could be measured against each other, Rockin' Robin Deakin's would take some beating.

Robin was born dangerously premature after his mother's waters broke three months early. Initially he was thought to be stillborn but after strenuous efforts from the doctors at Crawley hospital, he was revived and placed in an incubator. Weighing approximately one kilo, his life at this stage was highly fragile and as with all babies born so early, survival was not guaranteed.

Sadly, this was only the beginning of his problems. The position he had occupied in his mother's womb and the pregnancy's complications meant that he was born with severe deformities of his lower legs. Effectively, his feet were on backwards. To make matters worse, his left foot was affected by congenital talipes equinovarus or 'club foot' syndrome. If he survived, his parents were informed it was extremely unlikely he would ever be able to walk.

The tiny Deakin pulled through, and with the help of intense medical attention and after spending his first few months of life in hospital was eventually discharged and taken home. Problems with his legs would continue to affect his development and mobility however and by the time other children were taking their first steps, he was unable to do anything other than sit up.

It was decided that corrective surgery could offer the unfortunate infant the best chance of a normal life and from the age of one, Robin was returning for more long spells in hospital and a series of complicated and painful operations to correct his birth defects. Altogether he underwent more than forty operations. The procedures worked well on his right leg and by cutting and reconnecting tendons, sinews and ligaments, the foot there was returned to a relatively normal position.

Unfortunately, the situation regarding the left leg was more problematic and the young Deakin's run of tragic luck hadn't quite played itself out yet. At the age of three and after one particular surgery which involved the resetting of bones to rotate the foot, he was sent back home with a plaster cast on the limb so that it would heal correctly. After roughly five weeks of wearing the cast it had become uncomfortable and reached the point where one evening, Robin was in his bedroom, screaming with pain. His father, Lester, rushed in and as he pulled at the covers of the boy's bed, noticed a strange, rotten smell.

Sure that there was something badly wrong, Robin's father took matters into his own hands, grabbed a handsaw and some pliers and began the process of removing the cast. As pieces of plaster came loose, a dirty fluid leaked out of the edges and on to the floor. The room filled with a smothering smell of decay. It must have been difficult to bear for father and son, but as he removed the back part of the casing, with Robin howling in agony, the soft tissue of the boy's lower leg, which had turned a grisly, purplish colour, came away with it. Unknown to anyone, gangrene had set in. His leg had been starved of oxygen below the knee and had literally died, inside the cast.

As a result of this series of traumas, Robin Deakin still today has no calf muscle or Achilles tendon on his left leg. Pictures of him in his boxing shorts show a lower limb that is literally skeletal. He walks with a limp and is unable to run properly. Training is clearly affected. Psychologically too, he has never fully recovered.

'I used to get bullied a lot in school,' he says. 'Where I was brought up, around the Crawley and Horsham area, it's a small cliquey town and it didn't help that my dad was a bit of a bad-boy back in the day.'

Robin's father ran a hire-drive company but was also mixed up with some shady local characters, collecting money on their behalf.

'Because he had a reputation, it affected me. I was very shy as a kid, you might even call it cowardly, and I was in a wheelchair until I was six, but my older brother, Daniel, was often in trouble and kids used to pick on me because I was a soft target. It took a long time before I learned to stick up for myself.

'When I was in the wheelchair, as a little-un, I used to see other kids and think, "I wish I could be normal and do the things other people can do." Even now, I still feel like that sometimes. I can't wear shorts in the summer. Some of it is me, I realise that. I'm such a paranoid freak, if I was wearing shorts and someone walked past looking at me, I'd think they were looking at my legs and I'd be like, "What the fuck are you looking at you little prick?" straight away. I'd probably end up lumping 'em. That's just what I'm like. I get riled very easily.'

Robin started mainstream education late as he was in and out of hospital. He had a tutor who came to visit him on the ward and do pre-school activities with him. It wasn't until he could walk that he began to go to school.

'When I first went to school the other kids used to pick on me and I found it very upsetting, so my dad started bringing me to Horsham boxing club, to strengthen my legs, give me some balance and improve my confidence. Then I began looking at the other kids and thinking, "OK, you laugh and take the piss out of me now, but you wait." But you know, I was always crying, it was difficult to cope with all that when you're small.

'I always wanted to be a known person, whether it's the right way or the wrong way. I wanted the respect my dad had from being a tough guy. I even wanted it when I was a little kid. I looked up to my dad. From boxing I got that, although I'd never be a bully. I'd never do some of the stuff that my dad used to do, but I'll protect myself if I have to.'

Robin's repeated references to his father's past are mostly vague, hinting at some level of criminal activity. The reality is that at least in recent years, Deakin Sr has been involved in some fairly major stuff. On 6 March 2009 *The Crawley News* reported that Lester Deakin was found guilty and received a nine-month jail term for holding a man hostage and demanding a £27m ransom for his release. *The Crawley Observer*, covering the same incident, stated that Robin's father, with an accomplice, brandished various weapons including a rifle and a handgun while threatening to both shoot the victim and 'chop him into little pieces'.

Despite his obvious affection for his dad, Robin's voice wavers a bit. He clearly feels that to some degree, he grew up in the old man's shadow.

'I've always felt neglected, different, you know, growing up, my mum hated me. She still does now. When her relationship with my dad came to an end and he'd been knocking her around, she held it against me because I was close to him and she didn't really want me anymore. I never saw him hit her, but she used to come in with black eyes and stuff and we knew what'd been happening. I feel that I've always been the black sheep of the family. I've always been close to my dad, even though we bicker like cat and dog. We're both the same character. He thinks he's right and I'm like, "Fuck you, I'm right." Then we'll argue and fall out and not speak to each other for months, then we start speaking again. That's the way it is with me and my old man. But with my mum, she's never loved me. Not really.

'I'm always crying, to be honest. I still cry now, sometimes. I think, "Why can't I be normal?" You know I've got such a short fuse with people because I think that everyone's always against me. People in general, the boxing board, everyone. They're all against me. I've always felt that I'm not getting treated the same as everyone else, because I'm different.'

Robin's parents split up when he was six. For a time his childhood became deeply unsettled. He spent several months in and out of care before moving back with his mother.

'My dad was always having affairs,' he remembers. 'My mum used to say to me, "Your dad's always out shagging." I used to think, "Fair play to him!" She obviously didn't give him what he needed. Still today I don't really talk to my mum. But when my parents split up I used to live with her. I used to hate my dad being slagged off and you know people used to come round to my mum's for a cup of tea or whatever and they'd be slagging my dad off in front of me. I used to always cry and think, "Fuck off, that's my dad you're talking about." She always put me to bed early. The other kids would still be up, but it was like she wanted to get me out of the way. That's the way it was.

'My mum tried ringing me recently when I was in the papers. That's what she's like. She only wants to know me when my name is out there and she thinks I'm doing well for myself.'

From the age of nine, classmates knew Robin was training as a boxer. He used to come in to school with medals he had won at gym shows. In his first real, junior amateur contest he fought another Crawley boy by the name of Craig Clarke. It was a bout that would characterise Deakin's later career, in that both lads suffered knockdowns during the fight, but Robin was stopped on his feet in the third round. A year or so later, the two met again. This time Deakin won. In the meantime however, he had begun regularly to use his fists outside of the ring too.

'People heard that I'd lost my first fight and they used to come up to me and say "You're shit at boxing, you won't beat anyone, you've got spastic legs, you're a cripple" and I just thought, "You know what? I don't have to listen to this shit any more" and I'd be like, "You what you fucking prick?" and hit 'em.'

As a result Robin was frequently in trouble. Lester got tired of constant phone calls from teachers and managed to skirt the issue by telling them Robin had ADHD, although he had never been diagnosed or given any medication. Nonetheless, he was eventually expelled and had to find another school.

Robin also began boxing competitively more often, hitting his stride and picking up wins. Successes were reported in the local paper and other kids became aware of them, softening their attitude to him. He won the Southern Area schoolboy title and found that jibes and insults stopped.

At the age of 15, at which time he stopped living with his mum and moved in full-time with his father, he fought a boy called Todd Mills, who boxed for the St Mary's Amateur Boxing Club. Robin was stopped by a right hook in the second round, his schoolmates caught wind of the heavy defeat and once again, the taunts started. In his own, perhaps over-sensitive mind, Robin began to connect his performances in the ring with his relationships with other people outside of it. It seemed they only respected him when he won.

'I tried not to get in too much trouble out and about,' he says, talking of times when people would speak to him around the town. 'But sometimes it just happened. I've been hit in the street before and I've laughed. I love getting hit. That's the funny thing about me. It's an adrenaline thing, not knowing what's going to happen. That's why I love fighting.'

Deakin continued to be a decent level amateur and after moving to Crawley boxing club at 19 he was entered into an international competition in Limassol in Cyprus. 'I was always the underdog. Even *The Crawley News* made me the underdog, said I wouldn't get anything. I got a bye in the first round and I thought, "Wicked! I proved you all wrong!" I boxed Michael Blackburn who was a top Scottish amateur. In the second round he caught me bang on the bell. My spastic legs buckled and the ref's stopped it. After that I had about three months off then my coach asked me to come and fight out in Jersey. It was an open show out there.

'He said to me, "Look, you're not going to win, so just go out there and have fun." I thought "Fair enough" and I boxed a guy called Ben Murray. He was a big name in Jersey at the time. Anyway, I mugged him right off and [former WBO super-middleweight world champion] Steve Collins was there, the Celtic Warrior. I came into the ring and I was dancing, having fun, blowing kisses at the crowd. In the fight I was dropping my hands, sticking my tongue out. The guy was a nice boxer, but he hit like a girl, so I stood in the corner and let him hit me. He hit me three or four times and the referee gave me a standing count, I was just laughing!

'So anyway, I lost the fight, but got a standing ovation from the crowd. Afterwards Steve Collins asked me to go for a drink with him. He told me how much he enjoyed my performance and said he could get me a deal with Frank Warren. I got butterflies. I couldn't believe what I was hearing. People didn't believe me, they told me I wasn't good enough, that I was making it up, that Warren wouldn't sign me because I wasn't ABA champion.'

That year (2005) Deakin reached the ABA national semi-final where he lost to (future British super-featherweight champion) Gary Sykes. 'He was a level above me,' Robin recalls. 'He smashed me. But I loved it. I loved getting hit by someone at that level. Another time I boxed a guy called Alan Cutler and [Team GB boxer and Olympian] Iain Weaver was there to watch. I was waiting around before the fight and I could hear Weaver talking loudly, saying I was rubbish and I was going to get knocked out. And you know, I'm always slated, no matter what I do and I got a bit upset.

'I went and found my dad and I told him I would give up if I lost. But my dad told me to use it, all the anger I've always got inside me. In that fight I hit him with a left hook in the second round and knocked him spark out cold. He was out for about five minutes. I looked at Iain Weaver at ringside, straight in the eye and laughed, then I just walked out. I didn't stop or talk to anyone, I just went straight back to the dressing room, got dressed and left.'

After that fight, Steve Collins phoned Robin and asked to meet him again. Deakin made the journey to St Albans where Collins lived, met him for a cup of coffee and the Celtic Warrior suggested they go together to see Frank Warren that very day. The two drove down to the Sports Network office in Hertford and met the man who at the time, was still unquestionably the nation's number one promoter.

'No one had heard of Eddie Hearn back then,' Robin says. 'Frank still had Sky in those days and he was the top man all the way. He had an old fashioned jukebox and all this memorabilia in his office. There were pictures of champions everywhere and it felt like a dream or something. What he offered me was unreal – three-and-a-half grand for a four-rounder for my debut. I couldn't believe it. I'd hardly seen a tenner before. He said he wouldn't take nothing off me for the first year. He was a proper gentleman to me. I was getting more than Matty Marsh to turn over and he was ABA champion.'

It was a fairytale turnaround for a young boxer who hadn't been able to walk until the age of six. His debut for Warren's now-defunct Sports Network company took place at York Hall on 28 October 2006 in a super-featherweight bout against Telford's Shaun Walton, who came in with a record of 1-8-2. Deakin sold 400 tickets and took a 39-37 points win over four rounds. He hadn't boxed particularly well, which he put down to first night nerves, but all in all it was a promising start to his professional career.

His second pro fight would take place on a huge show at Wembley Arena in February 2007, on the undercard of a night which included Audley Harrison, Amir Khan and Dereck Chisora. It was the sort of beginning to a career that most young prospects would sell their mother for, Robin was being backed financially and given maximum exposure. This time he sold 700 tickets and appeared to be riding high, but sadly for Deakin, this was as high as his pro career would get.

'I was buzzing, but at the same time, it was difficult because I was very distracted. All the attention and ticket selling was taking away from my training and something else that I didn't realise almost until the night, I don't know what was going on, but I was super-feather and the guy I was going in with was a welter. He was quite a big welter as well, later on he ended up fighting at light-middleweight. I'm not sure what happened with the matchmaking for that one, Dean Powell rung me up and offered me it and I took it because I didn't know, but it made it a hard night's work for my second fight.

'To make matters worse, on the night they put me on first of the night, but there was a cock-up and when I got in the ring, the doors had only just opened and most of my fans missed it. I was boxing in an empty room, more or less. It all just gave me a bad feeling.'

Deakin's opponent that day was a Latvian by the name of Eduards Krauklis. At the time he was 0-3. Rockin' Robin battled hard against the naturally bigger man, but couldn't make a dent in him. At the end of the four rounds he found himself on the wrong end of a 38-39 decision from ref Bob Williams. Krauklis eventually retired several years later with a record of 2-10.

His other win was a first-round TKO over Ben Jones, who went on to win the English super-featherweight title. It seemed he only did well when matched against much lighter fighters. But despite any mitigating circumstances, just like that, for Robin Deakin, the good times were over.

'I'll be honest as well, I didn't train like I should have done. I thought, being promoted by Frank Warren, he would be my shield and I could get away with it, that I couldn't be beaten. So yeah, it wasn't a good night. The guy's record was shit. I should have beat him. I feel I did beat him. I felt the referee was against me. Bob Williams, he's a mug, I never liked him and I don't think he likes me. He mugged me off that night.

'But when I look back at those first two pro fights, I have a lot of regrets. It was there for me and I didn't make the most of it. I didn't perform well in either fight. I don't know why. I think sometimes it's because I was in the limelight from the beginning. Even my first fight was on TV. I was in the programme as being Steve Collins's protégé and a big hope for the future. I suppose it was a weight on my shoulders. I don't know what went on, looking back. At the end of the day I can't change it now.'

After the Krauklis disappointment, Robin took the decision to leave Frank Warren and the two mutually agreed to part.

'I left him because I thought I'd be on his back seat after the way the first two fights went. Graham Earl had already spoken to me about managing me and he said he could get me a deal out in America. I thought maybe that might work out better for me, so I phoned Dean Powell and told him that because of the loss and the way things had gone, I didn't think Frank would be making me a priority. Me and Dean had a long chat and I asked him if he'd give me my contract back. He agreed.

'So I went to Florida and trained there for five and a half weeks with Gus Curran. He was a top trainer and good friends with Pernell "Sweet Pea" Whitaker [world champion from lightweight to light-middle in the 1980s and 90s]. I trained hard over there and met a lot of people. In the end the famous promoter Lou Duva offered me a deal to stay in the States. Looking back, that was probably my other big mistake. My first was leaving Frank Warren, but having done that, I should have signed with Duva and given it a go in the USA. But I'd met a girl in England, fell in love and wanted to go back to her. I'm an idiot though, it was pointless, what a fucking tramp she was!'

Robin returned to England at the end of 2007 and, managed by Graham Earl, fought two fights far from home. In October he lost to Hyland in Belfast. Referee Paul McCullagh scored it convincingly 40-35 for the home boxer. Robin says he was 'robbed. I slipped in the last round and the ref scored it as a knockdown.' In November Deakin was stopped in the second by Ricky Owen in Irvine, Scotland.

'At that time I didn't really get how the game worked,' he says, 'I was still young and I thought I could just look at the opponent and if he was a Mickey Mouse twat then I'd beat him up. I'll be honest, I thought Ricky Owen looked like a tool, so I said, yeah, I'll take the fight. It was only eight days' notice, but what the hell. I flew up to Scotland and thought I was going to knock him out, but ended up getting stopped in the second round. He was a lot better than I thought he was, good fighter and a nice bloke as it goes.'

By this time, in early 2008, Deakin stood at 1-3 and it appeared his professional path was set. Yet there was still time for him to make a big impression in his next bout.

'I fought Vinny Mitchell, who was unbeaten, on a Frank Warren bill at York Hall, live on Setanta Sport. I was struggling a bit with the weight and Vinny Mitchell came in the gym and told me he was gonna put me to sleep. He was a bit of a prick, Vinny Mitchell, bit of a mouthy little chump. Anyway, I made weight in the end and at the weigh-in he's looked at me and said, "See you tomorrow to go sleepy-byes." That really fired me up, so I walked around Bethnal Green with Graham talking about the fight at about 11 o'clock at night. I took it all in, he really geed me up. On fight night, I went in there ready and dropped him heavily in the first round. I definitely won that fight. Vinny knows. He'd tell you himself I won that fight. I tell you right now, if I was a Warren fighter, I would have been given that decision.'

Referee Richie Davies scored a 37-38 win for Mitchell over four rounds.

'If I'd won that one, it could have been a turning point for my career,' Robin says. 'I would have been 2-3 and could have kicked on from there. But it wasn't to be. From there one thing led to another. But you know, it is what it is. I went on the road, but I don't cower away. I love a row. In that way I never fought like a journeyman. I'll come in and give it a go. I turn up and I think if you're a journeyman, you're bound to lose. You're in there, you're fighting these lads and give 'em a real beating, but lose by a point or whatever, it's hard, it disheartens me. I get down about it. Seriously, I cry even to this day. I could have had a good career. Boxing was my life. I think, "What did I do?" When money's involved, it turns hands. My record should be half-and-half. No way should it be the way it is. It's disgraceful my record. It's an embarrassment for the officials.

'But no matter what it says on paper, in my mind I'm a contender. I come in with a fresh tan, a fresh haircut and fresh gear. I always look good, whenever I come out. Why? Because people like you pay their hard-earned money to come and watch people like me. People pay their money to come and watch a fight, they don't want to see someone prancing around the ring, doing fuck all, covering up and all that.

'Don't get me wrong, someone like Kristian Laight is so clever, in his own way, such a good fighter and people ask who's the best journeyman, but there's two different types of journeyman. There's journeymen like me, that come in as a contender and have a row, or there's people like Johnny Greaves and Kristian Laight who are great journeymen, clever, don't get hit, very skilful. It depends what you like. But most people would prefer to watch me.

'Obviously, their way of doing it, you can have lots of fights. Kris could probably have 300 fights if he wants. My style, I couldn't have 300 fights, I'll be lucky if I get to a hundred. I'm going to do my best.

'I've passed the brain scan with flying colours. My speech is a bit funny, but it's gonna be. Twenty-one years of boxing, what do you expect? It's gonna take its toll.'

After his 11th contest, Robin left Graham Earl and signed with Mickey Helliet, claiming that Mickey enticed him via an online conversation. Even saying Helliet's name visibly riles Robin. 'He's a muppet, a fucking ginger fairy. He promised he would get me wins,' Deakin alleges. 'He said I was a good fighter.'

Yet by Robin's last fight on a British licence, in Glasgow in June 2012, which saw him retire on his stool after the third round with a broken thumb, his record was 1-48, his debut under Frank Warren remaining the only victory. He was called before the Board to explain his retirement from the fight and his run of consecutive losses. At the meeting his licence was withdrawn.

'They told me I wasn't taking it professionally and to be fair I wasn't. I wasn't training properly, although there were circumstances to explain that. I'd split up with my girlfriend and wasn't in the right frame of mind. When my ex-girlfriend, Katie, left me, I lost my house, I lost everything and I was sofa surfing so I never had a base to work from. To be honest, around that time my head was all over the place and I didn't really want to fight.'

But, Robin contends, 'Mickey would always phone me up and tell me he had a fight for me. I'd tell him I wasn't ready, that I was physically knackered. He would tell me that I had to take the fight, or I wouldn't get other work. From the beginning he would say to me, I'll get you a fight you can win, but you have to do this one for me first. There was always an angle with Mickey, always a way for him to pressure me into taking fights I didn't want.

'This went on for a good few fights, until I fought Phil Gill in 2010. That's when it all came out. Phil Gill was his fighter too and I tell you what, he was shit, but Mickey rang me and said he couldn't find an opponent for him and he wanted me to do it. I told him I was ill and I couldn't. I'd had a week off training with a virus, I had another fight the week after so I said that I couldn't afford to get stopped because I'd lose out on the other fight. So Mickey said that we could set it up between all of us so that Phil Gill would get the win but definitely wouldn't stop me and I'd get paid a grand.

'So I got in there, sick as a dog and lost on points to Phil Gill, all done to order, then I got back in the dressing room and Mickey gave me my money. I counted it and there was only £750 there. Even though I was the opponent, in the away corner, Mickey took a cut from me as well, so he was earning off both fighters that night.

I asked him about it and he said, "I've got to pay my mortgage." From then, I thought, "This bloke's having me on."'

Despite Robin's misgivings with his choice of manager, he states that he had signed a three-year contract and was stuck. He also says that he went to Mickey's office many times to complain and would just be laughed at. He didn't feel able to physically confront him for fear of police intervention or losing his licence, although it should be pointed out that Mickey Helliet was a decent light-heavyweight amateur himself and may well have held his own if they had come to blows.

'Towards the end, I did lodge a complaint against him with the Board,' Robin claims. 'But Mickey came to me and said that I couldn't fight for him while the complaint was there. He told me if I withdrew the complaint, he'd get me a fight. I was broke, so I withdrew the complaint and then three fights later I lost my licence.'

In spite of their professional differences, Helliet remained Deakin's manager until his final fight on a British licence in 2012. Eventually they parted company when Robin's licence was withdrawn, which voided his contract.

'The way it worked,' Robin recalls, 'the Board called me into the office. They said to me "Look, we've called you in a couple of times about your record. Things haven't changed. You're still going in there unfit." But you know what, the Board never looked at my manager, they looked at me. It wasn't that I was unfit, it's that I was being pressured to take fights even when I didn't want to, even when I was ill and unprepared. Going in like that, all you're ever going to do is survive and that's all that managers like Mickey want you to do.

'So while they're saying this to me, Mickey's sitting there on his phone, texting away, not even paying attention. I pointed at him and said, "This is who I pay 25 per cent to. Surely you should be asking him why I'm not given the right fights, why I'm always taking fights at the last minute. Why? Because I'm fighting his prospect for him, so he doesn't have to pay any another fighter and he can make 25 per cent off both boxers."

'This is what Mickey Helliet's all about. That's why he manages some prospects and some journeymen, so he can match them up together. They didn't say anything to him though. This is where the Board fucked up, where you see what the Board's all about. They took my licence away from me, even though I was doing my job. It's so they can make it look like they're doing something. It doesn't affect them if I lose my licence because I wasn't making much, but Mickey brings a lot of money in, so they wouldn't do anything to him because it affects their business. It's how it all works. If they really wanted to change things they'd sort out the guys like Mickey, but they won't because they make good money off him. It's you scratch our back and we'll scratch yours.'

The official outcome of the hearing was that Robin's licence was taken away to protect his health.

'When they took my licence away,' Deakin alleges, 'I spoke to Mickey shortly afterwards and asked him to speak on my behalf, to try to get my licence back. I was pleading with him and he said if I gave him two and a half grand I could have it. I asked him what the money was for and he said, "This business pays my mortgage. I'm not going to give it away for nothing."' After that, Robin says he gave up and began looking at other options.

His intention was to win on the German licence on 1 March, to demonstrate his more serious, professional attitude, then start the process of applying for his licence back from the BBB of C. Unfortunately it wasn't to be and he lost again. Unbowed, he intends to come again. If he eventually gets relicensed he says he will hook up with manager/promoter Steve Goodwin and from there he will be 'the real Rocky story'.

Outside of the ring Deakin's life now seems more settled. When we met he was living in a house owned by Mickey Norcross from TV show *The Only Way Is Essex* where he is looked after by Norcross's sister.

'She's making sure my diet's right and everything,' he says. 'She's like the mother I never really had. With this set-up, I think I can win the English title. Maybe even the British. I'm not interested in Masters and all that rubbish. All the fights I've had as a journeyman, I've always given a hundred per cent, even on short notice, unfit, whatever. All I want is a shot and that's what I'm aiming to get. If I could get that I could show everyone what bullshitters the press are.'

From now on Robin intends to train properly and fight every eight weeks. He hopes that if he picks up a few wins, his fortunes will change. At 28 he is certainly still young enough to come again.

'I feel that I've been cheated out of boxing. The board say they're trying to protect my health, but you know,' he claims, 'when Mickey was making me take all those fights on short notice they could have done something about it, but they didn't. They let all the fights go on. If I was that bad, as a fighter, that I lost my licence, Mickey must have been that bad, as a manager, to keep putting such a shit fighter in all those fights. But of course they don't look at it like that.'

Deakin says that he felt exploited.

'But I believe that everything happens for a reason. I was put on this earth to make an impression. And that's what I'm going to do.'

Since interviewing Rockin' Robin he changed his mind about his future career direction. He decided that boxing as a home fighter involved too much pressure and that rather than continuing on foreign sanctioned shows and selling tickets, his efforts would instead be concentrated on training with Matt Marsh at his gym in Woolwich. He is convinced Marsh can help him build on his strengths and work on his weaknesses, some of which are a result of his disabilities. Even now, he can't run properly because his left leg drags along the floor. His footwork sometimes looks imbalanced.

'This is why I use the ropes a lot in my fights,' Robin says. 'Because when I'm on the ropes, swinging from the ropes, I feel balanced. When I'm in centre-ring, I don't. But Matt will work on all of this with me.'

While training, Robin will be lobbying the Board to get his British licence back. He has already started an online petition to this effect. 'I'm at my best when no one expects me to win,' he said.

Due to the nature of some of the comments made by Robin regarding his former manager, Mickey Helliet, I felt it was only right to speak to Mickey and allow him to give his side of the story. For those who don't know, Helliet, a bilingual native of Watford, with French blood, is a young promoter/manager making great strides on the south-eastern scene. He runs a stable of roughly 80 fighters and his Hellraiser promotional company puts on shows at the Coronet in Elephant and Castle, the Camden Centre in King's Cross and several other venues.

He also promotes successful dinner shows through his other promotional arm, the Mayfair Sporting Club. Recently, he has taken his first steps into the lucrative TV market by striking a deal with the cable station Eurosport.

Mickey is a busy man, organising large numbers of shows and events, developing his own gym in west London and taking his fighters on international training camps, including a recent junket to Las Vegas for sparring in Floyd Mayweather's gym. Despite that, he found time to speak to me while eating dinner with his fiancée. He was open and responsive, speaking with respect and a little sadness concerning Robin, with whom he had recently had several vicious spats across various social media platforms. Despite parting company professionally back in 2012, their mutual hostility still seemed to frequently slide into internet abuse. Yet it was clear that the sourness in their relationship bothered him a bit.

'To be honest I can't remember how I met him,' Mickey told me. 'But at the time Robin had boxed about twenty times and obviously had lost all except one. He wasn't going anywhere as a professional and he needed some help. I remember having a talk with him and explaining that there was no point continuing to fight ex-ABA champions and top prospects like Crolla and Smith and all these sort of lads.

'I said I could keep him nice and busy and put him in with prospects, but you know, not the cream of the crop, the sort of prospects who might go on to pick up a Masters after nine or ten fights. The reason I said that is because although he could make more money in the short term by being used as an opponent for the top lads, he didn't have the skill level to make a go of it with them. What I was suggesting meant he could box nice and regularly and not have to take a hiding every time. The silly thing is, at the beginning he was very enthusiastic and grateful about the whole thing. Then after a while, he started complaining.'

Mickey went on to talk about Robin's contest with Phil Gill in November 2010, which Deakin said had been forced upon him and he had then been told to box to order. Helliet's recollection was quite different.

'Robin was always hassling me to find him as many fights as possible. He wanted the money. The truth is he begged me to make the fight with Phil Gill. He was broke and desperate. So I sorted it out, only for him to turn around on the night and say he was feeling unwell. I remember him saying, "If you pay me more money, I'll do it anyway." Then he asked me to go and see Phil and tell him to take it easy. You know, this was Phil Gill we're talking about and with all respect to Phil he wasn't a world beater. If it gets to the stage that you need guys like that to take it easy, you've got a problem.

'Anyway, our issues really came towards the end. I'd become worried about him, he was getting hurt too much, so I pulled him aside and said, "Look Robin, like all things, boxing careers have a start, a middle and an end." I know it's not easy, fighters never want to hear that, I boxed amateur myself and I was like a fish out of water when I finished, but that's the way it is. It was his end and he needed to accept it.

'I'd only been matching him with non-punchers or guys who were lighter than him and he was getting shaken to his boots every time. I'd tried to encourage him to be more defensive in his style but he just wasn't interested. The list of options for him was getting shorter and shorter. Who could he fight? And how could I keep putting him in there with a clean conscience?

'One of Robin's problems is that he's always traded on this "warrior" image, that he'll go in and have a tear-up with anyone and that's great, but it's not the way to have a long career. Look at the journeymen that have had 150, 200, 300 fights, they don't go in there gung-ho, swinging away. He was also totally unrealistic about his opponents. He always wanted to fight the best kids out there. To give you an idea, there was one time I put on a dinner show, it wasn't a well paid night for the boxers, but they didn't have to sell any tickets and I asked Robin to have a think and tell me who he wanted to fight. He came back to me with a lad who was 9-0 and being tipped as a future British title challenger. I told him to get real. He didn't need those sort of fights. He was just going to get hurt for the sake of a few hundred quid, but he didn't want to listen.'

Mickey paused to swallow a mouthful of food. When he spoke again his tone had changed slightly. It was softer and slower, as if he were choosing his words more thoughtfully.

'And yes, in the three years that I managed him I noticed that his speech had become more slurred. By watching him in the ring I saw his foot movement change. Obviously Robin's never had great feet because of his legs, but there was more to it than that. It's something I've always noticed about guys who get punchy. Their feet slow down and become a bit uncoordinated. He was showing all the signs. It got to the point where I just thought, I don't want to be a part of this anymore. I don't want to manage this guy while he carries on fighting and damaging himself. I couldn't see him improving and I didn't want to see him get badly hurt.'

Helliet insists that for him, the safety of his boxers is of paramount importance and it is for this reason that he did not oppose the Board's decision to remove Deakin's licence.

'So the last straw, I suppose, for him, was when we were called before the Board the last time and I didn't argue his case for him. I'd argued his case before because we'd been in there a couple of times, but not then. They asked me what I thought and I told them simply, "This is the end for him." And I took no pleasure from that. I know he probably feels he's got nothing else he can do. It's tough for fighters who reach the end of the road, really heartbreaking, but that's where Robin was. He needed to pack it in for the sake of his health.

'Afterwards he came to me again and asked me to go back and argue his case for him and I refused. I wanted him to retire. It would have been easy for me to go the other way. I could have kept putting Robin out there and taking £200–£300 off him every time he boxed. But it wouldn't have been the right thing to do. I don't think he's ever forgiven me for that and that's why we still have problems now, but I prefer it like that, even if he is always writing rubbish about me on the internet.

'I'd prefer that me and Robin fall out now than I kept him with me and in 20 years he's a vegetable and I have to face the reality that I contributed to making him that way. That's the way I am. I do care about my boxers and that's why I didn't want Robin to fight on. He might not want to believe it, but that's how it is.'

Clearly, both Deakin and Helliet have greatly differing perspectives on events and their own careers. All things are subject to personal interpretation, after all. The only ones who really know are Mickey and Robin, two young men brought together, then wrenched apart, by the business of boxing.

For me, Robin is one of those characters that you can't help but root for. No one could suggest he is an angel but his heart is clearly in the right place and he's kept it there despite life dealing him some truly shitty cards. We stayed in touch after we met and he updated me sometimes on his progress, so I have to admit it was with some sadness that I picked up my phone on 20 June 2014 and read the message he had sent me. 'They refused my licence application,' it said, simply. 'I'm crying my eyes out.'

Never one to allow setbacks to bother him for long, since then he has continued to conduct his business in his own inimitable way, awaiting another hearing before the Board in October. Lately Robin has zeroed in on Ohara Davies, a highly talented and unbeaten amateur from Repton ABC, currently 2-0 as a pro, as a potential opponent. An internet war of words quickly ensued, which descended into insult-trading within a matter of hours, with a throw-down being made, involving a fairly large sum of money, from Davies's loquacious advisor, Spencer Fearon.

While Robin remained unlicensed, a fight with Davies was impossible unless it was a behind-closed-doors gym affair, but the whole episode fascinated me. It seemed that even after spending the best part of two years in the boxing wilderness, not having won since 2006 and being pilloried in the national press, Rockin' Robin Deakin was still able to attract the attention of the sport's hottest young talents. And in that way, despite everything, he had to be doing something right.

8

On the Road with Mr Reliable

Kristian Laight

Lightweight/light-welterweight
Born: Nuneaton, Warwickshire, 15 July 1980
Active: 2003–present
Record: 9-180-7

I REMEMBER virtually the exact time that the idea for this book came to me. It had been forming in the back of my head for a while, but on Friday 9 September 2013, at about 8.30pm, it suddenly all came together.

I was ringside for the BoxRec News website at York Hall and found myself alone on the press table for the first time. The event was so low-key, it seemed even the hardcore boxing media had blown it off.

Former English welterweight champion Ryan Barrett, returning from a drugs ban, was the big name on the bill in a comeback fight against a Polish patsy who would barely throw a punch at him. There were only six contests on the card. Yet on that inauspicious evening, with the upper tier of the venue completely deserted and the rear of the downstairs only dotted with silhouettes, I witnessed something that changed the way I looked at a sport I had followed all my life.

In the fourth bout of the night, a light-welterweight match-up over four three-minute rounds, an Anglo-American prospect called Dean Burrell, with seven wins from eight fights, including six knockouts – an impressive record – was pitted against a fighter from Nuneaton with a very different set of statistics. At that time he stood at 7-158-7.

Kristian Laight then held the distinction of possessing the worst record of any active professional boxer in the UK. I was unsure what to expect and conjured images of a battle-weary, bent-nosed bruiser, like Anthony Quinn in *Requiem for a Heavyweight*. Instead, he emerged fresh-faced from the dressing rooms and jogged into the ring looking relaxed and happy. The crowd barely acknowledged his presence. His movements were loose, no hint of tension on his face. The very apt nickname, (although I didn't fully understand why yet) 'Mr Reliable', was visible across his waistband.

Burrell then entered, dreadlocks bouncing, Bob Marley's 'Buffalo Soldier' blasting from the PA, glossy robe worn over matching shorts. As a contrast, it could not have been more marked. The audience whooped and roared. He oozed professionalism and aspirational glamour from every pore, milking the acclaim. While he climbed through the ropes, raising his gloves, dancing, pivoting on his hips, I noticed something from my vantage point that perhaps only I saw. With the faintest of gestures, Laight motioned towards his opponent with one gloved hand, raised his eyebrows and shared a smirk with his cornerman. It was a gesture of weary amusement, a seen-it-all-before moment, as if he was implying, 'Who does this joker think he is?' Always inclined toward the underdog in any situation, I instantly warmed to him.

Burrell went on the offensive as soon as the action started, neat footwork creating angles, winging in hooks and body shots, trying to wear Laight down. He had fast hands and a nice balance to his work, but the man from Nuneaton soaked it all up comfortably. He kept his right hand high and tucked his chin beneath his left shoulder, like a tortoise with its head pulled in, meaning that he took virtually every punch on his gloves and arms. 'Hit him Deano, he's a dickhead!' the fans shouted, before becoming frustrated at Laight's defensiveness. 'Throw a fucking punch you tosser!'

In the second, Kris was finally caught with a perfectly-timed straight left, bringing cheers from Burrell's supporters. Instead of looking distressed, he swallowed it like a blob of ice cream, smiled and said, 'Good shot, son!' In the third Burrell missed wildly with a right-hand swing that would have taken Laight's head off if it had connected. While his opponent regained balance from the momentum of the miss, Kris waited, choosing not to hit the open target. Instead he shook his head disapprovingly, said 'Oooh!' like Kenneth Williams in a *Carry On* film and pulled a face of mock surprise. In the fourth, Burrell had his best moment of the fight, connecting with a huge left that sent a spray of sweat careening off Laight's head, towards the ceiling and across the ring. Kristian just laughed and danced away.

When the final reckoning came, the result was clear before it was announced. Burrell had won every round. Yet as the ring announcer relayed this to the audience, it was the man from Nuneaton who seemed the happier. The Anglo-American puffed out his cheeks and made gestures of quiet frustration. His fans appeased him by whooping some more. On the other hand, Laight grinned, congratulated his adversary, then jumped down from the ring and swaggered back through the rows of chattering spectators, shoulders rocking, a 'What are you looking at?' expression on his face. Everything about his performance had fascinated me.

Seven or eight decades ago, during the period referred to by boxing historians as the golden era, fighters were far busier than they are today. Willie Pep, for example, considered by many pundits to be the best featherweight of all time, fought 22 contests in 1941, a number unthinkable for elite boxers of the present, who usually have no more than three bouts a year.

While modern pros spend large amounts of time with trainers, increasing fitness and working on aspects of their game using sparring and drills, the great ones of the past honed their technique through fighting. The ring was their college, where some flunked out and some matriculated with honours. Unlike the young guns of today, who do whatever they can to protect an unbeaten record, the legends of history saw defeats as part of a learning curve.

It used to be an old piece of boxing wisdom, seemingly forgotten now, that 'You don't know how good a fighter is until you've seen him lose.' The world welterweight champion of the 1930s and 40s, 'Homicide' Hank Armstrong, for example, lost three of his first four contests. He grew from those setbacks and went on to establish himself as an all-time great. In the modern game it is likely he would have either retired at that point, or would be abandoning his title aspirations for a career on the road.

In this way, journeymen can be viewed as throwbacks. Despite losing more than they win, the sheer number of bouts they contest mean they have considerably more in common with the great ones of the past than modern champions. They are fighting men, for whom the hazardous environment of the ring, not the gym, is home. To walk out every week or two in front of crowds baying for your blood, opponents expecting to wipe the floor with you and officials contriving to make that happen, requires a particular form of bravery. Pep and Armstrong would have had it too, developed during their formative days. And there is no active journeyman for whom all this is truer than Nuneaton's Kristian Laight.

Laight is a truly prodigious grafter, known as 'Mr Reliable' for the fact that so far, in his ten-year career he has never turned down a contest. If you have a lad in need of an opponent, somewhere between featherweight and light-middleweight and you get on the phone to Kris's manager Jon Pegg, he will not let you down. In 2013 he amassed no less than 29 bouts, contesting four fights per month in March, May and June. A similar year in 2014 and he will break the 200-fight mark by autumn. At 33, thoughts of retirement are far from his mind.

Blessed with a tight defence and quick hands, Laight is always in tremendous shape, trains like a champion and unlike many of the young prospects he goes in with, he makes enough money from boxing for it to be his only form of income. Yet if you enter the name 'Kristian Laight' into an internet search engine it will not take long to find boxing related message-boards where his record is being discussed. The general tone is usually one of derision and disbelief that someone with such poor stats can sustain a career. He is compared to a footballer who can't kick the ball, a doctor who kills his patients or a hairdresser who makes customers look like hedgehogs.

'People on the outside don't see the politics,' Kris says. 'They just sit in their armchair and say, "Ooh, look how many fights he's lost." They don't understand what any of it means, really.

'Yeah, I've seen myself discussed on forums on the internet where people are talking about my record and saying I shouldn't be licensed, that obviously I can't box and I don't know what I'm doing, I'm putting myself in danger and I'm not going to lie, the first time I saw that kind of thing, it did actually bother me. You know, I was hurt by it, a little bit. No one likes being told they're shit, do they? But then after a while I got hardened to it and I thought, "They don't know the way the business works."

'Let's face it, prospects wouldn't fight prospects early on in their career. They're going to need opponents and I would like to think that I serve a valuable purpose in this game. It might be nice if more people appreciated it, but what can you do? They can say what they want. I'll do my job and they can do their job, work in an office or a factory or whatever, its up to them. Live and let live.'

If it wasn't for a slightly receding hairline, Laight would look younger than his age of 33. There are no visible signs of how he makes a living at all, apart from the fact that he is clearly in supreme physical condition. At 5ft 10in and walking around at just under 10st (135lbs) he has a long, lean physique and a waist that tapers away almost to nothing when viewed from the side. His face is unmarked and fresh-looking, his manner relaxed and open. He grew up in Nuneaton, where he still lives, near to his mother Jay-Louise, with whom he maintains a close relationship. She fondly recalls how he was as a child.

'There was never any sign he would end up as a boxer. I was a single mother and out to work a lot, but he didn't give me one bit of trouble. As a boy he was always good to me. He'd go out to play with his brother Joel and he would come back to see me. I'd ask him what the matter was, if he was hungry and he used to say he just wanted to check if I was OK. He was always doing that sort of thing. There was something a bit special about it.'

Kristian may have been an angel in his mother's eyes, but in reality he had the usual teenage issues.

'As a boy I wasn't really a violent kid. I didn't get involved in fights out in the street and that sort of thing. I suppose I was your typical lad, staying indoors a lot and playing PlayStation. Sometimes I went out with my brother too and played football or whatever. We watched boxing a lot back then and that's probably what got the thought in my head. Lennox Lewis, Naseem Hamed, Joe Calzaghe, all the guys from that sort of time, I used to watch them religiously.

'But you know, my dad wasn't around and I became a bit of a toe-rag, really. From about 16 I was out and about drinking, doing some drugs and all that stuff. I didn't like school and was a little bastard when I was there, nothing major, just silly stuff. I was always getting suspended for messing about and not giving a shit. I had some trouble with the police for possession of illegal substances and things like that.'

By the age of 18, Kristian was just another disaffected kid who had got himself into bad habits and left school with nothing. Another 1990s NEET (Not in Education, Employment or Training) for New Labour's government statistics.

'I was a chubby lad, back then, believe it or not and I was so bored. That's why a lot of kids get themselves in trouble. There's nothing else to do. So one day I just went down to Nuneaton Boys Amateur Club and started doing some training. Just for the hell of it. From the first minute I went in there, I loved it. I loved going to the gym and being with the other lads and it kept me off the streets.

'Something clicked and I knew this was what I wanted to do. So I trained for a year, had ten amateur fights, won five and lost five. I beat [European title challenger] Tyan Booth as an amateur, but the funny thing is, looking back, in my amateur days I was completely different. I was coming forward and attacking mostly, really gung-ho! Anyway I was approached by an old Nuneaton-based trainer, Sid Reynolds and he said to me, "What are you doing boxing for trophies? Come and box for some money." So basically his influence turned me into a professional and I trained with him then, managed by Jimmy Gill. I turned over[5] and I've more-or-less gone straight through ten years with no gaps, no layoffs, no time off.'

Maybe because of his rapid turnaround from 18-year-old layabout to 23-year-old professional pugilist, Kris admits to not initially appreciating the workings of the boxing world or his likely place within it. His first fight, at the Britannia Hotel in Canary Wharf in London, in 2003, was against James Paisley, who at the time had a record of 3-8 and retired three years later. Kristian was slated to box in the away corner but, failing to understand the game, fought proudly, went for the win and was disappointed to come away with a 60-55 points defeat over six two-minute rounds.

In his second pro outing he came up against Grimsby's Matt Teague. The fight took place two months after Laight's debut and Kristian weighed in 11 pounds lighter to meet Teague at featherweight up in Hull. Despite having to jump through all these hoops to make the fight, still the penny didn't drop for the novice Laight. Again, he put up a spirited performance.

Teague remembers that Kris was 'very tough and very hard to hit. Very awkward. He caused me problems, I really couldn't get through with much at all. I hardly hit him. He's a good looking boy as well and I thought if he stays in the game, that won't last.

---

5 'Turning over' is boxing slang for going professional.

Johnny Greaves, Peacock Gym, East London, January 2014 (Elisa Scarato)

Ernie Smith poses for the cameras after a bout at York Hall in 2007 (Phil Sharkey)

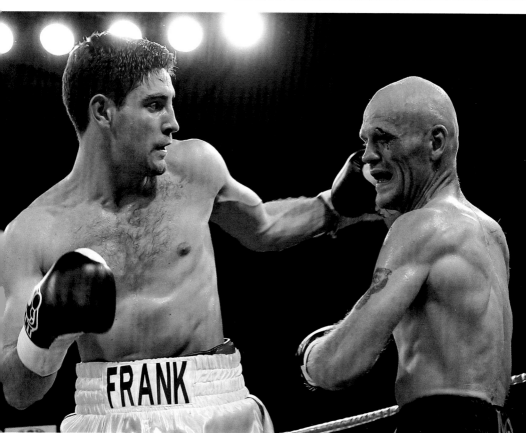

Frank Buglioni's left hook is blocked by Jody Meikle's glove during their bout at the York Hall in June 2012 (TGS Photo)

James Child, Goring-on-Sea,
1 February 2014
(Elisa Scarato)

Kristian Laight, Nuneaton, 7 June 2014 (Elisa Scarato)

Billy Smith celebrates his 100th pro
fight in 2010 and is presented a bottle
of champagne by super-middleweight
contender, James DeGale (Phil Sharkey)

Robin Deakin, Brentwood, Essex,
15 February 2014 (Elisa Scarato)

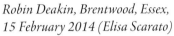

Johnny Greaves absorbs a heavy right hook from Dan Stewart in Swindon, February 2009 (Press Association)

James Child forces Joe McDonald to cover up during their bout at the Camden Centre in March 2013 (Phil Sharkey)

Bheki Moyo, South London,
8 February 2014 (Elisa Scarato)

Jody Meikle, Scunthorpe,
18 February 2014 (Elisa Scarato)

Rockin Robin
Deakin puts
Ryan Taylor
down in the
second round
of their bout
at York Hall
in January
2012. Deakin
had taken two
counts in the
first round
himself
(Phil Sharkey)

Super-
featherweight
John Quigley
finds no way
through
Kris Laight's
'tortoise shell'
defence in
Manchester,
October 2011
(Press
Association)

*Matt Seawright,
Tamworth,
8 March 2014
(Elisa Scarato)*

*Referee Bob
Williams calls
a draw between
Shaun Watt and
Bheki Moyo
(right) after their
bout at a dinner
show at London's
Savoy Hotel in
December 2011
(Phil Sharkey)*

*Jody Meikle doesn't
find his fight
with debutant
Jason Turner
too exciting in
Portsmouth,
February 2014
(Phil Sharkey)*

Max Maxwell, Birmingham,
15 March 2014 (Elisa Scarato)

Jason Nesbitt, Birmingham City Centre,
15 March 2014 (Elisa Scarato)

Jody Meikle before his last pro fight in May 2014. Three days later, he was back in jail. (Liz Phillips)

The camaraderie between Matt Seawright (right) and Aaron Fox is clear as they box a draw for the second time, in May 2012

Daniel Thorpe, Meadowhall, Sheffield, 19 February 2014 (Elisa Scarato)

Daniel Thorpe climbs up off the canvas in the second round of his fight with future two-belt world champion Amir Khan at the London Excel arena in October 2005 (Press Association)

Max Maxwell scores with the jab on his way to stopping Matty Hough for the Midlands area middleweight title in February 2008 (Phil Sharkey)

Max Maxwell pausing to admire his work after landing a right hook on his Czech opponent Stepan Horvath at the Civic Hall in Grays, Essex, April 2014 (Phil Sharkey)

Future Southern area welterweight champion Ahmet Patterson ducks low to avoid Jason Nesbitt's chopping right hand at York Hall in October 2010 (Phil Sharkey)

Billy Smith (left) as many on the boxing circuit remember him, after dropping a standard four-round points decision to Gareth Heard in May 2012. Just over a year later, he was dead (Phil Sharkey)

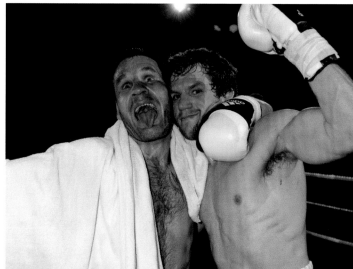

He's proved me wrong though!' Teague was given every round of six by referee Keith Garner.

Kristian continued fighting monthly or bi-monthly during his early career, hoping his luck would change. Despite always being the away fighter, he finally picked up a victory in his sixth bout against Jaz Virdee in Peterborough. Virdee sold the tickets but at the time was 0-4. After the contest he did not step back into a ring for two years. When he eventually did, his opponent was none other than Kristian Laight. He collected a revenge win on that occasion, although perhaps by that time, he was facing a different opponent, albeit one with the same name, as Kris explains.

'My first few fights I thought I could make waves. As the years go on you tend to learn about yourself and how everything works, but yeah, at the beginning I thought I was going to do something, be a champion, honest to God, I did. But I lost the first five and that changed things. I was always the away fighter but I was young and I didn't understand the politics, I didn't understand about ticket sales, I was a bit naive and I thought a fight's a fight, it doesn't matter what corner you're in, but then obviously I learnt how the game works.

'I had a few close ones, didn't get the decision and then I thought to myself, hang on! It was almost as if a spark had lit and I thought, "Right, OK, if that's the way it is, I'm just going to look after myself." And then everything came from there. I taught myself, bit by bit, how to be a decent journeyman. Every fight I go into, I learn from that fight, what the opponents are capable of, what you can expect next time and you just start getting used to everything. It's like a job and with any job you need experience to do it well. You progress into your role and learn what's required.'

In the decade-long career of Laight this moment amounted to something of an epiphany. If titles were not going to come along there could be another way to make a living from the game. After the first Virdee contest the regularity of his bouts began to increase slowly. He had two in April 2004 and two in June but still, from turning pro in September 2003 to September the following year, he fought only nine times. Busy by anyone else's standards but slow going for the boy who would become 'Mr Reliable'. As his reputation built, the momentum picked up. He had three fights in a month for the first time in May 2006, losing to Paul Holborn and Chris Long at light-welterweight, then to Akaash Bhatia down at super-feather.

For the next five years he continued fighting twice a month, with occasional threes and fours. With each contest he became wiser and more adept. By September 2011, when Kristian appointed Jon Pegg as his manager, he had reached a point where he rarely took a full-blooded punch and would utilise his reflexes, high guard or shoulder defence to block, slip or ride everything that came his way.

'Kristian is amazing defensively,' Pegg states. 'To be honest he's not so good on the offensive side but in terms of elusiveness he's one of the very best in the country. I mean that. I've told many people that. They find it hard to believe with his record, but it's true. I get youngsters in the gym that see Kris training and ask me about him. When I tell them he's lost 170-odd fights they start taking the mickey and I tell them, "You're not as good as him. You're not good enough to do what he does." People don't appreciate his ability.'

Early in 2011 Kris fought Chad Gaynor in Doncaster. Gaynor was renowned as a very stiff puncher and had stopped Johnny Greaves in the first round in his previous contest, a rare feat. Laight took him the distance.

In April 2012 he took on another unbeaten young fighter in Anthony Cacace who stopped three of his first five, including two first-round KOs. Again, Kristian took him all the way.

Perhaps his most impressive performance came against two-time world title challenger and current world number seven lightweight Kevin Mitchell, who he fought early, in his fourth contest in 2004. 'His single shots weren't so heavy,' Kris recalls, 'but his combinations were fierce.'

Laight was the first one to take him the distance. In fact, of Mitchell's first nine opponents, Laight was the only one to hear the final bell. Mitchell even stopped the famously resilient Jason Nesbitt by third-round TKO. In Mitchell's career to date, 26 of his 36 wins have come early, including title fights.

This defensive guile saw Kris frequently sought as an opponent. Anyone looking after a heavy-handed young fighter who needed rounds in the bank would seek him out. Pegg and Laight quickly formed an unstoppable partnership and from that point on, three or four fights per month became the norm, rather than the exception.

'Me and Jon, we don't like gaps,' Kristian explains. 'We like every week if possible. We always aim for 30 fights a year. The secret to it is having a good guy behind you. Jon's got all the necessary connections. He's matchmaking for most of the promoters around the country. That's why myself and Max Maxwell are the leaders at the moment, we're the busiest journeymen out there because we're both managed by Jon. Max keeps trying to say that he's the number one journeyman in the country, but he can get stood on. Everyone knows it me!

'Jon matches for Steve Wood and Errol Johnson who've always got shows on. He used to match for Frank Maloney [former promoter of heavyweights Lennox Lewis and David Price, now retired] and other promoters all over the UK.

'From my side, it's about being flexible. You know as a journeyman you can't be too precious about your weight class. You do what you have to do. I've taken fights at featherweight before and then sometimes I've gone up as high as light-middle. You either boil yourself down or beef up a bit depending on what's needed. But that's something else that people who just look at your record don't see. There's a lot of discipline in that. I might fight a lad at one weight and then a week later fight another lad at a completely different weight.

'People on the outside don't understand the training and dieting that goes into managing your body like that. And that's all part of being busy too. If I said I'm only fighting at light-welter, which is probably my natural weight, I would only have had a fraction of the fights that I've had. You just have to go wherever the money is.'

While in training for a lightweight fight, at Bedworth Civic Hall on 29 March 2014, for which he needed to shed three-quarters of a stone in a week, Kris outlined his daily diet. 'Breakfast is just a plain bowl of porridge. For lunch I'll have chicken breast on a brown bap with no butter and for dinner, minestrone soup with croutons and an apple. If I'm doing well with a few days to spare I may be able to have a snack of a handful of nuts and raisins here and there.'

This regime of deprivation would be maintained while running five miles every morning and doing a vigorous conditioning and padwork session every afternoon. He doesn't tend to spar. 'I don't need to, I'm in the ring every weekend anyway. But it can get to you a bit. Of course there are times when I'm starving and feeling weak and I could murder a bag of Doritos but I just think about the money I'll be earning on fight night and it's all worthwhile. Then once the weigh-in's done I can have a little scoff.'

Laight's highest recorded weight for a fight is 148.5lb, 5.5lb under the light-middleweight limit. He baulks at the idea of ever carrying any flab and insists he is only 'thicker set' like that. His lowest is 126lb, or 9st, bang on the featherweight limit, which he has done as recently as 6 December 2013. On 19 December he fought again and weighed in 10lb heavier, for a light-welter contest.

This sort of range from low to high (22.5lb) is the kind that many elite fighters will move through during their career. 'Sugar' Shane Mosley, for example, a three-weight world champion, started in 2003 as a 22-year-old lightweight weighing 136lb and now campaigns as a 42-year-old light-middle, weighing in at 152.25lb for his last contest. Such progression is common for a boxer whose build becomes naturally heavier during his late 20s and 30s. Yet for Kristian and fighters like him, there is no such progression. The normal process of nature and the advance of middle age is ignored. Body weight is simply chopped and changed to suit the opposition.

Inside the ring too, there is much more than good luck, or simply being prepared to turn up that goes into making a living in the way that Kristian does.

'You can't just decide you want to be a journeyman,' he says. 'There's a skill and an art to it. It's about looking after yourself in there, lots of movement, being crafty, knowing when to punch and when to step back, it's a fine art. You can't just go in there all guns blazing because you'll get cut. If you get cut, you're out for 28 days, British Boxing Board of Control rules, so that means no money for 28 days.

'People on the circuit often say to me, "Don't you find it hard?" and the truth is I don't. I keep myself in shape and for me it's just like going to work. I very rarely get nervous before fights. The only times there's a bit of nerves is for the kids making their debut or kids that I don't know about. With the decent kids, I know what's coming, but with ones you've never heard of there's that degree of unpredictability. You don't know what they're going to throw at you. For the good kids that I'm matched with, it's no problem, I'll keep my defence tight, use the ring and I've done it so many times its easy.

'One thing I often do is try to wind them up, you want them to get wild. If they're nice and tidy and you wind them up, they get angry and tense and they start telegraphing stuff and then it's easy. So yeah, I'll pull faces, I'll call him a pussy, or tell him he hits like a girl. It's about getting into their head. If it's a hard fight, you have to do that sort of thing. If it's an easy fight you can just go through the motions and you don't need to.

'I suppose as well it's all about having fun isn't it? It's a game, really. There may be a business around it, but when you get in there, it's a sport again. If you talk to them and pull faces it disheartens them. You may not beat them, but you can still have fun and try and deter them. I'm not really a dirty fighter, though. That's not my style. If anything, if I'm struggling I would tangle them up.

'I've been put over a few times by shots I didn't see and you know what? It's usually when I'm having a go back, I leave myself that bit more open and I've ended up on my bum. Then I think, what am I doing down here? Shit, get up! I've always made the count. Always. I've only lost five inside the distance in my whole time as a pro. And that tells you something. That tells you that I know what I'm doing.'

By early 2014 Kristian hadn't suffered an inside-the-distance defeat for four years, his last coming against the heavy-handed Dale Miles in Nottingham. To put things in context, ten of Miles's 14 career wins to date have been inside the distance, including one over British light-welterweight champion Curtis Woodhouse. Since then Laight had fought over 100 times, including bouts against James Dickens, who went on to win the English super-bantamweight title, Jon Kays who became English super-featherweight champion, Scottish lightweight champion Charlie King and two Southern Area light-welterweight champions in Tony Owen and Ricky Boylan. None of them could put a dent in him. A large part of this he attributes to the discipline and fitness levels he has brought into his game in the last few years.

'I never used to live the life. I've never been a smoker but I've been quite a heavy drinker and obviously if you're training seriously that's something you shouldn't do. I used to drink all week, even in the run-up to a fight, and you know, the night after the fight I'd have a skinful, but I was still doing my training and I'd get up and run, even with a hangover. But that's why in my early days sometimes I wasn't as sharp as I should be and once or twice I came in a couple of pounds over. I just drank too much, really.

'I've nearly got myself in trouble with all that. There was a time I was in the pub and my phone's rang and they said to me, "We're down at the Birmingham Inn Hotel, one of the kids has failed his medical, get down here!" And I'm on my third drink and I'm thinking, "There's a grand or so on the table, so let's go."

'I got my kit, had a few chewing gums, got in the ring and boxed. That was a tough one! I got through it, though. I weren't 100 per cent obviously, but I got through it. But yeah, I've taken plenty of fights like that, one hour, two hours' notice. I've been in the cinema, watching a film, you know, big bag of sweets, big drink and I get a phone call. I ended up boxing that same night. It happens all the time.'

Kris's old problems returned to haunt him in May 2014 when he suffered a TKO loss to novice light-welter Kerry Evans. With just under a minute remaining in the fourth and final round, Evans landed a huge right which put Laight down. Senses scrambled, Kris got up too quickly and wobbled badly in front of referee Clarke Joslyn, who immediately stopped the fight. It was his first stoppage defeat since February 2010 and it left him fuming.

'I'm annoyed with myself,' he said afterwards. 'Really fucking annoyed. I think I started believing I was indestructible. I've moved into my girlfriend's pub lately. I'm living upstairs and I've been drinking a bit too much again and taking my foot off the gas with training. Thought I could get away with it, but boxing always shows you what you can and can't do.

'To be honest he wasn't that special, the kid and I should have made it to the end, easily. I won't be making that mistake again. I've got five years maximum left in this game and I'm going to make them count.'

Stoppages may be a rarity for him but the constant piling up of losses has attracted the Board's attention. Between December 2008 and January 2014 Kris fought 113 times, winning just once. He was called in twice to see the area panel in that time but found that an honest approach served him well. He explained candidly about his role in boxing and his rationale was accepted.

'They know it already,' Kris says. 'I just say that I'm going in as the away fighter and I'm not getting decisions and they all nod and accept it. They wouldn't come out and say it publicly but they know how the game works. They've got to be seen to be trying to do something about it, haven't they? So they pull in a journeyman every now and then. It's easier than tackling the real problem.

'In all fairness though the Midlands area are very good, they're the best area board. I've heard the Southern and the Central can be a bit harsh. They can be a bit quick to take people's licences away, but the Midlands see me fight on shows and put on good performances, they know the score. They just say something like, "Come on, try a little bit harder" but it's just for appearances really.'

On 30 January 2014, Kris bucked the trend in a fight at the Millennium Hotel in Mayfair, London, being awarded an almost unheard-of points decision over unbeaten prospect Craig Whyatt. Feeling sharp after his winter break, Laight threw far more punches than usual to take the decision by one point. What made this event particularly strange was that many at ringside felt Whyatt had won.

Even Jon Pegg said, 'I thought Whyatt won it by a point, or maybe a draw. I was very surprised when they gave it to Kris. Lots of people were complaining afterwards but I was telling them that it's so unusual for a close decision to go to the away fighter that no one can complain. The amount of times Kris has been on the wrong end of close decisions, he deserves one sometime.'

Immediately afterwards, however, Laight faced the consequences. He was scheduled to fight again on Friday 7 February but the prospect he was due to face pulled out a day before the contest, depriving him of a wage. Two weeks later another young hopeful scratched. Altogether it was nearly a month before Kris boxed again, against Charlie Payton in Hull. 'That's what happens when you win fights,' Laight reflected, ruefully. 'The kids' managers have backed out because they're scared of losing.'

The contest against Whyatt had been his first win for 16 months. 'It's a funny one with the wins,' Kris says, 'I must admit, a couple of them I've been fortunate. At least four of them came from an old referee, Lee Cook, who was very fair. You can get fair referees, they're very rare, but you can get them. Lee's out of the game now, sadly. With him, if it was a tough fight and an even fight, he'd sometimes give an away win, which not many others do.'

To add to the win Kris picked up in January, he took another points decision over novice Aaron Flinn (1-4) in March. This made the first part of 2014 his most successful start to a year since turning pro. 'I'd better make sure I don't get any more for a while,' he said, laughing. 'I'll never work again!

'To tell the truth, the thing that links together all the wins I've had is that beforehand I've known in my own mind that I've had a good chance of winning them. I used to look into their records and look at their amateur backgrounds and whatever, but now I don't tend to do that so much, but I have an idea from what people tell me. Now I just go in there and do my job.

'What I tend to do now is have a good look in the first round and if they're strong or if they're sharp then I'll just go into survival mode. But if I feel there's a chance and they're not dangerous, then I'll put it on them. I guess over the years I've learnt to take a safety first approach.

'Basically the whole home fighter thing is massive in boxing and a lot of people on the outside don't get it. It's a lot to do with the promoters. The officials are paid by the promoters, I'm not saying that they're told to favour the home fighters, but there's something going on there. If it's a 50-50 fight, nine times out of ten it'll be given to the man who sold the tickets. That's just the way it goes. That's the system. If you're bringing money in, you get looked after. It's all about money, isn't it? Everywhere, money speaks.

'As a journeyman you get to see it from the other side. There have been many times in my career when I have been given a bit extra and told to take the kid around. Again, people in the crowd don't realise that's happening, but it's very common. It happens more than people think. With that sort of job, it's like I'm in charge but I'm moving him around the ring and letting him score a few points. People don't understand how that's different to what I do normally, but if I'm in there with a talented kid, I'm surviving and trying to spoil his work and stay out of his way.

'With one of these kind of jobs, they know the kid isn't up to much, but he's probably a big ticket seller and they need guys to look after him for his first few contests, just to make sure. The last thing they want is some lad who's shifting four or five hundred tickets a time to lose, get disheartened and quit.

'There's all sorts of things like that. Sometimes managers will set something up so the lads will fight twice. The first time I'll give him the win, the second time he'll give me the win. You can do that with two journeymen and that way you keep the Board off both of your backs because you both pick up a W to go on your record. Believe me, this kind of stuff goes on all the time.'

Despite the vagaries of his vocation, Kris does not regret his decision to go down the journeyman route. He is at home in the role, withstanding occasional moments of doubt. He wishes he had understood the business before he started, but even if he had, isn't sure he would have lasted as a home fighter for very long.

'I'll be honest, my heart goes out to all the prospects out there because it isn't easy, doing what they do. I'm fighting soon at Bedworth Civic Hall which'll be nice [in the contest in which he beat Aaron Flinn]. It's a ten-minute drive from my house. I've got a handful of tickets to sell but I'm getting a wage anyway because I'm in the away corner. I don't mind shifting a few tickets and people will want to come because it's obviously close.

'It's not the first time, I've sold tickets before, for fights in Birmingham and things like that but it's such a hassle and it takes your mind off what you've got to do. I'd much rather just pick up my kit, go to the venue and do my job. Selling tickets is hard graft, believe me and if you're under pressure to sell a hundred or whatever while training and dieting you just don't need it.

'I do think perhaps though, if I'd chosen the right team behind me, as in promotional and managerial team from the beginning, maybe I could have had a few more wins, but in the same breath I wouldn't have boxed as often as I have and I wouldn't have made a living out of it. I would have just been an average ticket seller. And there's a lot of those around!

'They might have nice looking records, but loads of those boys are struggling. I've never needed another job. I've got a little sponsorship with Fridge Freezer Direct that buys me kit and things like that, but this is all I do. That's why I've had to learn to look after myself. If I get suspended with an injury, I literally have no money coming in.

'Sometimes I do wonder if life would be better if I had a "normal" job with paid holidays, sick pay, a pension scheme and all that stuff. You know there are times when you have to get up and go for a five-mile run and you just don't feel like it. But then fight night comes along and I remember how much I love what I do. It's a buzz. Where else am I going to get that?

'And look, I know what I've got inside and I definitely believe there's a Midlands Area or at least a British Masters title in there for me. I've had two British Masters challenges before and I've lost both by three points. But one of them, I had a week's notice to do a ten-rounder with Jay Morris [in May 2010]. So with the right training and looking after myself I could definitely do it. It's something I've always said I want. Before I retire I want a belt of some description. The Midlands Area would be more prestigious but I'd take a Masters. As long as I get something to put on the wall!

'I'm aiming for 300 fights. I'm still relatively young, I'm only thirty-three. I don't take a lot of shots. I still feel fresh. In my eyes I've got another ten years left. If the Board permit it, I can see myself fighting into my 40s.'

Part of the human condition is that all of us, to some extent, become what we do. Spending most of your time engaged in a particular activity shapes who you are, defines your sense of self and how you look at the world. In this way, Kristian has become a consummate journeyman professional. He is probably the best example around – a committed, dedicated fighter who trains and disciplines himself according to his role, earning a solid living from an unforgiving business. He is such a fixture on the UK circuit and has fought so many young guns on the way up that around his weight classes, until you've been in with him, you can't consider yourself a real pro. Yet even in this well established position, there are things that play on his mind.

'I have one massive, massive worry every year and that's my brain scan. So far, I've never had a query on it. I know a few other lads that have had the results come back and it says you've had a change in your brain and that's got to make you stop and think. In my whole ten years as a pro, mine has always been fine. You know the blood tests don't worry me, but that stuff scares the crap out of me.

'Obviously you see the guys who've gone on too long and how they've ended up and it is a difficult one, but I think a lot of it's to do with defensive style. Most of these kids who end up punchy, they're going in all guns blazing and taking a lot of shots. If you're crafty and you stay out of the way, it's less of a problem. With me, even the shots I do get caught with, I ride most of them anyway.'

Kris shifts on his seat a little awkwardly as he says that. The thought of sustaining serious injury doesn't rest easy on his mind. He is still living a bachelor lifestyle, some might say carefree, younger than his years, handsome. Slurred speech, shaking hands and a shuffling gait would not be a good look. Being a journeyman is his job, though, a job he does extremely well in his own way, a job that gave him direction when he needed it and paid him well.

'That's it,' he says. 'That's what it's about. Boxing is about money. It's about tickets and it's about money. End of.'

DEVON
• CARE FREE PRO!
• JOURNEY MAN PRO!
• DEFENSIVE EXPERT!

9

The One Man Riot

Jody Meikle

Super-middleweight/light-heavyweight
Born: Riddings, Scunthorpe, 8 May 1980
Active: 2011–2014
Record: 7-45-2

Scunthorpe

Named after the Viking who founded it and populated since the industrial age by iron- and steel-workers who lived in its rows of small terraced houses. A proper northern corner, squeezed by recession and Greenpeace-listed as a toxic hotspot due to pollution from heavy industry. It was known only to me for its less-than-illustrious football team and the fact that every time I see its name, the word 'cunt' jumps out at me from the first syllable – not exactly a ringing endorsement. From now on though, I will forever associate it with a truly intriguing character.

Travelling up there was laborious, even at night. We left home at 7.30pm but the A18 was closed after Doncaster and we were diverted down a country lane where we got stuck behind a cattle truck doing about 20 miles per hour. This dragged the final leg of the trip on past midnight.

As I struggled to stay awake behind the wheel, with my wife poking me in the ribs and firing questions at me to keep me alert, I thought about the men making such journeys every weekend, up and down motorways, before and after fights. This is their Friday or Saturday night. A moment of intense adrenaline and danger, like a hit of cocaine, under the spotlights, sandwiched between hours of dusky, motorway tedium. It is a pretty crazy way to make a few quid.

Jody Meikle's name had originally been suggested by one of his best friends in boxing, Johnny Greaves. The two shared the same manager and occasionally worked each other's corners. 'I taught him everything he knows,' Johnny had told me, grinning. 'He's the next great entertainer.' When I mentioned it, Meikle accepted Johnny's explanation with a wink. 'Yeah, he did…I love Johnny and I really used to love watching him fight. Me and him are cut from the same cloth.'

If anything however, Jody has taken the act one step further. He is the only fighter I have come across who has been deducted points during a bout for the official reason of 'excessive clowning', against Tobias Webb in Swansea, in September 2012. Pictures of him in action generally show the first two rows of spectators howling with laughter. Nobody takes the piss like the 'Riot'.

In boxing, nicknames are like opinions – everybody has one, often even trainers, managers or in the case of Steve 'Big Daddy' Bunce, journalists. Sometimes they can be evocative and descriptive, like Ray 'Boom-Boom' Mancini, Mike 'The Body Snatcher' McCallum and my personal favourite, perhaps because legend has it he boxed my great grandfather, Jimmy Wilde, 'The Ghost with a Hammer in his Hand'.

On the flip side, some boxer monikers seem hastily or carelessly applied just for the sake of adding something to a licence. Herol 'Bomber' Graham was a lovely stylist but never a particularly big hitter. Tony 'TNT' Tubbs had quick hands for a big man but sported the contours of a baked potato and was usually anything but explosive, while Johnny 'The Entertainer' Nelson was involved in some of the most tedious fights in living memory during his early career.

A few hours in the company of Jody Meikle however, or watching highlights of his antics, would be enough to convince anyone that the 'One Man Riot' suits him absolutely perfectly. Backstage at York Hall in April 2014, prior to defeating debutant Aston Mount, he could be seen on the pads with Adeel Gul, Kristian Laight's cornerman, being cheered on by the other red corner boys, practising special combinations that involved right and left hands, headbutts and elbows.

Jody was born and grew up in a part of Scunthorpe known as Riddings, which has a notorious reputation and is described on a North Lincolnshire Council website as 'a deprived estate with high unemployment and social issues'.

'It was like the Bronx,' he says, smiling. 'Police wouldn't go down there. It was so rough even the rats carried flick-knives. It was a place where you'd sink or swim. If you were driving around, you could tell when you were coming into Riddings by all the boarded-up windows. They've tidied it up a bit now, but back then it was proper dodgy. There were always fights in the street and robberies. Perhaps this may sound corny, but there was a real community spirit as well. I miss it in some ways.'

He was the youngest of seven siblings, although he only shared a father with one of his sisters and the others were much older. His parents split when he was still a baby and his father moved to South Africa, where he recently died. Jody doesn't remember him at all. In the absence of his dad, Meikle was brought up by his mother Pam and stepfather Craig, who moved into his mother's house as a lodger when he was four.

'My mum was a tough old bird,' Jody recalls. 'I remember one time a TV licence man came round and looked through the window. Me and my sister were watching TV and we didn't know who he was. As far as we knew there was a strange man looking at us so we called out to mum and she went out there with a broom and laid him out in the garden! That's what she was like.

'To give you a better idea – there was a woman in the area who used to abuse her baby, beat him up, mistreat him, all that sort of thing. My mum couldn't stand anything like that, she was actually a foster carer and used to take kids under her wing. Anyway, social services gave her this baby, Peter, to look after for a while and she got really attached to him. After a time, they took the baby off her and gave him back to his mum. The thing was, after they did it, this woman burnt the poor little sod with cigarettes. It was horrible. My mum vowed after that, that every time she saw this lady she would smack her. And she kept her word!

'There was one time we were on our way to go swimming, just walking through the centre of town and all of a sudden my mum has flown across the road. She must have been 45 at the time and pretty overweight, but right then she was Usain fucking Bolt. It turned out she'd seen this woman who'd abused the baby and she just sprinted over and bashed the hell out of her on the pavement. It was mental!

'Another time she chased her down the street and knocked her over a wall. The police came to pick her up for that on an assault charge, but within a couple of hours she was back home. They let her off because she played the innocent old lady routine. She had arthritis so they didn't believe she could have done it. That's what she was like. She said she would batter this woman whenever she saw her and she did, until her dying day.'

Jody's undying love for his mother is clear and whether it's a genetic or an environmental link, as he talks about her with such affection, parts of his own character, which may seem mysterious, become more clearly defined. His past is a curious mix of violence and tenderness. Children are a massive part of his life. He has three: a son, Ben, who lives with him; a daughter, Evie, who he has regular contact with; and another son, Charlie, who lives in southern England and he sees only rarely.

Photographs of them adorn his living room and his eyes soften when he talks about them. On social media he frequently puts up pictures of kiddie day trips and family treats. Ben even comes to his fights. He is a tough guy but a model dad at the same time, having inherited his devotion for children and family from his mother.

His relationship with Ben, his younger son, seems particularly special to him. Ben had lived with his mother until two years ago but she was raising four other children from different fathers and Jody didn't feel the boy was receiving enough attention.

'He set a fire in his house,' Jody recalls. 'His mum rang me up, 1 January 2012, I will always remember the day, about eight in the morning and said I had to come and get him. I went around there and Ben was saying "I don't want to go, I don't want to leave my brothers and sisters." She turned around to him and said, "Fucking tough you're going!" I went mental at that. What a horrible thing to say to your own son.

'But since he's come here he's settled right down. When he first came to live with me, he wasn't doing well at school and he was on the Special Educational Needs register, now he's in top sets for maths and English and they all comment how happy he is. He comes to watch me box sometimes and he loves it when I mess about. There was one fight recently, in Peterborough, and I was in a mood beforehand and wanted a tear-up. Ben asked me if I was going to clown around and I said, no, I'm going to take it seriously and try to win. He went, "No, don't dad, come on, be funny!"'

As a youngster growing up in a rough area, Meikle recalls being bullied but he avoided trouble and kept a low profile, even going as far as to describe himself as 'quiet'. It was not until he reached his teens that the first signs of the mayhem that would engulf him appeared.

'I remember at about 11 or 12 getting bullied because I had a massive head. I've still got a big head now. But at that age I used to look like an orange stuck on a toothpick. Honestly, I was a right skinny, little dweeb and I had this big head, so I used to get bullied all the time and there were times it would actually hurt me, I'd be crying.

'Anyway, I remember one day, I was in year nine and these year elevens were picking on me. This one lad was giving it and giving it and giving it and I just flipped, steamed in there and windmilled him. I pinned him in a corner by a wall and absolutely battered him. I was knackered after about ten seconds and was hoping a teacher would come along and break it up. In the end, someone did. I was proper relieved! I needed rescuing as much as the other lad did.

'But from then I got some confidence. I saw what I could do and I became the bully hunter at school. If there was an older kid who'd pick on all the younger ones, I'd go and have him!'

Jody's reputation blossomed and he grew enthusiastically into the role of school hard-case. 'It's funny though,' he says, 'people looked at me then or even now and say, "Jody, he's tough and he's hard" but that's not really true, I was just daft, I wasn't scared of anything. I don't know why.

My big brother Trev used to box [Trevor Meikle was a welterweight who retired in 1997 with a record of 21-40-6, having won the Central Area title] and I used to mess about with him. He always used to say if I was in a street fight to headbutt the guy on the bridge of the nose. That was one of his tips. So I guess he taught me a thing or two, although he never really taught me to box, but I don't know where the lack of fear came from. Maybe it was growing up with my mum.'

By the time Jody had entered his teenage years scuffles in the school yard had spread into his home life and the street.

'There was a big family that lived near us called the Teambys and I was only 14 at the time, but they'd threatened my sister. Anyway, Craig, my stepdad, went down to sort this bloke out with a mate of his and I tagged along, but when we got there they were waiting and lobbed petrol bombs at us. It all went a bit mad after that, but I remember chasing after them, chinning one of them and smashing a load of windows in their house.

'That was my first charge from the police. I got done for violent disorder. To be honest, it defined what happened to me later in life, I suppose, because I'd always thought I'd go in the army, but because of my arrests for things like violent disorder, it couldn't happen.

'The funny thing with that particular case was I remember standing in the dock and Craig, my stepdad, was standing next to me and was being sent to prison. I was in floods of tears, not because I was a young lad in the dock at crown court, but because my stepdad was being sent away. I started calling the judge a bastard and all sorts. I was lucky not to get done for contempt of court.'

He smiles ruefully. 'But yeah, it screwed me up and meant that when I went to try and enlist in the Royal Engineers after I'd finished school, when I was 17, I still had the conditional discharge hanging over me. They told me to wait until the discharge was spent and go back, but that very night I went out with my girlfriend at the time, Kirsty, brilliant girl she was, and out of nowhere, she's come up to me in this club and smacked me across the head.

'Her mate was stirring shit and told her I'd been pulling some lass. She really went for it. She was beating the crap out of me! Of course, I couldn't hit her, she's a lass and the bouncers were just standing there, laughing. My brother and me were well known around the town so they were enjoying it. "Look at that chump Meikle!" they were saying. "He's getting battered by a bird!"

'Anyway, after they finished laughing they've thrown her out and I've gone outside to remonstrate with her, to see if she's all right. She's started hitting me again. So I grabbed her arms and these three lads who were standing by have seen it, decided to be heroes and started kicking off. So I thought, "Right, fair game! I can't hit a lass but I can hit you bastards!" So I chinned two of the lads and the other ran away, but I was proper pissed off by then and I thought, "You're not getting away from me!"

'So I've chased after him down the side of this nightclub, like an alleyway, which was quite dark. I bumped into him and then someone's tapped my shoulder from behind. I span around without thinking, swung an arm and sparked this bloke clean out with a lucky punch. But sod's law, it was only a copper, wasn't it? Couldn't believe it! So obviously I got charged with that one as well and that was the end of my army career. I was only a week away from getting in, but that was that.'

With the focus of enlisting in the armed forces gone and being a known face around Riddings, Meikle could easily have followed the same path as many other local lads. Huge numbers of boys his age succumbed to substance abuse and addiction, some also getting involved in dealing for quick and easy money. He is proud that he avoided that particular pitfall. The temptation was certainly there and as a renowned tough guy, he wasn't short of offers but it was a route he did not want to take.

Run-ins with the law continued throughout his teens and 20s, however, becoming almost the focal point of his life. Bar fights and street scraps happened weekly, sometimes involving makeshift weapons. Viewed by Humberside Police as an out-of-control youth, it was only a matter of time before incidents led to jail time.

'The first time I went prison I was 19,' he says. 'It was for biting a kid's ear off and spitting it in his face. I was in a bar and had got into some bother with these two lads. They were going to glass me, so I nutted one and grabbed the other and as I wrestled with him, I've just bit his ear, I don't know why, just one of those things you do instinctively. Anyway, we've fallen over, wrestling on the ground and a bouncer's come along and pulled us apart. His ear came off in my mouth, so I spat it out and it went in his face. The guy's still only got half an ear now. I see him around sometimes. I was on remand for three and a half months for that one. I got probation and a bit of community service as well.'

Always on the lookout for ways to satisfy his thirst for adrenaline and on completing his first spell inside, Jody became embroiled in the world of football hooliganism within the small but infamous firm of Scunthorpe United FC. Even today, the club still has one of the worst records for banning orders of anywhere in the country.

He talks about meet-ups with Millwall in his home town and a pitched battle with local rivals Doncaster Rovers in a Yates Wine Lodge near their ground, during which he attacked rival fans with a chair leg. On another occasion, in Huddersfield, he slipped out from the police cordon shepherding Scunthorpe fans to the stadium and ended up running at a group of 50 Huddersfield supporters on his own.

'I only did it because there were so many police about,' he says. 'I knew they wouldn't let me get killed.'

When in court for the enforcement of a football banning order shortly afterwards he fondly recalls the PC witness statement which read, 'Mr Meikle is apparently scared of nobody and is even undeterred by large numbers.'

He was duly barred from attending United's matches, but being Jody Meikle, he ignored the ban and continued going anyway, finally being tumbled after going in the home end during a match at York City. He was seen by a policeman who knew his face and escorted from the stands. Outside, in the car park behind the stadium, Jody lost his cool, fought with several officers and was promptly rearrested and charged.

'I don't know what it's all about, really,' he says. 'I've always had a problem with authority, anyone who's trying to tell me what to do. The police fit that category. Even doormen do, they all know me around Scunthorpe. One time I was about 21 and went to a place called Club 2000. I got there and this big lump of a bouncer told me I wasn't allowed in, so I looked at him and said, "Shut up, you fucking idiot" and just walked in. He knew better than to try and stop me.

'The club was owned by a local guy, a horrible, slimy fella who was always messing around with underage girls. I found him in a room with a couple of lasses who looked about 16. So I approached him and asked him why I wasn't allowed in and he blanked me. I found that annoying, so I grabbed him and slapped him around the face to get his attention and he's shouted, "Get him out of here!" at the top of his voice. Anyway all the doormen, all these big lads, they're all looking at each other going, "I'm not getting him out."

'In the end about seven or eight of them have got together and jostled me towards the exit and I've absolutely lost the plot, raging. I nutted a glass door and put it through, grabbed a doorman through the hole, dragged him outside and started punching his head in.'

Worse was still to follow.

'Anyway, the main time I went away was after going on a stag do to Scarborough and I met a lass. I remember the day so clearly because England were playing Sweden in the World Cup the next day in Japan 2002. So I was chatting these two lasses up and this doorman comes over and says, "That's my mate's missus." I looked up and said, "Do I look like I give a shit? Now fuck off."

'He obviously took a bit of offence at that. A bit later I went to the toilet and he followed me in. I knew what was coming so before he could take the initiative I've grabbed him, put the nut on him, banged him and knocked him down. Afterwards I went back out and continued talking to these girls and this guy's come flying out and he was a big unit. He was angry as hell and I had to do something to deter him, so even though it's a bit naughty, I hit him three times around the head with the base of a bottle. He grabbed hold of me by the collar, so I headbutted him again and knocked his teeth through his lip. He finally left me alone then. He had a fair bit of hospital time afterwards and had to have quite a few stitches.'

For this latest violent assault, Jody found the judge was no longer in a lenient mood. His prior record was considered and at the age of 22 he was sentenced to four years. Even this was not enough to make him stop and consider a change of approach. During this incarceration Meikle was moved 23 times due to repeated disorder inside. His son, Ben, was born while he was behind bars and Jody states that he found having to miss the birth and his boy's early development emotionally challenging.

'My way of getting through it was to kick off as much as I could,' he says. 'For a while I was in Walls prison in Hull and it was one of those private jobs run by Group 4. To be honest most of the officers were an absolute joke. When you're in HMP a lot of the guys are ex-military and they're tough, but these guys were just old codgers, mainly. There was a guy in there who thought he was the hardman on the wing, an ex-Hell's Angel and he'd bullied this lad and beat him up really badly, so I went and found him, he was lying on his bunk and knocked seven bells out of him. I was just hitting and hitting and hitting him. There was claret everywhere. I had to hit him until he stopped moving because if he got up, he would have come after me. I thought for a minute I'd killed him.

'Afterwards, I went out, playing all innocent and reported it to the guards, I said, "Look, I don't know what's happened but someone's been beaten up in there. He needs help, urgently." The whole wing got banged up and doctors and nurses were pulled in to carry him away to an outside hospital. By the next day, they'd figured out it was me. Someone probably gave them my name, but when they came to take me away I wouldn't have it. I was fighting with the screws. It took them two hours to get me from my cell to the block which was round the corner.'

Fortunately for Meikle, the times when a governor was able to add extra days to a difficult prisoner's sentence were over and new regulations meant an outside judge had to be brought in to do it, meaning it rarely happened. Otherwise he could very easily have found himself serving far longer than his original term. As it stood he only earned himself six extra weeks of time, but was upgraded from Category C to Category B, meaning he was relocated to Dovegate prison in Staffordshire, where the inmates were generally serving longer sentences for more serious offences.

'It was a mental place,' he says. 'They were big-timers in there and it was like a crazy holiday camp. My mate had a PlayStation 2 and we used to sit in his cell and play football manager games. I had a little still underneath my bed and I brewed alcohol down there. Every weekend, we'd sit about, chat shit and get absolutely rat-arsed. The screws knew what was going on and they let it go on to keep the peace. But there were a lot of tough cookies in there. I had the shortest sentence in the place and there could be a real hostile atmosphere at times.

'One weekend, we were all smashed and the prison officers came in, picked on this kid for no reason and pushed him off his seat. I'd had a few too many so I chinned two of them and sparked them out. More came along, dragged those two off and they closed down the wing. All the officers just left. Now that made even someone like me apprehensive. All these big-time boys suddenly started walking down the stairs with bags over their faces, so they couldn't be seen on camera. They knew there was no staff and they had the running of the place.

'There was a real feeling like absolutely anything could happen. It was pure anarchy. They locked the wing down for two days and in the end, when they came back, they hauled me straight down the block. They gave me a bit of a pasting in there and after a couple of days they've come bursting in at about six in the morning and started whacking me.

'I fought back and managed to push them out of the cell, but then they came back in with bloody riot gear on and dragged me out and put me on a bus.'

Jody was transferred to Lowdham Grange, near Nottingham, a Category B prison of roughly 1,000 inmates, and was not welcomed by the staff there who had heard of his activities at Dovegate.

'At Lowdham I actually tried to keep my head down, but the screws knew I'd been fighting with officers at Dovegate and they had it in for me and kept trying to wind me up. So in the end, I thought, "Stuff it, I've had enough of you bastards." I went into their office, there was a screw in there. I lobbed him out and barricaded myself in. I stripped down to my boxers and found a bottle of washing-up liquid by a sink. I covered the floor in washing-up liquid, so when they tried to come in they were slipping all over the place and I'd shove them back out. I was in there for about a day in the end, just to piss them off.

'After that I was transferred to Hull prison and ended up chinning up the governor. He deserved it, though. Me and this other lad had barricaded ourselves in a cell for about 22 hours and when we finally came out, the officers were there and the governor got hold of me and smacked my head in. He absolutely battered me. I laughed at him and promised him that one day he'd get it back. He sneered at me, "I've heard that off bigger and better people than you, Meikle" which was a bit of a challenge, really.

'So one day I was on the phone to my mum and saw the governor coming. I said goodbye quickly and called out to him. He started to walk my way and I've launched at him and cracked him in the chops, straight off, before he knew what was coming. I was scrapping like hell with him and he's pressed the alarm bell and the screws have all come running in and given me an absolute hiding. It was the best hiding I ever took in my life because I managed to put one on him! That bastard really had it coming.'

On release from this sentence, Jody's problems on the outside continued unabated. Repeated incidents in the town centre saw him barred from most Scunthorpe pubs and bars by court order in 2006. Predictably he breached the order, continued drinking where he liked and was arrested for it in 2008, whereupon he was given a suspended prison sentence and an Anti-Social Behaviour Order. The memory brings a smile to his face.

'Ridiculous!' he says. 'I was on pubwatch and got an ASBO. Twenty-fucking-seven years old and they gave me an ASBO! Who's ever heard of that?'

His third spell in prison came when he was 29, as a result of trying to break up a fight. His girlfriend at the time and mother of his youngest child, Charlie, was sadly caught up in the scuffle. As Meikle broke the fight up she was punched in the face by one of the men involved. Enraged, Jody beat the hell out of him.

The guy gathered some friends and followed Jody home so he went inside, got a cosh and came back out to confront the group. Before long they scattered and he went back in the house to relax. Unable to beat Meikle physically however, the lads decided to phone the police. Tired of his constant misdemeanours, the cops were quick to charge him with assault. He was convicted and sent away once more.

Again, Jody talks of the emotional strain of imprisonment. He found it a difficult period, leading to the break-up of his relationship. His ex moved away and Jody lost touch with his son, something that affected him deeply and still does today. The swirl of anguish was stirred further by the fact that at the time his mother was suffering with cancer of the oesophagus and didn't have long to live.

'I got given 12 months and my mum was hoping to see me again when I got out,' Jody remembers, his voice wavering slightly with emotion. 'She asked me to promise that I wouldn't kick off or do anything to make my sentence longer.'

He began his term in Hull, then was transferred to Moorlands near Doncaster, 'I was just keeping my head down, going to the gym and stuff.

'They let me out one day to see her. I was taken home in a prison van and they blocked the road off. The house was crawling with police! Just for me, on a 12-month sentence. It was barmy! Anyway, the next day, she passed away. They were bad times. I lost my son, my mum died and I was banged up.'

He was taken to attend his mother's funeral in handcuffs and even now, six years later, he becomes visibly agitated as he recalls how he was unable to help to carry his mother's coffin because the officers would not free his hands to do so.

'I went back to prison and I was fuming,' he says. 'I told a couple of lads that I was going to get the security officer because what happened at the funeral was his fault and the bastards grassed me up. So before I knew it, screws came in, twisted me up, slung me in the block and transferred me to Lindholme.'

With his mother's passing, his promise to her was no longer valid and at Lindholme, also near Doncaster, Meikle again began to conflict with officers. As he had done previously at Dovegate he picked a moment to attack and barricaded himself into the governor's office, where he caused damage worth several thousands of pounds. He was in there for seven hours and after making a series of random demands aimed only at causing as much inconvenience for the officers as possible, he eventually gave himself up.

By the time he had completed this third custodial sentence, Jody was 30 and had a string of convictions for violence behind him. Something was needed to break the cycle or his life was only likely to head one way.

'If I hadn't got into boxing, I'd probably have ended up killing someone,' he says. 'I would have. God knows where I'd be today.'

Boxing ran in the family and he had been dabbling in the noble art for years. Following in the footsteps of his older brother, Trevor, he fought five amateur contests as a 15-year-old, losing the lot.

'I just messed about and took the mick,' he says. 'I thought it was funny to piss about and in all seriousness, I was knackered. You never realise how hard boxing is until you have your first fight, so messing about was another way to get through it. My opponents were hitting me and I was just laughing at them and mucking around. I was like that all the way through the juniors. In my last junior fight a guy stood up on the ring apron and shouted, "This isn't boxing!" I told him to shut up and pushed him off. They banned me from the club for that.'

After that, Jody drifted away from the sweet science for more than a decade because he 'discovered beer'. He played football in a couple of local teams, but kept getting sent off. From there, he graduated to rugby and played junior level for Scunthorpe. Again however he found the limitations of the game's rules a touch too restrictive. 'I kept getting sent off from rugby as well. If a kid tried to get rough, I'd always get rougher. The referees stopped putting up with it after a while.'

From there he gave up on sport a little bit. 'I thought maybe I'd just stick to drink and women,' he says, smirking. He did so for 12 years, during which time he was banged up for six. Like so much in his life up to that point, his eventual return to the ring was related to his troubles with the law. Between his second and third prison term, at 27, Jody was back in crown court after another fracas with a doorman.

'I didn't care about boxing originally. But when I was going to get sent away again, I said I'd go back into training to get a reference off my amateur coach, to make out I was channelling aggression in the right direction. I didn't really have any intention of boxing seriously, if I'm being honest, but the judge loved it and gave me a suspended sentence, so at that time I went back, just to keep up appearances.

'I trained with Leon Dobbs who in my opinion is useless. As far as I'm concerned he's the laughing stock of Scunthorpe and to be fair, he didn't teach me anything. I just fought how I wanted. But anyway, I trained three months with him and got carded. I fought Shane McPhilbin [later to become British cruiserweight champion] in my first senior amateur fight. I stopped him as well!

'He won't thank me for saying it, because he can't take it and he still denies it, but I did stop him. It was a lovely finish too, an elbow right in his eye! He squealed like a little girl and I got disqualified. The funny thing was the referee only gave it to him because I owned up. He was going to give it as a legitimate stoppage but I admitted what had happened.'

Between January 2007 and October 2010 Jody contested 40 amateur bouts as a senior at super-heavyweight, of which he won 12. He was tough as hell, could withstand punishment all night long and relished the confrontation, but was uncultured and lacked technique. Rather than bulking up with weights, Jody competed at the higher weight limit because he 'was eating and drinking whatever I liked'.

Among those he traded blows with at this time was the future European Union heavyweight champion Richard Towers, who stands 6ft 8in and weighs 235lbs. 'He was such a big bloke and every time he hit me I saw stars. That was one of the only times I was in the ring and thought, "What the hell am I doing in here?"

'Another time I was actually due to fight [current British number one heavyweight] Tyson Fury. I'm gutted that never came off. He was going to come over to Scunthorpe to fight me but it fell through. It would have been great to say I'd done that.'

Jody's attributes were not particularly well suited to the amateur code and before long he was plying his trade on the EBF (European Boxing Federation), an unlicensed circuit running in central and northern England. He had 15 fights there with mixed results, again fighting at heavyweight, but his time on the EBF came to an end when he was slated to fight Paul Venner in Middlesbrough. Inexplicably he started drinking during the day, continuing in the car on the way to the venue and even after he arrived.

'I don't really know why I did it,' Jody says. 'I was just in the mood for a drink, I suppose.'

By the time he was due to step in the ring, Meikle had been on the lash for ten hours straight. He was in no state to even make a pretence of professionalism, walking unsteadily towards his opponent, hands by his side, laughing and goading him on. The home-town crowd quickly became extremely hostile and Venner was irritated enough to headbutt Jody openly. Rather than disqualifying Venner, after the restart, the referee warned Meikle. 'Behave yourself or we'll have a riot on our hands,' he chided.

At the end of the contest, which wasn't really a contest in the normal sense of the word and more an exercise in Jody seeing how far he could push his luck, a win was declared for the local boy. Despite this and wary of the venomous atmosphere, Jody was advised by security to leave via the back door. He refused and went out of the front. Outside the venue he was greeted by an angry mob of Venner's followers and was informed by a representative of the EBF that he was no longer welcome to box on their circuit.

Having caused problem after problem in the amateurs and managed to get himself barred from unlicensed boxing, Meikle's future as a prizefighter did not appear too bright. He stopped training with Dobbs at this time and moved to the St Paul's gym and then Brigg, both in the Scunthorpe area before using personal contacts to find his way to the famous Ingle gym in Sheffield.

'I loved training there,' he says. 'I had some problems at the time. My boy, Charlie, who I don't see, was very ill in hospital and it looked a bit dicey for a while. Training with the Ingles really took my mind off it. I think it was then that the penny started to drop a little bit. I started to see how boxing could work for me and I began to really enjoy the discipline of training hard. My weight started to come down, which was better for me and suited my frame.

'Anyway, this was about 2010 and I began to toy with the idea of turning pro. I was staying at John Ingle's house and obviously I was working back in Scunthorpe, as well as seeing my little boy every day, but he let me stay there for training purposes. I asked him about the rent and he was always saying, "It's OK, I'll get it off you when you box." Anyway, I really wanted to turn pro with the Ingles, but I appreciate they've got much better kids than me down there and I knew I wouldn't be top of their list of priorities.

'So I'd filled in the forms and everything and was waiting to go in front of the board. I was itching to get going by this point and Dominic's come out and said, "Oh no, not this time, we'll try to get you in next month." And I just started to think, "Bollocks to this." I'm living there in someone else's house, training every day and although it was top quality training and I think I was at my best when I was with the Ingles, I wanted to get started and they were holding me back.

'I'd been told about Carl Greaves because a mate of mine knew him. I'd been down to Carl's gym a few times and sparred one or two of his lads. I got his number off Shane McPhilbin and phoned him up. I explained the situation with the Ingles and he said it was OK, I could sign with him as long as I hadn't got a contract with them. To be honest, I had, but I told him I hadn't and he sorted everything out for me quickly. I went before the Midlands Area Board and that was that.'

Jody's first pro fight was against Justyn Hugh in Newport, Wales. Hugh was 6-0 at the time. Meikle obviously boxed in the away corner and lost every round on the official card but loved every second of the bout. 'I couldn't stop smiling,' he says. 'Getting up there in front of a decent audience, being paid well for it, I really had a feeling like I'd found my niche.'

For his second paid outing he found himself at Wembley Arena, on a Mick Hennessy-promoted show that included Tyson Fury and Ashley Theophane. He was booked to box the big-ticket-selling Greek Londoner Andreas Evangelou, who was making his debut, over four three-minute rounds. 'I found it unbelievable,' Jody says, 'that a kid from Riddings could end up boxing in a huge venue like that. I just kept looking around and grinning to myself.

'The trouble that night was that John Ingle had the hump because I'd blown him off by turning pro with Carl. He started moaning about the money I owed him for rent. I had every intention of paying him, but he rung me up,' Jody alleges, 'threatening me, telling me a certain person would come looking for me, so that got my goat a bit and I said, "I tell you what, you better make sure that certain person kills me, because if he leaves me alive, I'll come after you. I'll be round your house to even the score." I was fucking furious.

'To be honest I was going to pay him once I'd had my first two or three fights and got some money together, but he pissed me off so much I told him, "You're not getting your money now, you can fuck off." Anyway, the Ingles were there at Wembley with some of their boys and of course, sod's law, the way the money was worked out on the night, they were the ones supposed to be paying me. My mate Lee Murtagh was doing my corner that night, really good mate of mine and I was warmed up, ready to go out, just got a sweat on and John Ingle walked in with a right face on. The place just went quiet.

'There were other lads in the dressing room, Matt Seawright and Jason Nesbitt were in there. Me and John had a massive row. He said he was going to take the money out of my purse and I told him if he took the money out of my purse, I'd punch his head in. I went mental. Lee went out and got security and the security boys actually came in and took John Ingle out. And you know what, after all that, he never took anything out of my purse and I never gave him a penny.

'Anyway I got in the ring to fight Evangelou and I was buzzing from all the aggro. John Ingle's sitting there giving me the evil eye from the first row and I was winking at him and all sorts. I just thought, you know, they could have earned money out of me, the Ingles, I know I wouldn't have been one of their superstars but I would have been out every week and they could have done something with me. It's their fault at the end of the day. I've spoken to John since then and he's been all right about everything. I think he knows he was in the wrong.

'So that's how it all began for me. I never started with my head in the clouds. I always knew I was going to be a journeyman. I'd heard stories from my brother, who had a mixed career, but was on the road for some of it and he'd been ripped off left, right and centre. He was mismanaged and used. Keith Tate robbed him blind, apparently. That's how it is in boxing, there's a lot of bad people in it. But I really trust Carl [Greaves]. He's honest with money and he doesn't mess me about. He's more of a mate than a manager. We're quite close. That's all you can ask for, really.

'I've told Carl from the beginning, I want tough fights, I don't mind getting punched, it's bread and butter for me. Me and Shane McPhilbin always say every time you get hit, you get better looking! And the truth is I'm not in it for the money. They money's great, of course, but that's not what brought me into it. I get a decent wage from roofing. What really makes it all worth it is when you see people laughing and enjoying themselves at ringside. I know I'm not the greatest of boxers, I've got a decent chin and that's about it but I can still entertain people and make them enjoy their evening and that's what I love.'

Jody's durability ensured that his first 14 fights all went the distance, including a solitary win over Elvis Dube in Cleethorpes. The 15th proved a salutary lesson on an away-day in Tenerife, against Adasat Rodriguez. The fight was offered at two days' notice and Jody had to lose a stone in 36 hours to make weight. He simply starved himself.

'I didn't eat or drink anything, not a crumb, not a drop,' he says. Naturally, as the bell sounded for round one, he was frighteningly drained and weak.

Boxing is full of metaphors for life and there is an old saying in fistic circles that the most damaging punches are the ones you don't see. Jody came out for the first round, was feeling his way into the contest and suddenly found himself on his back.

'I thought I'd slipped,' he says. 'I got up at about seven or eight and the ref waved it off. I was furious, kicked a stool across the ring, called the ref a cheating bastard, called the doctor a cunt, all sorts. Don't think they understood me to be honest, they were all Spaniards. If it'd been in England I'd have been in loads of trouble. Anyway, I watched the video afterwards and he caught me with a beautiful hook, bang on the button. I was out cold for a few seconds, that's why I didn't remember it. So I knew from then that I could be knocked out. Everybody's human. I learnt from my mistakes that night.'

Another 12 fights down the line, Jody was matched with Ricky Denis Pow from Alicante. Pow had a record of 7-0, including six stoppages. One of those was a first-round crushing of Rodriguez.

'That was a tough one going in mentally, because I knew what he'd done to Rodriguez but when we got going, the reality was he couldn't punch at all, that guy. I've no idea where his six knockouts came from. At the end, the ref Clarke Joslyn said to me, "If you'd gone for it a bit more, you could have beaten him," and he's right, I probably could have, but why would I want to do that? I'm in with a kid who is 7-0 with six stoppages and if I beat him, where does that leave me? Who's going to call my manager looking for an opponent then?'

This same philosophy was plainly visible when Jody took on Bournemouth novice Jake Gosling at the Guildhall in Southampton on 22 March 2014. Meikle was dismissive of his opponent's power and clowned constantly. In the fourth round he wobbled the youngster with a powerful right hand, leaving him tottering like a baby giraffe for a good ten seconds. Rather than follow up, Jody stepped off, laughing, allowing the lad time to recover. Speaking afterwards Meikle explained, tongue firmly in cheek, 'No, I don't think I really wobbled him, he just decided to do a bit of breakdancing.'

In its ringside fight report BoxRec News wrote that Jody 'was playing about constantly but could have easily won this fight if he could be bothered'.

'The reality,' Jody explains, 'is most of the time you're not going to win anyway, you know I'm going in there with guys like [former English and British super-middleweight champion] Tony Dodson and these guys have been dedicating themselves to the sport since they were kids. They're miles ahead of me. I'm just a daft bloke who'll fight anyone. So yeah, maybe a lot of the time I won't try as hard as maybe I could do, but what's the point? There have been times I have gone at it and really had a go and the referee's still given it the other way and you think, are you watching the right fight?

'I went up to Scotland and absolutely battered this kid up there, Davie Drummond. I hammered him. He looked like he'd been in a car crash when he got out of the ring. And of course, they gave him a draw.

'All the home-town decisions, I've wondered what's behind it. I don't know if its corruption but you do question if the refs are told to lean towards the home fighter, because it happens all the time. You know this thing of protecting the ticket sellers, the promoters obviously do it but it does seem like the officials do it too and I'm not sure how or why that works.

'But there's other ways of looking at it. Like most things in life, its up to you how you view it. I've had quite a few lads break their hands on my head. Me and Andrew Pattinson [another journeyman] always used to say that if they break hands on your head then it counts as a win. So that's about another five or six wins on my record!

'But I've been in with some good lads. [English super-middleweight champion] Callum Smith was the best I boxed. I was due to rematch him in Blackpool live on Sky, but the TV people said the fight wasn't competitive enough and dropped me. They pulled in this kid from Latvia, Pujonisievs, who was basically a fat welterweight and got knocked out in about three punches. I thought, "That's justice right there! Are they seriously telling me I wouldn't have put up a better fight than that?"

'And look, obviously there's other times where you're paid a bit extra and asked to give someone a move about. This sort of thing goes on all the time. Of course it does. You know most of the time when that happens, you're already booked in for the fight, then when you get there they tell you that's what they want. For most journeymen, they're not going to turn it down if the money's good. It's a part of the game.'

I saw Jody's participation in this side of the business first-hand when, two months after I interviewed him, on Saturday 21 April 2014, I was at York Hall for RingNews24 at a show billed as the 'Return of Smokin' Joe'. Sadly, the evening had nothing to do with a psychic event involving the great heavyweight Joe Frazier, who died in 2011, but Brentwood super-middleweight Joe Mullenden, who uses the same nickname and was topping the bill in a challenge for a Masters title.

Jody was on the card, the second fight of the night against a light-heavyweight debutant who had a noisy contingent of supporters in the building, ensuring he entered the ring to a huge welcome. Even before the action began, however, the novice gave signs of being some way out of his depth.

During the pre-fight introductions, while Jody danced around, making faces and gestures at the screaming fans in the upper tier, the home fighter, who appeared soft and fleshy at the weight, shifted nervously from foot to foot. Whether or not he froze on his debut only he can know but from the first bell he was beaten easily to the punch. A mischievous glint appeared in Jody's eyes as he quickly discovered he was not only tougher but technically superior. He could do whatever he wanted and I knew from prior experience what was coming.

From the opening exchanges the bout became the Jody Meikle show, in which the One Man Riot went jubilantly through his entire repertoire of tricks, much to the chagrin of the ticket-buying supporters. He danced in and out of range, stuck his chin out, grinned and made faces at his opponent, kissed him on the cheek in clinches, staggered around theatrically pretending to be wobbled by his desperate punches, patted him on the arse, made the wanker sign at his fans, leant on the top rope and spoke to people at ringside, including several comments directly at me, windmilled with one hand while punching with the other and so on.

During the third round, referee Bob Williams paused the action and told Jody to 'stop pissing about' but did nothing to try to enforce his command and the last minutes proceeded in the same way as the first, with the ticket seller utterly downcast and demoralised by the end.

The home fighter had done so very little throughout the bout that Williams had no choice than to award the decision to Meikle, but his scoreline of 38-39 deeply flattered the debutant. Being generous, he could have been given a share of one round, which would have made a score of 37-40. Jody made a face of mock surprise as his hand was raised and jumped down from the ring apron to where I sat at the edge of the press table. I stood to congratulate him on the win and the sheer slapstick lunacy of his performance. He grinned, 'I wasn't supposed to win that one!'

A couple of days after, he gave me slightly more detail on how the night had panned out.

'The lad had sold a fair few tickets, but they were a bit concerned that he couldn't cut it so when they brought me in as the opponent for his debut, the matchmaker paid me extra to look after him. The problem was he was dog shit! I don't know why a promoter would sign someone like that. I couldn't have done any more to lose except diving on the floor, and I don't do that for anyone. When a fighter's that bad, sometimes it's harder to lose than win. That's the way it was in that one. Even the matchmaker didn't complain. He could see I did my best to throw it away!'

Unfortunately, by the time I watched Jody clown his way through those four hilarious rounds, he had already made the shock announcement that he was retiring from boxing in May. Publicly he gave the impression that the decision had been made for the sake of his family and his health, but the reality was that other forces were at play. Try as he might, the One Man Riot had not yet escaped the chaos of his past.

His last offence, committed in summer 2012, still hung over his head as this book was being written and despite occurring nearly two years previously, had only just been brought to trial. He had involved himself in a dispute between several youths in a bar and acted initially as the peacemaker. As the incident played itself out however, Jody was struck with a bottle, causing him to retaliate, attacking one of the young men, who he suspected to be under the influence of cocaine.

'I knocked him down about six or seven times,' Jody said. 'He must have been off his head because he kept getting back up. I actually busted my right hand that night. My last five fights of 2012 I fought one-handed, didn't tell anyone because I wanted the money, but my right was fucked.'

The whole incident was caught on camera and in a sign of the times, the case became complicated by the fact that the individual that bottled Jody was an Iraqi. Unfortunately, during the commotion, people standing by could be heard referring to the lad as a 'Paki'. As a result of this slur the offence was classified as racial assault, which carries a maximum term of ten years.

Once arrested, Jody knew that his prior record made such a sentence likely. Rather than plead not guilty and risk a prison stay of that length, meaning he would miss his daughter's early life and his son's ongoing development, Meikle followed his barrister's advice and entered a guilty plea, making one-and-a-half to two years or a suspended sentence the most likely outcome. He hoped for the latter but either way he knew he would be disqualified from boxing, having already received a six-month suspension in 2011 because he didn't notify the Board of his previous convictions. This disappointed him deeply although he hid it from the world. He hadn't intended to leave the sport yet and the charm of his performances was winning him admirers up and down the country.

Rather than wait for the inevitable and the Board's withdrawal of his licence, Meikle decided to take matters into his own hands and announced he would be retiring after a contest at North Kesteven Sports Centre on Saturday 17 May. For the first time in his pro career, like his friend Johnny Greaves, for his final bow he would box in the home corner and sell tickets, eventually battling to a typically entertaining draw with Hampshire's Sam Couzens.

As the final bell rang, British boxing lost one of its most entertaining performers and Jody lost the part of his life, other than his children, that meant the most to him. Regardless of the circumstances surrounding it, it was impossible not to feel saddened by the turn of events. Unintentionally, this chapter has become the postscript to Jody Meikle's boxing career.

It was a career that saw him have 62 fights in three years. In that short time he was consistently one of the nation's busier journeymen, unquestionably its funniest and provided value for money to paying customers up and down the country. In his own way, Jody left an indelible mark on the sport.

'I've loved it. All of it,' he told me. 'Everything about it. I never even worried about ending up punchy. If it happens, it happens. What's the point in worrying about it? It's not going to help and you know what, if I died in a boxing ring, it wouldn't be a bad thing for me. I know that may sound ridiculous, but that's the way I feel. The Board insurance would have meant my kids would be looked after and it would mean I died doing something I love. And hopefully I'd get to see my mother again. If they'd let me I would have fought until I was 90.'

Jody had intended to put his experiences to good use by working with young offenders and going to university to do a criminology degree. He still hopes to make that happen. There is a bitter irony in the knowledge that prior to his last offence coming to trial, he had made contact with his local police force to try to find some youngsters to work with.

Like boxing records, criminal records do not tell the whole story. Just as the numbers 8-51-3 provide no indication of the levels of sheer joy Jody brought to small-hall boxing fans, his lengthy list of previous convictions and now four prison terms don't provide a rounded picture of his character. The court clerk's ledger will tell us that in a sentencing hearing on the morning of 19 May 2014, Jody Meikle, an offender with a long prior history of violent disorder, was given 20 months, to serve a minimum of ten, for racial assault.

Many people would read that line and form an instant judgement but when I read it, I remember a humble man, thrilled to be interviewed, who spoke in silly voices while playing with my one-year-old daughter and talking of his own children with such pride, a man who made me and many others laugh, who gained wisdom from his mistakes and wanted to contribute to his community. He will be behind bars when this book goes to print. It would have been easy for the turn of events to send him spiralling into depression and self-pity. But that would not be Jody Meikle's style.

'Look, my kids are the most important thing,' he told me on the phone, as the hearing loomed, disguising the tension in his voice. 'I love boxing and it's been great for me, but they come first. I took one on the chin and pleaded guilty to guarantee a short sentence, so I can get out and carry on being their dad. If this is the end, it's not come in the way I wanted, but that's the way life is sometimes.

'I've loved every minute of my boxing career – let's make that clear, every minute – but for me, it's never been about winning or even the money. People don't get it, but it's about having fun, enjoying it and making others enjoy it too. When the crowd are having a good night, it makes me happy. That's why I do it and in that respect, I'm retiring unbeaten.'

The last I heard, in early June 2014, Jody had spent a week back in the familiar surroundings of HMP Hull. He had then been transferred to the nearby Wolds prison, where he had an altercation with another prisoner and was placed in the block. He moved on to HMP Humber in East Yorkshire where he settled down, was able to use the gym on a daily basis and vowed to stay out of trouble to ensure an early release.

In the ring, in the nick, in the street; always a one man riot.

10

'Undefeated in the home corner'

Matthew Seawright

Welterweight
Born: Bathgate, Scotland, 8 February 1978
Active: 2007–present
Record: 5-91-5

THE away dressing room for a night of boxing at the Meadowside Leisure Centre, Burton on Trent, on 2 March 2007, was quieter than usual. The rhythm of a rope slapping floor tiles echoed around as super-featherweight Shaun Walton skipped in one corner with heavyweight Luke Simpkin, already gloved up and waiting for his moment, looking on. Three other fighters sat on the benches of what was usually the gents' swimming changing room, having hands wrapped or speaking in lowered tones. Smells of sweat and bleach mingled in the air.

The door suddenly swung open, bringing with it the rumble of the audience from the hall and the daddy of all journeymen, Peter Buckley, a 38-year-old veteran of an incredible 279 fights, swaggered in having just lost by a point in the first bout of the night. 'Business as fuckin' usual!' he grinned, then, looking at Simpkin said, 'Good luck big man.' One of the runners stood at the door motioning to the heavyweight that it was time for him to walk.

Buckley was keen to get home but headed to the far end of the room where a short, heavily-tattooed Scotsman in black shorts shadow-boxed vigorously. 'Everything OK, Matt?' he asked. The younger man, his stablemate, training and sparring partner, was making his debut, face tense, throwing his hands to relieve anxiety. 'Aye,' he replied. Buckley felt for him. He remembered what it was like. 'You'll be fine,' he said.

As Buckley headed off to wash and change, another figure entered, a tall, hulking, bald man in jeans. The nervous Scot saw him approach and stopped moving. The big guy, known as 'Nobby' Nobbs, was trainer to him and Buckley and an important figure for him that night. He came closer, smiling broadly as usual.

Through the walls came the muffled sound of the bell. The heavyweight bout had just started. He was on next. His heart sped a little. It was a loaded moment, pregnant with tension, possibly the last chance to receive some advice before his maiden ring-walk. He wondered which words of motivation his manager would choose. He didn't want to admit it, but he felt like he needed a lift, a bit of inspiration. He listened keenly as Nobbs leant in.

'You'll probably lose tonight Matt,' Nobby said. 'On points, most likely. Now let's get some gloves on you.'

Seven years on from that night, on an unseasonably sunny Saturday in March, durable Scottish bruiser Matt Seawright opens the door to his Tamworth flat wearing a sort of knee-length, racing green, high-collar parka. His head is shaven, as usual, his black skinny jeans finish above the ankle and on his sockless feet are what appear to be some kind of slip-on desert boots.

I try not to show it, but I'm a bit taken aback. Flamboyant dressing might be par for the course for pimped out, mack-daddy champeens in Vegas, but not jobbing journeymen in the West Midlands. I can't work out if he more closely resembles a Bond villain or a Mod/*Enter the Dragon* hybrid, how Noel Gallagher might look if he had just spent six months training at a Shaolin Temple. Matt's five-year-old son, Brandon, full of energy and jostling for attention, scurries around his legs.

Guys become journeymen for different reasons. There are some, among those featured in this book, who feel their talents perhaps deserve better, but the boxing business forced their hand. They fight while holding themselves in check, often on request, to preserve the status quo. There are others who feel they belong at small-hall level and are happy to be there, grateful to the sport for affording them the opportunity to compete and earn regular money. Matt Seawright falls into the latter category.

In the ring Seawright looks a stocky, thick-limbed welterweight, but when clothed he seems slighter of frame. His face has the tight stillness of someone in supreme shape and anyone who has seen him fight knows that he is always in championship condition. His eyes are wide and intense, but relax, becoming gentler as he recalls his early years in West Lothian in Scotland, where he grew up in a village called Blackridge.

'It was just a typical small village where everybody knew everybody else,' he says. 'It was a little bit rough to be honest. Every other lad you look at around there has got a slash mark somewhere, it's one of those kind of places and like everyone else, I got in some trouble.

'Basically there were lots of little parts and each one had their own neighbourhood gang. They were fighting over drugs and other bits and pieces. You know if you're in one gang, you're not allowed to go in certain areas and all this sort of rubbish, postcode rivalries. I got mixed up in all that silliness.

'I was doing a few other stupid things too. Nothing too serious, you know, robbing clothes off clothes lines. If I fancied a top, I'd just be like "I'll have a bit of that" and take it. Nicking bikes, petty theft I suppose you could call it. As I got a bit older, things with the gangs got a bit out of hand and it got to the stage that my mum and dad were scared for my safety, so they shipped me down here

[Tamworth in Staffordshire] to my aunt's house to get me away from all that.'

Matt isn't sure what attracted him to the gang lifestyle but to make matters worse, he went to school in a different area and become involved with a gang around there. This caused problems with lads on his home patch who felt he should have been affiliated with them.

'I guess I just wanted to be recognised as a hard man or something,' he says, laughing gently. 'You know what it's like when you're a kid. But then it all just spiralled out of control. The last straw was one time when I was on my way home from the youth club. I didn't actually know this but every week, my dad would wait at the bus stop for me coming home – every week. He realised that things were going on and he was looking out for me. He didn't want to find out that I'd been stabbed or something.

'Anyway, I got off the bus, looked down the road and before I even knew what was happening there must have been about 20 lads running at me and I thought, "Oh shit! I'm going to have to do one here." So I just started pelting it up the road. I didn't look back, just running hell for leather.

'Behind me I heard this big noise, like a car skidding, engine growling and I thought it was more of them turning up. So I started going even faster, carrying on through the housing estates, over walls, through gardens and all that. I got into the house and about five or ten minutes later my dad turned up. It had been him who was in the car and he told me as soon as he'd started the car, lights on, loads of revs, all the lads scampered.'

Fortunately for Matt, his father was known locally as a tough character and his arrival had saved his son from serious harm. However the whole episode was enough to convince Matt's parents that he needed to leave the area. He was only 14 years old.

'I was a bit of a rough kid,' Matt remembers. 'Always involved in scuffles, I think I had a bit of a chip on my shoulder, a bit of an attitude really. And to begin with I brought it with me when I came down. When I first moved to Tamworth I went to a school called

Woodhouse and within the space of a week I'd had a fight. I didn't tell my aunt or anything but looking back it was just the kind of stuff you expect, you know. I came down here, I didn't know a soul and I got a bit of grief for being a Scottish kid in an English school. They used to take the mick out of my accent and all that stuff.

'After that I made a decision to start chilling myself out a bit. I didn't really want to go back to Scotland and I knew if I stuffed it up down here that's what would happen.'

It was then that Matt had the idea to enrol at a local karate club with the idea of training in martial arts.

'I was always a big fan of Bruce Lee, still am, love him and I wanted to emulate him. A mate of mine at the time kept going on about boxing but it didn't interest me. I wanted to concentrate on karate and kung fu. Anyway, I'd been doing martial arts for a year or so and learned the basics but my mate really persisted, trying to convince me to box, so one night I went down to Tamworth Amateur Boxing Club with him, just to shut him up really.

'I was 15 at the time and because I already had a bit of a martial arts background, I had a different outlook on it to a lot of the other kids. I had a little go at sparring and loved it, so that was it. I got into it straight away. It's hard to explain, but I just felt at home doing it, if you know what I mean? From then, I never looked back.'

Matt may have been fortunate in that the club he joined is one of the best-managed and most progressive boxing clubs in the country. Having started in 1969, in a room above a pub in the Glascote area of the town, Tamworth ABC initially offered boxing training to boys two nights a week. Such was its popularity that before long it began to offer sessions every night.

By the time Seawright joined, under the guidance of coach Alan Keast, the club had moved to new premises on an industrial estate and was developing a track record of helping disadvantaged youngsters and those excluded from education. Matt thrived in this environment, becoming one of the club's main faces. Over the next four years he had 20 amateur contests and won 15.

'I was happy as an amateur and had no real thoughts about turning pro,' he recalls. 'But that changed the night Jimmy Vincent came down to our gym [Jimmy Vincent was a Birmingham welterweight who fought twice for the British title between 2003 and 2005]. His younger brother trained with me and he came down to meet the boys and give us some advice. One thing led to another and I had a little spar with him. Afterwards he took me to one side and said, "You want to forget about the amateurs and go pro."'

Jimmy Vincent was trained and managed by Norman 'Nobby' Nobbs, something of a legendary figure in British fighting folklore prior to his retirement at the end of 2007. A former nightclub bouncer, who worked at a fruit and vegetable market by day, Nobbs found a niche in the UK boxing scene by providing what the great, recently-deceased promoter and matchmaker Mickey Duff referred to as 'fodder'.

At the peak of his notoriety, Nobbs claimed to be able to provide an opponent for any boxer on 30 minutes' notice. His reputation in the game and his ability to keep his fighters busy and making money meant that he felt entitled to take a higher than usual cut on the earnings of every member of his stable, which included, at various times, Peter Buckley, Jason Nesbitt, Howard Clarke, Karl Taylor, Hastings Rasani and Arv Mittoo, all well-known journeymen.

Matt says, 'So Jimmy Vincent asked me to come down with him to Nobby's gym in Aston. I went down there and trained for seven or eight months. It was a funny time, because I intended to turn over then and go into the pro game but I just didn't end up doing it. I was still a young lad and didn't have the commitment. It's one of my few regrets in boxing actually. I wish I'd stuck at it when I was 19.'

Instead Matt drifted away from the game, got a job and indulged in regular young-guy activities – going out, partying and getting drunk. 'I lived like that through most of my 20s,' he says. 'But at some point around 27 or 28 I just started to feel bored. What I was doing wasn't exciting anymore. I didn't want to carry on as just an ordinary person, doing ordinary things, working nine-to-five and getting smashed at the weekends. I had visions of myself ending up as a bitter old man, looking back on my life and always wishing I'd given it a go. Boxing had always been in the back of my mind so I went back to doing some training.'

This change of direction led to a reunion with Nobbs. Matt went back in the gym, got himself fit and eventually signed professional forms at 29, ten years after he had first considered it.

'The funny thing, although I was turning pro with Nobby and the reputation he had, I honestly didn't give it serious thought. I hadn't really been keeping up with the boxing scene in the time I'd been away from the game and just had a very naïve view of how it all worked. Nobby even had a sign over the gym door that said "Losers Unlimited". That's what he used to call his team of boxers! I just thought it was some sort of joke. He was always messing around and taking the piss. It may sound silly, but I didn't want to be a journeyman to begin with. I wanted to go as far as I could go, but I didn't understand a thing about professional boxing. Not a thing.

'Pretty much everyone in the gym was a journeyman and looking back, once I understood a few things, even the training was geared towards it. Really, Nobby was more interested in just getting you out there and making some money than anything else but to be fair to him he did teach me a couple of bits that have stayed with me. I do have that to thank him for, but you know, with Nobby it wasn't like, "Put your shoulder here, turn your body like this, move your foot that way and let the right go." All the training he did was teaching you how to survive, he didn't teach you how to win.

'It was how to grab on, how to waste a bit of time if necessary, when to walk around the ring and you know, he'd have me sparring with Peter Buckley and people like that. Peter was a master at all that stuff. So that was my grounding as a professional boxer.'

Matt's debut opponent was Derby's Jack Perry who at the time stood at 2-0 and had picked up a points win over Kristian Laight in his previous contest. Matt was in the away corner, but didn't know what that meant.

'The thing I always remember about that night,' Matt says, 'was what Nobby said to me just before I went out. You know, it was my debut and I was pretty edgy, nervous, excited, all of that, so I expected a little pep-talk, you know, a bit of Cus D'Amato-type stuff or something. What he said really took me aback. It baffled me more than anything else. I was really confused. I thought, "There's me, I've done all this training, ready to go in there and go for the win, why's he's saying that?" And as I was walking to the ring, all of that was in the back of my head.'

With his pre-fight psychology effectively destroyed, Seawright didn't fight as well as he would have liked to have done. Still, he felt the outcome was not a fair reflection of what transpired.

'In the end, Nobby was only half right. I lost, but not on points. The referee [Shaun Messer] stopped it, second round. It was a terrible, terrible decision and to this day I don't know why. I sometimes fight with my hands down, and use my elusiveness to avoid punches. I still do it now. I remember the ref telling me to keep my hands up and I continued fighting my way. There's nothing in the rules about keeping your hands up. Loads of famous fighters have fought like that. Ali fought like that most of the time. The kid caught me with one and he's jumped straight in and stopped it. One shot. I wasn't wobbled or in trouble or anything.

'To be honest the experience of that first fight really did my head in. First up there was what Nobby said to me beforehand, then there was the refereeing. I honestly think referees used to take one look at you walking to the ring with Nobby and just assume you were there to lose. So I came away thinking, "What was the point in that?" It put me on a bit of a downer. Obviously over time, boxing has educated me and now I understand what goes on but back then I didn't have a clue.

'There's lots of dodgy stuff in small-hall boxing. But you get used to it, it's a job like anything else, you know. And it's not all from the promoters and managers.' There is absolute sincerity in his voice.

'There's plenty of lads being paid extra to move someone about, for example. There's boys on the circuit making good money doing that. It goes on a lot, of course it does, but hand on heart, it's not for me. I wouldn't even know how to go about it. I'm not getting on my high horse or anything, if other lads take a bit of extra cash to do it, that's up to them, but I'm not very good at faking so I'd probably do it really badly and make it obvious. You know, people can make whatever judgements they like from this, but to be honest I've tried to win every fight I've ever been in. I always go in there and give it my best.

'People might look at fights where I just couldn't get in range to land much, but it's not because I wasn't trying. A lot of the time as well, you know you're not going to get the decision. That's just the way it works. It depends on the promoter, but most shows if you're in the away corner, you have to knock them out to get a draw.

'If I'm being completely honest there have been a couple of times when I have had personal problems and haven't been training as hard as I should do, which has affected my performance, but whenever I've done that, it's not been a good experience. I learnt a big lesson from those occasions because a professional boxing ring is not a nice place to be when you're not in shape.

'During the little period I had when I wasn't training right, I fought a lad in Scotland, Eddie Doyle [in Motherwell, December 2008]. I wasn't fit and to be honest, I was terrible. But I've fought that lad on two other occasions and it was totally different. So I know better than anyone how important training is. Now I'm always well prepared and ready to go. I make it my business to be.'

He certainly does. Seawright is not a journeyman who is so at ease with his role that he can turn up after a night out, or smoke cigarettes just before competing. At 36, he is in absolutely awesome physical condition with ten to ten and a half stones of muscle packed on to his 5ft 6in frame.

'I've always kept myself fit, even before I started boxing, but now it's something that I feel I have to do. It doesn't get easier as you get older, but I don't like that feeling of going in the ring thinking in the back of my head that I'm not fit enough to get through it. For me being a good journeyman is about having the right mindset. You need to be mentally focused. And if you want to make a go of it, you definitely need to be in shape, 52 weeks a year, no ifs and buts.'

As his fitness levels have peaked, Matt has maintained the awkward style learnt during his early days at Aston, the influence of Nobbs still visible. After fighting Matt at the Coronet, in south London, on 6 July 2012, while being interviewed by iFilm London, welterweight prospect Johnny Garton remarked, 'Seawright's very tricky, he'd clinch and grab my right hand so I couldn't hit him. He kept tying me up.'

A year earlier during Matt's contest with Rob Hunt, the TV commentators for Eurosport remarked, 'Hunt is being manhandled and pushed about by Seawright. He's been made to look average and Seawright has made him miserable for four rounds.'

Both fights resulted in points defeats.

Matt works nights for an engineering company, manufacturing parts for the building industry. In order to keep himself in the necessary condition to box regularly he fits training in around his shifts. He generally finishes around 7.30am and runs between five and eight miles immediately upon clocking off. If he's not fighting he does a sprint session at the weekends. The gym is saved for three or four afternoons a week, before heading off to work. He doesn't tend to spar, focusing instead on bag work, pads, strength and conditioning. It is a demanding schedule, with no let-up, that requires incredible discipline.

'When you're fighting every week or every other week you don't really need to spar,' he says. 'Sparring puts miles on the clock and when you're a journeyman having 100-odd fights in your career, the last thing you need is more miles. At 36 you have to stay on it. If you let yourself get out of shape at my sort of age there's no way you could get in there. But it's not a problem for me. I love training and I'd probably do it even if I wasn't boxing. I like to feel fit. The bit that kills me is the dieting. You know, the way I look at it is that I can eat what I want when I'm finished. I can get fat then, but it does get to me when my son comes around and he's sitting there eating sweets and chocolate biscuits and all sorts and I've just got fish and rice for days on end! It drives me potty.'

Matt's somewhat squat build makes him a stockier competitor than many of those he faces, with shorter, thicker limbs. Normally, given such a set of characteristics, his only chance would be in swarming his opponent and turning the fight into a toe-to-toe brawl. At range, the taller man will win almost every time. He rarely takes the initiative in his fights however, often fighting off the back foot, ducking low, waiting for his opponent to move forward, then counter-punching.

'Look,' he says, 'I have to have the journeyman mindset. I'm going in there to keep things tight and survive, to fight again in the next week or two, but even though that's always at the back of my mind, I still give it my best. What people have to understand is that doesn't mean I'm going to go rushing in and try to flatten everyone. You can't fight every week or every other week and have a brawl. It's different in the red corner, it's a job, it makes money for me, so that's how I treat it but at the end of the day, the Board are watching and if I don't look like I'm trying, they could take my licence off me.'

Despite his admirable honesty and lack of pretension, Seawright bears the brunt of a great deal of public criticism, perhaps even more so than other fighters in this book. He doesn't clown to win the crowd over like Meikle or Greaves and around the circuit, he conducts himself in a quiet, dignified manner, rarely drawing attention to himself. Interviews, publicity or media presence are minimal, even on the web. It is maybe for these reasons that he suffers such vitriol.

Some typical opinions lifted from internet discussions suggest, 'Matt Seawright is a punchbag, the only thing he is experienced at is getting beat.' 'What a stinker, all you get is four rounds of holding' and even, from the YouTube video of Matt's fight with Rob Hunt, 'Matt Seawright is the shittest boxer I've ever seen in my life!!! What the fuck is this doughnut doing in a boxing ring??!!' Matt sighs when confronted with such comments.

'Of course people look at my record and say I'm crap. I know that. Or they may watch a performance where I'm on the back foot and spoiling, not appreciating that I took the fight at one day's notice and have got another one the next week, so I have to fight a certain way. It used to upset me a bit, early on, but now it doesn't really concern me. The bottom line is that those kind of people are uneducated about boxing. It's as simple as that.

'A real boxing fan knows what it's all about. The sad thing is there's probably more people out there that don't understand boxing than do. The general public who might watch a big fight on a Saturday night on Sky or whatever would look at a record like mine and not understand what they're looking at. They haven't got a clue and that's fine, but if they haven't got a clue they shouldn't comment! I don't go around spouting off about things I don't understand. One of the problems with the internet now is that everyone feels they can throw their opinions around.

'One side to it is me playing my role as a journeyman, the other is the number of fights that I've won, but haven't got the decision. Really, you wouldn't believe. I reckon with fair scoring I'd have about another 25 wins. I fought a lad called Joe Collins in Manchester [June 2013] and it was just a blatant robbery. I won every round. Ryan Rhodes was commentating for Coldwell TV and even he said that, at the end of the fight. But of course, it couldn't work like that and they gave it to Collins by a point. It was the worst decision of my career.

'There was another one when I fought a guy called Danny Johnston in Wolverhampton [February 2009]. Same again, I won every round, maybe not quite as convincingly as against Collins, but it was my fight by a mile. The ref gave it to him by a point again though. Those are the two best examples, but there's loads more.

There's plenty of times when I know I've won and so does the other guy and I can sort of accept it because I know how things work, but those two genuinely gutted me because I won them so clearly.

'It's all part of being a journeyman though. You have to be philosophical about this sort of thing. If a lad is selling three grand's worth of tickets, obviously the promoter doesn't want him to lose because he wants him to sell all those tickets again in a couple of months' time. You would think, in an ideal world, you've got a fight and whoever wins, wins. I'm not saying I'd be a world champion or even a British champion, but when I win a fight, I should get that decision, but it doesn't happen like that.

'The easiest way to explain how the game works is to look at my record closely. In my whole career I've had three fights as the ticket seller and in those I've had two wins and a draw. So I'm undefeated in the home corner! Ninety-odd losses, but not those three! To anyone with their head screwed on, that tells its own story.'

It is to Seawright's credit that he speaks without bitterness. He holds no animosity towards the Board, fight officials, or the business of boxing in general. If anything, it is the opposite, he is very appreciative of the part boxing has played in his life and the extra income it has afforded him.

'Look, its brilliant and I love being involved. I'd say the only thing that annoys me sometimes is the attitude of some of the young lads, starting out. Most prospects are good lads, but then you get these guys who pick up a few wins and they're walking around like they're Joe Calzaghe, putting crap all over the internet and you think, "Have a word with yourself." They're only in that position because the promoter has put them there.

'I don't claim to be a world-beater but the difference between me and a kid who wins a Masters or an Area title but goes no further is basically just that they sell tickets and I don't. It hasn't got anything to do with quality. Half of those kind of lads, as soon as they get beat once or twice you never hear of them again. I must admit, that does annoy me, these boys who think they're the dog's bollocks but they've never been tested.'

When I interviewed Matt it was 16 fights since his last win, which came against Karl Ferguson in Newcastle in May 2013. His longest run of defeats had fallen between November 2010 and May 2012, during which time he lost 23 consecutive fights. Two of those were first-round knockouts, against debutants Billy Cayzer and Dale Evans. Unsurprisingly, Matt was called to justify himself before the Board during that period.

'It was all right at the last meeting actually,' he says. 'I've been to see them twice. With the stoppages the Cayzer one was genuine, he hit me in the ribs and I thought my tonsils were going to come out! Proper winded me. As soon as I went down I just spat my gumshield out because I knew that was the end of it. But the one in Wales against Evans, my shoulder went, so I took a knee. I was counted out like that.

'That's all it was and when I explained that to the Board they were fine. It's not nice when you get called in there though. You feel like you're in court. I guess they have to pull somebody in every now and then just to cover their own backs. People complain about guys like me with losing records and they have to be seen to be doing something. But the truth is you don't need to explain to them about home and away fighters and ticket sales. They know it all already.'

The week after we met, Seawright was awarded a bottle of wine and a certificate by Dave Roden from the Midlands Area Board to commemorate his 100th fight, in which he lost a 40-36 decision to Billy Mullan at Aston Villa's football ground. Yet even at 36 and with a century of fights in the bank he doesn't see any need just yet to start thinking about retirement.

'As long as I'm fit enough and able enough, I'll carry on,' he says. 'I don't have a specific figure in mind. I'll just keep plugging away and we'll see how it goes. I still feel fresh. I feel like an 18-year-old. I look at guys like Jason Nesbitt and Sid Razak, they're both 40 and still going and that gives me inspiration.

'Of course the possibility of brain damage is always in the back of your mind. Of course it is. But you have your medical every year with a CAT scan and all that. That's why if I feel I can't do it and I'm taking too many punches, then I'll stop. It's not just about me, it's about Brandon. I don't want him growing up with a dad who can't talk to him.'

His relationship with Brandon's mother finished two years ago but Matt has a shared custody agreement and sees his son for a few hours every day, as well as weekends. He takes the lad on days out and buys him presents with his ring earnings, as well as indulging his own slightly avant-garde fashion tastes.

'For any lad who's having a few problems like I did, I really would recommend getting into boxing,' he says. 'I've been in no trouble at all since I've turned pro. It's all the training and discipline. If it wasn't for boxing I don't know where I'd be.

'So I would never say I regret my career. Of course I could look back and wish I'd done some things differently, but I don't really like to do that. Perhaps in an ideal world I wouldn't have started out with Nobby Nobbs. He was a great guy in his own way but he only operated with one business model. I didn't understand it at the beginning. I didn't understand his corner of the market. Nobby could have managed Mike Tyson when he turned pro and he would have lost on bloody points! That's just how it was with Nobby.

'But look, I've got a lot to thank boxing for, it's given me a good living, I've got a flat, a decent lifestyle, helps me look after my son. More than anything else I enjoy the structure, having to train and keep myself fit and ready. You know, it's got its faults, like anything, but I love it. I really do.'

11

I could have been a contender

Daniel Thorpe

Light-welterweight
Born: Sheffield, 24 May 1977
Active 2001–2011
Record: 23-113-3

Rawling: 'He's a switch-hitter, Thorpe.'

McKenzie: 'Already this is shaping up to be quite an interesting, entertaining fight.'

Rawling: 'Right hand got through from Thorpe in that little exchange. Thorpe does have speed. He's got good lateral movement too, like a lot of the Sheffield fighters…And he's landed again! Another left hand from Thorpe.'

McKenzie: 'Make no mistake, this is a definite step up in class for Amir Khan…Thorpe's been around the block. He knows every bad trick and every good trick in the book…Khan isn't used to this kind of treatment. He usually intimidates his opponents, but Thorpe has no respect for Amir Khan's reputation.'

John Rawling and Duke McKenzie commentating on Daniel Thorpe's fight with future two-belt world champion Amir Khan, live on ITV, 10 December 2005.

If you know your British boxing and you think of the famous Ingle gym in Wincobank, Sheffield, you will most probably conjure an image of fancy-dans in silly shorts, tormenting opponents while bouncing around with their hands down. Fluid footwork, switching between orthodox and southpaw stances and punching from unusual angles are all familiar trademarks.

The awesome Herol Graham, Ryan Rhodes, Johnny Nelson and of course the uniquely gifted 'Prince' Naseem Hamed all emerged from Ingle's tutelage to ascend to the highest levels of the pro game. Today the production line is still in evidence, churning out classy performers like Kell Brook and Kid Galahad alongside exciting prospects like Adam Etches. Yet like all boxing gyms, Ingle's also produced less-celebrated names.

Despite not being a famous figure outside the circuit, the mention of Daniel Thorpe elicits interesting responses from people in the game. When he is referred to, they smile wryly or whistle through their teeth, as if there is something about him difficult to express in words. 'He could really fight a bit,' Kris Laight said when I told him I had arranged to meet Thorpey. 'He was always a good fighter, but he chose to be a journeyman.'

Former Premier League footballer and British light-welterweight champion Curtis Woodhouse tells a story about his first steps as a professional boxer.

'I was 25 at the time, but obviously a total novice in boxing terms. I was training at Dave Coldwell's gym, got in to spar and did four two-minute rounds. I knew Dave was working with [two-time light-middleweight world title challenger] Ryan Rhodes and [world number four welterweight] Kell Brook, but I didn't know what either looked like in person. So I got in there, did my rounds and got hit from pillar to post. He absolutely battered me, cut my mouth, wobbled me a few times, my nose was bleeding and everything. It was very one-sided.

'Dave sat me down afterwards and encouraged me to keep going. He said it was going to be hard to start, but if I stuck with it, I would get better. I appreciated Dave's kind words and I asked him, "That kid I was sparring was brilliant, who was it?" He said, "Yeah, he's a good little fighter is Danny but he's not won a fight in over two years." It was Daniel Thorpe. And after what he'd just done to me I thought, oh shit!'

Thorpey started early. He was born on the Parson Cross estate in north Sheffield, an area that has always had a run-down, anti-social reputation, having been created by the great slum clearances that occurred in many major British cities between the wars. Still now, one of Sheffield's more notorious gangs are known as the Parson Cross Crew and there have been several recorded incidents of shootings on the estate in the last few years.

Daniel was not a typical street kid however and was, in fact, worryingly withdrawn, rarely speaking to anyone. His family moved to the nearby Wincobank area when he was six but his introversion seemed to be deepening. His concerned parents decided it was time to act. As luck would have it, Daniel's grandfather was an old acquaintance of Brendan Ingle and spoke to the legendary trainer about the boy's predicament. Perhaps a bit of boxing would give the kid some confidence? At seven years old he was taken on a short walk, around the block to the famous gym to find out.

'The first time I went down there [the Ingle gym] I was introduced to [British and European middleweight champion] Herol Graham,' Daniel recalls.

'He was in his prime at the time and everyone expected him to go on and win a world title. It's funny because as a lad I wasn't that bothered. He was a big hero in Sheffield but I didn't really follow boxing. I was too shy to speak to him and just looked away. I didn't realise it then, but obviously I was being given a massive opportunity. What a great start in boxing – to be able to train somewhere like that as a kid, with fighters like that around you.'

He started going to the children's sessions every Saturday morning. In the early days boxing drills and practice were only a small part of what went on. Ingle's coaching methods were unconventional, to say the least.

'It was all about building your confidence up,' Daniel says. 'Brendan was brilliant at that. Half the time we didn't even do any boxing, really, he used to get us up singing and dancing and stuff like that. He used to make us stand in the middle of the ring and talk about ourselves, with all the other lads watching. It still took a good four or five years to get me talking, but it worked in the end!'

Among the boys starting around the same time as Daniel were future British and European middleweight champion Ryan Rhodes and Naseem Hamed, who was two years older and would go on to establish himself as an all-time great of the British ring, winning three of the four major world featherweight belts.

As time went on, Brendan would start to mix elements like circuit training and sparring into the sessions and the boys bonded into a team. Within a year of first walking through the door, Daniel was attending the gym for sessions after school on some days as well. By the age of ten, he was training every day. He had his first contest at 11.

'Back then, the Ingle style in the amateurs was absolutely hated,' he recalls. 'The old boys all wanted everyone to box a particular way. Even when Naz started they had it in for him. Brendan used to have us in big flashy green and gold dressing gowns and he used to tell us to shadow-box and dance around as soon as we got in the ring. It was clever really, it was all about projecting an air of confidence and giving our opponents something to think about. Compared to them, we'd look really professional. Ryan and Naz used to somersault over the rope as well, even as kids! Later on people said they nicked the idea off Chris Eubank but it's not true, they were doing it in the juniors before anyone saw Eubank do it.

'It's great memories though. Of all the kids in the gym me, Naz and Ryan were big mates and were the top three of a similar age. They used to call me Battlecat, from the cartoon *He-Man* because when we sparred I was ferocious and used to get stuck right in. I had so many great spars with Naz.'

After several years of boxing as a junior amateur, Daniel found his confidence and began to make a name for himself. He believes that if he had remained committed his life story could have been very different. But at 13 he got in trouble – as so many young men have, over a girl.

'There was this lass who lived near the boxing club,' he says. 'Blonde and pretty. I met her and fell totally in love. My boxing got put on the back burner. We even ran away from home together, it was all like something out of a bad movie! Anyway, that started a bit of a slide really.

'Without the discipline of boxing I started to get in a bit of bother and by 15 I was having some trouble with the law. Me and a couple of mates, we just used to go around and pick fights with lads we didn't like the look of. You know, I'd just go up to someone, call him a twat and smack him. I think I was abusing the boxing really. I'd learnt things in the gym that I was using in the wrong way.

'I went through a bit of a phase and I wasn't a very nice kid at all at that age. I was thieving and boozing and got my collar felt a few times. At school I became a lippy little fucker and didn't give a shit. I just think when you start off as someone with no confidence and then you get a bit, you don't know how to handle it and you abuse it. Brendan Ingle did great things for me, so it's not his fault but as a teenager I took the wrong lessons from what he taught me.'

Daniel left school at 16 and enrolled on the Youth Training Scheme as a joiner, but didn't last long as there wasn't enough money in it. His father then got him a job with an engineering firm which he kept for about a year before getting the sack. From there he took a position at a foundry within the famous Sheffield steel industry.

The harsh realities of moving from job to job and scraping a wage provided food for thought and by 18 Daniel had begun to miss the camaraderie and sweat of the gym. He went back to resume training.

'It was good to go back and great to see the boys again. Obviously they'd come on a lot and were on their way to becoming stars, Naz was already European champion, but I was smoking every day and going out clubbing, popping a few Es on the weekend and all that. I used to be a regular at Niche, which was a big club in Sheffield back then. I enjoyed those days,' he says, laughing. 'But I think they took their toll a bit. I wasn't fit enough and I found it hard to keep up.

'So I had a couple of amateur fights when I was about 18 but Brendan could see that I wasn't dedicating myself and obviously he had other, much bigger fish to fry at the time, so I ended up drifting back out again. I've never been a fitness freak or anything and with all the drinking and pills I was doing on the outside, boxing wasn't really a goer.'

At 19, like many lads going out in the 1990s, Daniel succumbed to chemical romance, meeting the girl who would become the mother of his first child while under the influence of MDMA. His daughter, Bridie-May, was born a couple of years later and life instantly became harder. He continued working odd jobs but the young couple found paying the bills a struggle. With worries over rent and nappies on his mind, it was natural that he would turn back to boxing as a means to support his new family.

He took a job at a machine knives factory where he made friends with a colleague by the name of Andrew Facey. Facey was also a boxer (he would later go on to win the English light-middleweight title twice and beat three-time world title challenger Matthew Macklin) who trained at Ingle's gym after moving up to Sheffield from Wolverhampton.

'Me and Andrew had a good chat about it all and he was telling me how much money he was earning. He was fighting four or five times a year and getting a grand or so each time, maybe two grand if it was on a TV show and that obviously sparked my interest.

'I started seriously thinking about going back down and talking to Brendan. Then by coincidence, not long after that I bumped into John Ingle in the street and he suggested that I come back down to the gym. We had a proper talk and he spoke to me about fighting in the away corner and the money I could earn.

'By then I was 23 and I looked at Naz and Ryan and what they were doing [Hamed had already fought 16 world title fights by then, winning the lot, Rhodes was British champion and had lost a challenge for a world title] and I thought I'd left it too late to start off as a prospect but looking back now, if I'd got properly stuck in at 23 I could have done something.

'So it was a strange start to my pro career, really, because I came in with the intention of being a journeyman but was training every day with the Ingles and using the foundation of the skills I'd learned as a kid. My training partners were the same guys I'd trained with as a lad and they were stars, so at the back of my mind was always the thought that I could do something.

'I always felt I was good enough. I got myself properly fit within a few months and there was often this little battle going on in my head between just accepting the journeyman role and trying to go for titles. That's probably why I picked up a few more wins than most journeymen do. The mental side can be hard when you're in the away corner, because the money's great, but I don't care what anyone says, we all like to win. When you get a win, it's a brilliant feeling and then you think, shall I give it a go?'

The uncertainty in Daniel's mind over which professional path to take, coupled with his obvious talent, led to mixed early results. He drew his first contest against Brian Gifford at the York Hall in September 2001. Gifford was also a journeyman with a record of 1-9 and the idea was that Thorpe would provide him with another 'W' for his tally. Strangely, the contest was televised live on the old BBC Saturday afternoon sports show *Grandstand*, meaning a slightly higher fee. Daniel boxed superbly for the first two rounds, dazzling Gifford with typical Ingle gym tactics, switch-hitting and sharp movement.

'The thing I always remember about that first one, we were going down to the changing room and Dominic Ingle, who was with me, asked one of the runners or someone organising the night, "Are we in the winner's corner?" The guy told him, "No, you're not." I was listening to them talk like that and couldn't believe it. After they'd finished speaking, I turned to Dominic and I was like, "What do you mean winner's corner?" He replied, "So the referee knows which hand to raise." He might have just been messing around, I don't know, but that always stuck in my head. It's pretty much how it all works, if we're being honest.

'Anyway, John Ingle told me afterwards that someone phoned him up during the first two rounds and asked who I was. They said I was brilliant, that they could throw some money at me, that I was like another Naz! Then in the third round they phoned back and said, "Nah, forget it, he's fucked." It's true, I tired badly in the second half!'

Despite that, Daniel felt he should have been given the decision. In his second fight, two and a half weeks later, he did win, on a dinner show in Cleethorpes against a journeyman called Ram Singh, for which he sold 20 tickets. He then also picked up victories in his fourth, seventh and ninth fights. Unusually for a journeyman this gave him a record of 4-4-1 at the start of his career.

'At that time I had a problem because obviously if I wanted to fight as a prospect, I'd need to sell tickets and because of my lifestyle, being out in pubs and clubs and things, people who knew me didn't take me seriously as an ambitious fighter. The most tickets I ever sold was about 50 and that was for a Central Area title fight, but I think as well, although I understood that I was fighting in the away corner, I didn't get how it worked with journeymen.

'I didn't realise that it would actually benefit me to lose, so I guess I was still learning how the game worked and how I was supposed to play it. No one sat me down and told me to go in and duck and dive and stay out of the way, so I just did what I felt like doing.

'I also sometimes think during those early days the Ingles might have been feeling me out a little bit. They were maybe putting me in even fights to see how I got on. Perhaps if I'd been going in and knocking all these guys out they would have pushed for me to build a career as a prospect.

'My third fight, with Mally McIver, was an absolute barnstormer. It was an Ingle show but it was in Dewsbury, which was McIver's home town and he was a massive ticket seller so he was boxing in the home corner. He was one of the two lads I boxed as an amateur when I was 18 and he'd absolutely pasted me back then because I was on the disco biscuits and all that. He was a pretty good kid too.

'So there was a bit of history there and we just went toe-to-toe pretty much, but they gave him the decision. McIver was 6-1 at the time and I wonder if I'd won that one, if Brendan or someone might have tried to push me down the other path.

'Anyway, around then, John Ingle had a word with me and suggested that I register as self-managed. The Board had a rule that you can't box someone who has the same manager as yourself, I don't know if they still do. By doing that I'd be able to box on Ingle shows as the away fighter against other Ingle boxers. I suppose it was from then that I really started to take on the journeyman role and I started getting chucked in with good names on TV shows.

'Obviously, if you're fighting quality boys and taking fights on late notice you're going to be very unlikely to pull it out of the bag so you end up going into survival mode a little bit.'

It was in Daniel's eighth fight, against a debutant called Jackson Williams in Norwich, that the realities of his position in the boxing world were made clear.

'That one was the first time I was told, directly beforehand to lose on purpose,' he says. 'I was told to just look after him and let him win. They gave me a little bit of extra money for that.

'To be honest, throughout my career I was asked to do that sort of thing pretty often. I did it with that lad, I did it with Nadeem Siddique [another debutant he first fought in November 2002] and a bunch of other kids. I actually fought Siddique three times and every time it was the same deal. He was a massive ticket seller so they wanted him well looked after. In fact one time when I fought

Nadeem, we drove up to Scotland together, boxed each other and then drove back down together.

'He knew I was being paid just to go in and move around and on the way home he's on his phone and he was talking to his family and mates about the fight, bragging and giving it loads and I was thinking, hold on, you knew what was going to happen before it even started!

'I remember on his debut I was walking to the ring and all his supporters were giving me absolute dog's abuse and I felt like turning around and saying, look, I'm letting him win this! The truth is I could have smashed him to pieces at the time, but I was being paid to do a job.'

It is perhaps understandable that Thorpe was asked to fight like this so often. For the men managing young prospects, Daniel was never one of those journeymen you could feel completely at ease with and was known to have the ability to give anyone a tough night.

In April 2003, for example, he fought another debutant called Stephen Mullin on a Matchroom show in Liverpool. The promoters made the mistake of not slipping Daniel a few extra quid to look after their boy and paid a heavy price. Mullin was tipped as a hot prospect having had an excellent amateur career including ABA victories, but Daniel read his man perfectly, came around the outside with a right hook, put him down and stopped him after a minute and a half of the first round.

'The problem was with that,' he recalls, 'the work started to dry up. When I was losing I was getting sometimes four fights a month and the money was fantastic, but then I fought McIver again for the area title and won. So obviously because I was Central Area lightweight champion, people thought I was taking it seriously again. That's when it really kicked in for me and I realised that winning wasn't doing me any favours because I couldn't get any work.'

Winning the title and the lack of away corner fight offers led to another little spell of ambition. Daniel won three of his next four bouts between claiming the belt and defending it, including victories over fellow journeymen Jason Nesbitt and Peter Buckley, taking his record to 12-26-2.

'I thought I might as well, really. Perhaps it could have been the launchpad to have a go at the British title or something, but then my first defence was against Stefy Bull in Doncaster and I got robbed. It was on their home show and I lost by one point. That was after the ref had deducted me a point for something silly. On those sort of shows, when you're away and there's something on the line you really have got to knock them out.

'That stuff always bothered me, but I don't know where it comes from. I guess it's just to help promoters out. I don't know if there's any backhanders going on but it wouldn't surprise me. If fighters are being given backhanders then it's not impossible to believe that officials are. I don't doubt there's some crooked referees, but whether it's all of them, I don't know. At the end of it, the promoters want to keep their lads winning don't they, so they can keep selling tickets.

'I used to sit and have a drink with a lot of referees, like Howard Foster, Mickey Vann and Richie Davies and sometimes I asked them about this sort of thing. They never said it in so many words but the impression I got was because they see you as a journeyman, they think you're not really bothered if you get the win anyway so it's easier just to give it to the other lad and keep everyone happy.

'In my experience, the boxers themselves want to fight. Most fighters are happy to fight anyone. You've got to have a bit of that attitude to want to be a fighter in the first place. But it's the promoters that create all this side of it because they think they'll lose the golden goose if their boy gets beaten a few times, so they set up soft fights or guaranteed wins to build them up.'

After losing his belt to Bull, Daniel suddenly found that offers for work as an away fighter started coming back in and from that point on, the confusion he had felt in his early career disappeared. He was a journeyman and content to be so. He won only six of his next 20 and from there, victories became more and more rare.

'I learned that it's good to win one now and then. Occasionally I even won two on the bounce. But whenever I did that, the phone stopped ringing. If you look through my record you'll see I never won three in a row. It's not because I couldn't, it's because I knew if I did that my career as a journeyman was finished.'

Shortly after the Bull fight, offers for fights live on Sky television began to arrive, usually Frank Warren-promoted. The fee for these contests would sometimes be as much as £3,000 and Daniel didn't want to risk losing such valuable paydays. 'Warren was always the best payer,' he says. 'By a mile.'

As a result, Thorpe shared the ring with some of the best Britain had to offer around his weight class at the time, including world champions Gavin Rees, Ricky Burns and Amir Khan, and two-time world title challenger Kevin Mitchell.

'The first time I fought Gavin Rees, [in Cardiff, in June 2003] I was still training with the Ingles and to be honest he just obliterated me in about 30 seconds. I remember seeing him at the weigh-in and he didn't look like much and I thought, "I'm going to piss all over this kid here," but he was top-drawer. He came out at first bell like a little bull and he hit me so quickly with so many hard shots. He was a really good body puncher.

'By the time I fought him again [in Newport, March 2006] I was training with Dave Coldwell and I just wanted to prove something to myself. I took him five rounds that time. To be fair he'd been out for a while and weren't really at his best but it made me feel better about myself. I didn't like getting taken apart. Losing is one thing, but when you've been outclassed it's not a nice feeling.

'When I fought Kevin Mitchell [in Preston, October 2005] I was in my best shape ever and because Dave [Coldwell], who was my manager at the time was friendly with Frank Warren, we got put up in the home fighters' hotel which was some proper fancy place. After the weigh-in I found I kept walking past him in the corridor. I tried to speak to him, just in a friendly way, to say hello and all that but he wouldn't have nowt to do with it. He was just glaring at me every time I walked past him and I thought, "He looks a right wanker, this bloke!"

'In the fight I did quite well but Dave pulled me out at the end of the fourth. Mitchell would probably have battered me in the end anyway but I was really trying for that one. I wasn't just in defence mode. The thing was, the minute it was stopped he came straight over and told me it was a pleasure to share the ring with me and how much respect he had for me. He was actually a really nice fella. I think the business beforehand was just his way of dealing with pre-fight nerves.'

Prior to his bout with Amir Khan, Daniel was interviewed by *Sporting Life* in an article headlined, 'Thorpe plans to make a Name for Himself'. The opening line of the piece read 'Daniel Thorpe plans to ditch his journeyman status for good by handing Amir Khan his first defeat.'

Thorpey smiles warmly as he remembers. 'The fight with Khan was a funny one. I loved every minute of it. He was an Olympic silver medallist and the new big star of British boxing. I knew full well I was going to get pasted but to tell the truth I think I could have gone the distance with him easily. The thing was that we had a plan to try and jump on him. No one had put him under pressure yet in his career, so we thought we'd give it a go and maybe he'd crumble.

'It wasn't how I normally boxed at all, but there was a chance to make myself a superstar if I could knock him out. Or at least earn myself a big money rematch. I'm sure if I had beat him they'd have signed me for a rematch and paid me to go down, which would have been worth my while!

'Anyway, the thing with Amir Khan was just the accuracy and speed of his punching. It really was unbelievable. The individual shots weren't that heavy, I wouldn't say he's a big puncher whatsoever but they were all so well timed and half of them were just too quick to react to. He was the best I've boxed by a mile, other than Naz, but obviously I only sparred with Naz. Naz was a phenomenon.'

In the end Daniel held his own in the first round, even managing to put Khan under pressure in the early stages before suffering a flash knockdown. The Olympic medallist upped the tempo in the second, however, put Thorpe down twice and forced a stoppage.

On other occasions, Daniel managed more than flashes of success against big names. Two weeks before the Khan fight he boxed Commonwealth Games gold medallist Haider Ali in Walsall. Ali was tipped for big things but by the midpoint of the third was finding it harder and harder to deal with Daniel's switch-hitting attacks. He was frequently backed into corners and particularly open to the left hook, with which Thorpe tagged him repeatedly.

With pressure increasing in the fourth, Ali sustained a hand injury and rather than face further punishment, retired on his stool. After that, the amateur star's career never caught fire and he ended up quitting the sport four months later, with a record of 5-3-1.

Thorpe also fought two-weight world champion Ricky Burns on eight hours' notice in 2004, after the Scotsman's original opponent scratched out through injury. Even with that sort of pre-fight preparation, he was good enough to give Burns an almighty scare.

'With that fight,' he says, 'I was working nights and I got a phone call at ten o'clock in the morning off John Ingle. I'd only been in bed about an hour. He said, "Do you wanna fight in Scotland tonight?" I said, "Yeah, no problem." He replied, "Great, your flight's at two o'clock, get yourself down to East Midlands Airport. I'm busy so you'll have to go on your own."

'So I bombed it down to the airport, had a bit of sleep in the departure lounge, then went and boxed. I remember I forgot my gumshield and had to borrow one off some other kid. Anyway I wasn't feeling at my best, but in the first round he kept walking straight at me, so I stepped inside and hit him with a right hand – lovely shot and down he went!'

In the end Daniel found himself on the wrong end of a 59-55 points decision over six rounds, but several observers felt that he had done enough to claim the victory.

In February 2006 Thorpe fought a draw with Ashley Theophane who would go on to lift the British light-welterweight title. Towards the end of his career, in September 2010 Daniel went in with Commonwealth lightweight champion Derry Matthews, losing a six-round points decision. He insists he could have won if he had wanted to. 'I could have stopped him in the first round but I stood off,' he says. 'The Board tried to stop me taking that fight as well, but even by the end, when I was getting fed up with it, if I wanted to I could give anybody a good go.

'To be honest a lot of the lads I fought weren't as good as they were cracked up to be. Once I went into full-on journeyman mode I would go in there, realise they couldn't hurt me and just mess with their heads.

'That sort of thing always worked well for the kids who are having their debut, because they came out and they've sold all these tickets, they might have beaten loads of lads in the amateurs, then they're boxing me, I've lost 40 out of 50 fights and they think they're going to knock me out in the first round. When I'm tagging them, spinning them around, calling them a wanker and smiling, it drives them crazy.

'But my main thing was to be elusive. You see some of the kids that go in and have a war and take lots of punches and everyone's patting them on the back and saying what great battlers they are, but where are those sort of guys going to be in ten years time when they can't wipe their own arse? Getting in fights like that, it's not good for you, especially if you're doing it every week. I never had a scratch on me at the end.'

After looking promising in patches, Thorpe's career petered out. He lost 41 fights on the bounce between November 2008 and February 2011, the vast majority on points and with four losses coming by stoppage. During that run he won only three rounds. Having finally accepted his role as paid opponent and with the spark of ambition extinguished, he lost motivation, stopped training and began turning up for contests half-fit.

This approach drew critical attention from the Board and after retiring on his stool at the end of the second round in two consecutive bouts in Glasgow in early 2011, he was called in and had his licence withdrawn. He didn't protest, accepting the decision grimly.

'I don't really have any quarrel with the Board. I do think there's too many of them that never fought and it would be better if they were all ex-fighters, but when I look back at it now,' he says, 'I mean my whole career, I do regret it. I regret all of it. I regret not taking it seriously. I enjoyed being a journeyman but towards the end I was just taking the piss.

'Even now if I could go back to it, I could get another five years out of it, easily. By the last couple of fights, I went in there, fiddled about in the first, didn't do too badly but then was nearly spewing in the corner at the end of the round because I was that unfit. I'd just had enough of training and all that stuff. You know making weight was such a pain in the arse, although I was good at it. It gets to you after a while, especially when you're losing every week anyway. There wasn't one fight in my pro career when I came in overweight, but when the Board explained to me what they thought, I didn't see the point in arguing. They were right. I think in a way I wanted out by then.

'So if I'm being honest about it, I regret not giving it a proper go from the start and I regret not living the life. I suppose my main regret is not doing anything with my money. I just pissed it all away. It's difficult to talk about it and make it sound right and for people reading it, it may seem silly, but when I go back to those early days as a kid, training with Naz and Ryan, you know I more than held my own with them.

'Naz was always a little bit special but back then, there wasn't that much between all of us, talent-wise. I look at guys like that and what they achieved and I think I could have done something similar. I really think if I'd had the sense to dedicate myself from an early age I could have gone all the way in the sport, but I never had that will to just churn it out day after day. You need that, to be a champion. It's as much about character as talent and I didn't have the right character.'

Despite his lack of passion for boxing in his later years, the loss of his licence didn't signal the end of his days in the ring. Daniel still dabbles now and then, participating on the EBF unlicensed circuit, although it's not something he would necessarily recommend.

'I just do it for the money. Not that I'm struggling, but it's a bit of beer money or whatever. Since retiring from the pros I've had six fights on the EBF and won one,' he says. 'The one I won, I did a few tickets for it and I beat a kid, but the truth is he went down on purpose. That's what it's like on unlicensed, the money's crap, it's dangerous and it's pretty much all fixed. I'm going in with kids I could beat with my eyes shut. They're absolutely useless most of them.

'On the other hand, I fought a couple of kids that were going on 14 stone and they've hit me once and I've just thought, sod this, and gone down. Most of the time I've been told to take a dive beforehand anyway, so I've bounced around a bit then jumped on the floor in the first round. I'm not getting my face smashed up for £150! Every time I get out of there I think I'm not going to bother doing that again, then I get a phone call and its quick and easy money. Same old story!'

Through everything he remains a boxing fan. 'I'll always watch it on the telly. I'm always reading about it on the internet and stuff. I've thought about getting involved in the training side, but it's probably not for me, really. I'm not a leader, managerial type. I never have been. Maybe I could be a cornerman or something.

'I've got some great memories from boxing. Sparring with Naz was something else. It was more or less impossible to lay a glove on him and when he got older and grew into his strength, he had unbelievable power. He could hit you from two inches away and knock all the wind out of you. You could have as tight a guard as you like, leave a tiny gap and Naz would find a way to angle his body and punch through the gap, but even when he threw these weird punches from funny angles, he had such power. He was unbelievable. He could really take some stick as well. He'd go toe-to-toe with [WBO cruiserweight world champion] Johnny Nelson in the gym and they'd be really giving it some.

'He ended up being a genuine legend of the game and I was in there with him. I saw him first-hand every day. When I think of things like that I do miss it, but it's all over for me now. If they did a journeyman prizefighter and invited me, I'd definitely come back and get in shape for that. I'd put everything I've got into it. I've been talking about it for years. It would be great for TV, wouldn't it? Look, journeymen fight for money at the end of the day. If you offer them a big enough carrot you would see some cracking fights. But other than that, my pro days are done.'

Daniel has three kids; Bridie-May who is 14 and two boys, Cole and Cain (5 and 7). All live with their mothers but he sees them three or four times a week. 'I'm not very good at relationships,' he explains. 'But my kids are really important to me.' His main income now comes from working shifts as a fettler at Sheffield Forgemasters.

The disappointment in Daniel's voice as he reflected on his career reignited my thinking on journeyman psychology. I worried about him continuing to fight unlicensed for peanuts, despite his insistence that he didn't really need the money. Why else would he continue to do it? He certainly didn't sound as if he was enjoying it.

As I watched this softly-spoken man stuff his hands in his pockets and walk away, through the crowds at Sheffield's Meadowhall shopping centre, I found it strange to think that he sparred daily with Naz, went to war with Amir Khan and knocked down Ricky Burns. Thorpey the fighter seems a long way below the surface of Daniel as he is now.

It made me wonder about the importance of self-belief. It is a sporting cliché but it seemed to be all he had lacked. Its absence had left him with many unanswered questions. When he looks back, it isn't all those losses that trouble him, it's not knowing

– not knowing how well he could really have done. For a fighter with such a long career behind him, he is in perfect health, an achievement in itself, but his unfulfilled ambition nags him. I got the impression he was struggling to let it go.

'The great thing about boxing is you can be bottom of the pile,' he had told me, 'then beat two or three kids and suddenly find yourself in the top ten. A little run is all you need. I think that's why I always had that dream in the back of my head, the dream that I could be a champion.'

12

'These boys can't beat me!'

Max Maxwell

Light-middleweight/middleweight
Born: Clarendon, Jamaica, 26 July 1979
Active: 2006–2014
Record: 19-47-3

O
N 28 February 2008, at the Civic Hall in Wolverhampton, 'Mad' Max Maxwell stopped Matty Hough with a two-fisted flurry in round three to win the Midlands Area middleweight title, moving him to 7-1. A fluent, athletic, boxer-puncher, managed by former WBC world super-middleweight champion Richie Woodhall, he was capable of poking opponents around with his jab or sitting down on his shots and hurting them. At that stage he looked set for a career as a contender, possibly more.

Two years later, after a mixed run, he was brought in as an opponent for the rising star of the light-middleweight division, Blackpool's Brian 'The Lion' Rose. Technically tight and well-schooled in the European style of high-guard-and-jab, at the time Rose was gliding gracefully through the domestic pack on his way to a British title challenge. Most tipped him to dominate but Maxwell's natural competitiveness ensured he stayed in the running. In the early rounds he held his own in the jab exchanges, while trying to engineer openings to disrupt Rose's delicate precision.

'He's dropping his right from his chin when he throws the jab,' Woodhall said to Maxwell between rounds. 'Wait for him to lead and chuck the right over the top.'

Max followed his man around for five rounds to get the timing, then during the first knockings of the sixth he pressured him towards the ropes and unleashed a ferocious, beautifully-timed, arching right hand. It impacted Rose's chin like a wrecking ball, sending him face-first to the canvas.

With the count at seven The Lion staggered to his feet like a wino, was asked to step forwards by referee Steve Gray, made a pawing gesture with one hand and lurched to his right and back to the floor. The official had no choice. With the home crowd silenced, the fight was waved off. Maxwell celebrated passionately while Rose was given oxygen. Against the odds he had collected an impressive TKO victory and re-established himself near the top of the domestic hierarchy.

Boxing is a business that forces young men to make difficult decisions and like two paths that converge in a wood, before spreading diagonally in opposite directions, Maxwell and Rose's careers separated completely after that night in May 2010. Despite the defeat and with careful handling, Brian Rose regrouped and picked up the English light-middleweight title within six months. He went on to win the British title and defend it three times, including a revenge points victory over Maxwell, claiming the coveted Lonsdale belt outright. In October 2013 he then took a controversial split decision over tough Argentinian Javier Maciel in a WBO world championship eliminator.

As this book was being written, Rose was preparing for a challenge against that organisation's world champion, Demetrius

Andrade, which would prove ultimately unsuccessful, the American stopping him in the seventh. Since knocking Rose out, on the other hand and while the Blackpool man would climb almost to the very top of the boxing ladder, Maxwell would win only five more contests, soon embarking on a run of 36 straight defeats.

Max Maxwell is perhaps unique among the current crop of professional journeymen in that he switched into the role halfway through his career and is still regarded as a top-calibre opponent, someone who can be called up and used as a dance partner for an elite fighter at the drop of a hat. Daniel Thorpe, during his pro journey, certainly during the early part of it, was thought of in the same way. The requirements of being asked to go in with young, nondescript novices to give them a little test or being expected to fight Olympic medallists or former world champions on short notice are very different. Yet even this kind of 'high-end' journeyman work is still subject to the vagaries of the boxing business.

By way of example, on Saturday 22 March 2014, a week after I had met Max at his home near Castle Bromwich in Birmingham, he was booked in as an opponent for former WBC world light-welterweight champion Junior 'The Hitter' Witter in Sheffield, on the undercard of Kid Galahad's successful European title challenge.

On the Wednesday before the fight, Max came down with a serious chest infection and was bed-ridden. He was reluctant to lose out on a wage but by Friday night hadn't slept for two days due to coughing fits, was on antibiotics, had not left the house or trained for 96 hours and had accepted that he would be unable to contest the bout. He sent a message to Witter's promoter via Jon Pegg, informing them that sadly he would have to pull out.

On Saturday morning, 12 hours before the allotted time for first bell, Max received a pleading phone call from a member of Witter's team. They had been unable to find another opponent, Witter really needed a bout and a payday and if Max would agree to show up they would arrange things with Junior and ensure the fight would not be too tough. The former world champ would gently box his way to a points win and Max could take his money and go home.

Lured by the cash, Maxwell agreed, and dragged himself, about 20 per cent fit, to the venue, only to find once the bout started that Witter either hadn't been told of the agreement or had chosen to ignore it.

Witter went after his man, winging in volleys of spiteful shots, going all out for the stoppage from the very first round. Max hung on, in serious trouble at times, gasping for breath and aching from head to toe. He survived on pride only, losing every session of a bruising and painful six-rounder. That he made it to the final bell at all speaks volumes for the strength of his will.

Afterwards, he was justifiably annoyed. He had done Witter a favour by hauling himself out of his sick bed to turn up for the fight, but if the former world champ had been successful in his attempt to force the stoppage against a severely weakened opponent then Max would have been suspended and unable to fight again for several weeks, damaging his livelihood.

This is the side of the sport that the general public don't see or understand and the boxing media don't mention. Immediately after the bout, *Boxing News* tweeted to their 48,000 followers, 'Former World Champion Junior Witter boxed with style and flair to control Max Maxwell throughout the six rounds.' The report in the magazine the following week was similarly laudatory of Witter's performance. If it hadn't been reported here, the back-story to that fight would never have been told.

I arrived at Maxwell's house at about ten on a Saturday morning. He lives on a small estate, 15 minutes' drive from the centre of Birmingham and emerged, blinking, from his front door, dreadlocks hanging around his shoulders, shoeless and in a vest. The impression I had was that I had got him up. That evening he was scheduled to fight a six-round light-middleweight contest in Reading against local boy Tamuka Mucha (7-0). Max was struggling to make the weight and had not eaten since having a half of grapefruit the previous afternoon. 'I can't keep doing this 11st business,' he told me with a surprisingly warm smile. 'I'm getting too old for this shit!'

Max, it is fair to say, has a reputation as something of a Casanova. Former female light-welterweight world champion turned promoter and pundit Jane Couch MBE posted a series of interviews with him on the web, during which light-hearted banter frequently descended into open flirting. 'Max I have to say you're looking really fit,' she simpers in one, while chewing on a piece of gum. 'After this fight, you have to take me out. Everyone knows you're my favourite boy in boxing.' Max smiles and bats away her chat-up attempts with laconic charm, but they make for awkward viewing.

My wife, who came along to the interview to take pictures, was quite taken with how photogenic he is and just to emphasise the point further, a lady friend waited for him upstairs while we spoke, sitting on his bed. If standard boxing wisdom is to refrain from sexual activity prior to fighting, it didn't appear to be something that Max took too seriously at this stage of his career. Although, with weekly bouts, as Jody Meikle had remarked, 'If journeymen never had sex before fights we'd all be born-again virgins.'

Max's early years were spent in Jamaica and he still carries a rich Caribbean undertone beneath his Brummie accent. He was born in Clarendon, in the south of the island and lived there until he was 11 years old.

'To be quite frank,' he said, smiling, 'I came from a poor background. Life growing up in Jamaica was very hard. You know there were times when there wasn't enough to eat in the house, sometimes I'd be going to school without lunch and that sort of thing. My mum had mental health issues as well, but she was very hard-working and doing whatever she could, you know cleaning people's floors, all sorts of jobs, so I'm very thankful to my mum, but that's how it was in Jamaica in those days. A lot of people were struggling.

'My dad was here and there. I didn't know him too well and it wasn't easy, but we survived and I did what I had to do to get on. You know I look back on those times with mixed feelings. From my memories I don't think Jamaica was as rough as it is now. You didn't have all the gun crime and everything that you hear about these days. But there were things going on.

'I remember being like ten or 11 and I used to go to the dance halls and pick up empty bottles of Coca-Cola and beer because you could take empties back and sell them. I was out at like one o'clock in the morning around clubs and dance halls doing that stuff. That wouldn't happen here! I do sometimes wonder if I'd stayed there how I would have turned out, you never know, but I guess there's a chance I would have been led down the wrong way because it happens to a lot of young guys over there.

'But, at the same time I had lots of fun as a kid in Jamaica and although it's true that we didn't have much, that's one of the things that's made me the person I am. When you come from something like that and you've had it hard and then you come to England, you can really appreciate it. I don't really understand how people moan about life here. You've got everything you need. I see people who are homeless and I just think, "Why?"'

The problems in Jamaica were enough for mother and son to decide to make the move to England in 1991. To begin with they both lived with Max's grandmother who had already resided in the Birmingham area for many years, but Max's mum soon moved out for work reasons, leaving him in the sole care of his grandparents. This arrangement came to an end when Max was 13 as he struggled to cope with the discipline imposed by his older guardians.

'In England, I settled in quite quickly, you know my school was very mixed ethnically and it was just a case of whether you were hard and could have it or not. If you weren't, you'd get picked on. I was always able to look after myself so I fitted in fine. I used to finish school and that was it, I'd be out playing with my mates.

'The problem was that my grandparents were deep Christians and had very old-fashioned, strict views on what children should and shouldn't do. You know they'd be out preaching at the weekend and all this, going to prayer services several times a week and I'd be expected to go with them. So this one time I'd been out playing and I didn't get back until nine o'clock at night. They didn't approve of that. When I got home the door was locked! I knocked, but they didn't answer. That was it. They'd shut me out.

'I'm not going to lie, that did affect me personally. I mean I was still only a young boy, in a foreign country and I couldn't understand it. I hadn't done anything, really. I was just out playing. I could understand if I was out every night. I wasn't taking drugs or anything like that. I had to go back to my friend's house and sleep there. After that, my grandparents wouldn't have me back and unfortunately my mum's mental health issues had got worse and she couldn't take me either. Social services looked into it and they took the view that if you're responsible for a child's welfare, you can't lock them out of the house. So one thing led to another and I ended up in care.

'I have to be honest, I was really lucky. I know some people had bad experiences in care but my foster mother, Sue Farmer, was a great lady and I have so much to be grateful to her for. Obviously I realise that things could have turned out badly but I settled down with her and my life started to go really smoothly from there. And I think, because of everything I'd been through, when I was 14 I was quite mature for my age. I'd had a lot of experiences and learnt from those experiences. For example, the whole black/white, racism thing didn't really affect me because my foster mother was white and she was such a great lady so I got to see things from that side.

'Anyway, I checked out how the system works and I found out if you're in care in this country it only lasts until you're 16, then you end up getting housed in a hostel and I really didn't fancy that. So I was trying to think of options. One day I was at a mate's house and his dad was going on about being in the Navy. He was saying, "I used to go all around the world, I had a bed to lie in, a woman here and a woman there" and I was like, "You what?" So from the age of 14 I knew what I wanted to do.

'I spoke to the Navy at careers day and they advised me to wait until I was 18. Sue told me I could stay with her until then, even though she didn't have to. That's the kind of woman she is. She helped me so much.'

Max is able to talk about his childhood difficulties with a smile. 'It's funny,' he says, 'because at the time I didn't feel hurt by it, I think I just blocked it all out and took it in my stride because I was used to taking things in my stride, but now sometimes I think about it and it does bother me. You know there's times when I haven't seen my grandmother for a while and she says to me, "Why don't you come and see me? What have I done to you?" and I think "You locked me out the house and had me put in care! What do you mean, what have I done to you?" So yeah, it's like the last few years that it's all come flooding back a bit.'

Max fulfilled his childhood ambition and joined the Navy as an engineer at 18. On enlisting he was sent to HMS *Raleigh*, a shore-based training establishment near Torpoint in Cornwall, for basic training. Once there he quickly caught the eye of the fitness instructors. His natural athleticism marked him out as a cut above his peers.

'They thought I was the best thing since sliced bread,' he recalls, laughing, 'until it came to swimming. I couldn't swim at all back then. I was like, come on, that's the way it is with black people, most of us don't swim! But it was good I excelled at something because I probably wouldn't have been up to much as an engineer. I wasn't that interested in engineering in truth.'

After ten weeks at *Raleigh* and some intensive swimming lessons, he passed out and was sent to HMS *Sultan*, in Gosport, Hampshire, a training centre for Naval engineers. It was at *Sultan* that he met the man who would provide the inspiration for his future. PT instructor Q. Shillingford had a glittering career as an amateur boxer, representing England internationally and winning a variety of accolades. From there he became a successful and highly regarded coach, ultimately being awarded an MBE in 2014. The illustrious PTI quickly took a shine to the young trainee.

'He just randomly came up behind me in a PT session and punched me on the side of the ribs,' Max remembers. 'I looked at him and he said, "Never let your guard down." I was like, "OK, cool." About ten minutes later he did it again. "I told you," he said, "never let your guard down."

'So I waited about two hours until the end of the session and I sneaked up behind him and got one in on him. I gave him a big grin and said, "Never let your guard down." So he turned around to me, all serious and said, "OK Maxwell, boxing gym, six o'clock!" And that was an order.

'I turned up, I'd never boxed before, he put me in a headguard and a pair of gloves and I was straight in the ring with him. The funny thing was I held my own. I was just moving about and windmilling really, but it sort of worked for me.'

That little taster was enough to convince Shillingford that he had a talent on his hands. Max suddenly found that the PTI was relieving him of cleaning duties and other odious tasks to allow him to come back to the gym and train. Maxwell was more than happy to play along and soon was sparring and learning every evening. At 19 he was a relatively late starter but with natural athletic ability and intensive attention from Shillingford, he mastered the rudiments quickly and began to develop more advanced skills.

'That's one of the things I think, when I sit back and I look over the little career that I've had,' Max says. 'I think, what if someone had grabbed hold of me when I was seven or eight and started training me? I came into the sport so late, but I still did pretty well. You know especially when I've been around sparring the lads that are world class and have been to the Olympics and all that kind of thing. I competed with them and I wonder how far I could have gone.'

Max's first amateur fight followed within months and took place on HMS *Sultan*. It was in a Navy v Cambridge University event and he won comfortably on points against an opponent in his 20th contest. From there, things developed rapidly. He was

Navy champion in his first year and spent a sizeable chunk of the next seven years boxing.

'If you're on the Navy team, they look after you,' he says, grinning. 'Probably six months a year I was taken off my ship and just based at *Sultan* with the boxing squad, living like a professional. We'd train twice a day, have our meals, get relaxation time and at the end of the month, you'd get your wages as well. To be honest, it was a perfect way to start.

'I'd be on a ship, halfway around the world and the Commodore would get a phone call asking for me and I'd get flown back to England to train, then put on another plane to go out to America to box. It was a great life and a fantastic time, but there was one thing missing from life in the Navy – women!'

In his time boxing for the Navy, Max had 35 amateur contests and won 27. He eventually left, after seven and a half years, to pursue his interest in the fairer sex, initially doing some work as a supply teacher, covering PE in Birmingham schools. Unlike his Navy career, life and love on the outside weren't all smooth and within a few months he seriously entertained the thought of re-enlisting.

'The Navy was all I knew, really,' he says, 'but I didn't like the idea of going back and everyone making fun of me because I couldn't hack it on the outside.' Pride made him persist and before long, the 25-year-old civilian Max began to settle into life on shore and considered the prospect of boxing professionally.

'I actually met Jon Pegg at a football match,' he recalls. 'He was talking to one of my mates, saying that Richie Woodhall was opening a boxing gym in Telford. So I ended up going down there on the Monday. To tell the truth I'd watched a little bit of boxing but I didn't really follow it, so the name Richie Woodhall didn't mean a lot to me, but I went down there, did a few bits and pieces and Len Woodhall, Richie's dad said to me, "You're OK, we can do something with you."'

Max turned over with Richie as his manager and debuted in Wolverhampton in October 2006 as the home fighter. Unfortunately, first-night nerves got the better of him.

'One thing about me is that I've always got nervous before fights. I suffer with it really badly. I think that night was particularly bad because it was my pro debut and I was so keen for it to go well. Boxing as an amateur just seemed like a fun thing, a hobby almost and for me the pros did seem like quite a big deal. When Richie realised how nervous I got on fight nights he used to sit in the dressing room with me and talk to me about anything other than boxing – women, music, Jamaica, whatever he could think of just to take my mind off it.'

On the night Max burned up so much tension in the first two rounds that he ran out of steam. Despite that, he remains convinced that he did enough to win but instead he found himself on the wrong end of a 38-39 decision against Crawley's Anthony Young. Although disappointed, the debut loss did not set him too far back and he went on to pick up seven consecutive victories, all fought in the home corner, culminating with his Midlands Area title win over Hough.

'The truth was,' Max says, 'although I started off as a prospect, I was being looked after by the Woodhalls a little bit. I wasn't a very good ticket seller, you know the most I ever sold was 50 and that was for my British title shot, most other times I only sold a handful. If I didn't have Richie and Len behind me and supporting me, it probably wouldn't have worked in the way that it did.'

It was this that led to the decision to start going on the road and boxing in the away corner. As much potential as Maxwell had, and he still believes to this day he could have won more titles, certainly on the domestic scene, he was simply not financially viable as a home fighter.

'It was Ken Purchess running it all back then. He started me off on a grand a fight and that's going back six or seven years ago. Guys are still getting a grand a fight now.

'Between him and the Woodhalls they kept it going at the beginning. You know basically what it meant was that other lads on the show were selling the tickets to compensate for me and Ken was alright with that to start with, but after the first six or seven fights, Ken realised he wasn't going to get rich quick from me and things changed.'

Purchess was a bit of a character on the Midlands scene who would turn up to shows on a Harley Davidson and cultivated an image as a sort of Brummie Don King. However he didn't have deep enough pockets to continue to indefinitely bankroll a boxer who just wasn't selling tickets.

'Ken was a really nice bloke,' Max maintains. 'But I think he just thought boxing was a lark.'

After the area title victory, Ken and Max agreed to part so that Max could follow his own path. In an alternative reality he may have looked up, towards an English or British title fight, instead he began boxing in the away corner. His record started to change straight away. Max felt there was an immediate difference in his treatment by the officials, leading to the loss of his title in his first defence and then seven of his next ten fights.

'Without being disrespectful to any referees, I just think they know where their bread is buttered. There's been plenty of times when I know I've dominated fights. For example I fought a guy called Chris Black in Scotland and was given a draw but I beat him hands down. Another one was Sam Webb who I fought in London. Now he was signed to box for the British title. I dropped him in the second round, cut him with a punch in the third and for most of the fight he was just running away from me. I couldn't have won that fight more clearly. Of course they gave it to him though and he went on to become British champion.

'The week after the Webb fight, I boxed a guy called Thomas McDonagh, nice boxer but cannot punch to save his life. He couldn't break an egg. McDonagh tagged me with a stiff jab and the referee stopped the fight in the first round! So you know what, they've obviously seen what happened to Sam Webb the week before and they've thought "we can't have any of that". Look at McDonagh's record, he hasn't stopped anyone. It was an absolute joke!

'I fought Thomas Doran who's managed by Ricky Hatton and this one was beyond funny. First round, I hit him so hard and wobbled him badly. I went in to finish him and the ref has pulled me back and given him a standing eight count! There is no such thing as a standing eight count in professional boxing unless he is being held up by the ropes, or his gloves have touched the floor, but he was in the middle of the ring and still standing. After that, every time I hit him, he wobbled again. It was only a matter of time until I got him out of there. Then he hit me with one good shot, I took a step back and the referee jumped in and stopped it. Couldn't believe it! That one was Howard Foster, the same ref who stopped Groves against Froch, maybe he likes his early stoppages, but they do seem to happen on the side of the home fighter.

'The first fight with Brian Rose was already during the part of my career when I was keeping busy without picking up too many wins. I was out on the road and fighting very regularly, but at that time I was still taking it seriously. Always in good shape and going for the win, no matter what. The fight was nip and tuck all the way. Richie kept saying to me, "Throw the jab and right hand over the top, he's open for it." So I tried it a few times and at the beginning of the sixth it landed big.

'Now at the time Rose was signed to fight for the British title and everyone was saying that I should get a shot because I'd just knocked him out. This shows you just how corrupt boxing is! After that, Brian Rose came back, rebuilt his career. He got an English title shot before I even got a shot at anything, then he got his British title shot. You know, then to be fair to him, he was man enough and he gave me a rematch, beat me on points and it was a fair decision, you know.

'I didn't agree with the scoring [Rose won by eight rounds on two judges' cards and seven on the other], I thought it was a bit wide, but he did enough to win it. You know, fair play, he's a very tidy boxer, Brian Rose. Looking at it, he's a good kid, but he's not world level, but the promoters love him because he sells tickets. He can sell Blackpool out on his own, so because of that he's always been looked after and given every opportunity possible. That's the game. That's how it works.

'Brian Rose is a nice guy and I wish him all the best. If he does manage to pick up a world title I'll be cheering for him, but the only thing I don't like is that every time he's on Sky or whatever, they always mention me and say I was the guy that knocked him out, but that he was having psychological problems at the time. That bugs me, because they're trying to say I didn't beat him fair and square, which I did.

'We can all have problems, but if they're that bad then you don't get in the ring as far as I'm concerned. Once you step through the ropes you leave your problems behind and get on with it. If you're not ready, you do what David Haye does and pull out, simple as that! I would appreciate it if Brian Rose could come out and nip that in the bud because I don't like it. They are trying to make me sound like a mug and it's not fair really.'

Since losing out on the British title to Rose and accepting a late-notice challenge for the English championship against Erick Ochieng which also didn't go his way, Max had a think about his place in the business, which led to a conversation with Jon Pegg. At the time he stood at 16-13-3. He had started in professional boxing without a great deal of direction and his four years of fighting out of the away corner had produced mixed results, but it became clear that title challenges were going to be harder and harder to engineer.

'Look, to be honest the Ochieng fight was on a big bill at the London Olympia and they offered me five grand just before Christmas so I took it. But I went into that with a journeyman mentality, maybe for the first time. I'd been ill and off training, but the money was so good I couldn't turn it down. You know, I don't want to take anything away from Ochieng, but if I'd been given proper notice and I'd trained well for it and all that, it would have been different. I just thought of the money, stayed defensive and survived really. It was a taste of things to come!

'After that I spoke to Jon and told him I was going to retire. I meant it too, I was going to retire there and then but suddenly the phone went and I got offered four grand to go out and box in

Poland. I thought, "Four grand, OK then!" I was boxing this kid called Jonak, he's ranked in the top ten in the world and at the time he was 35-0. I went out there and played with him. It was easy work. I tell you what, if someone like that can have a world top ten ranking then anyone can. It just shows you how much of a mess boxing is.

'So after that I said to Jon, you know what, I'm gonna have another year, have loads of fights, go in with a journeyman attitude and survive and make as much money as possible, then call it a day. And my year's up soon. I box every week, give the lad a workout and take the money. That's all it is to me now.

'And look, people will have figured this out for themselves, but most of the time I'm going in there and just having a move about. That's the deal. Half these lads I've been in with in the last year or so, they're not all that. These boys can't beat me! Their managers and everything know that. You know for instance I boxed Lee Noble, a Sheffield lad and when they told him he was fighting me, he was worried, you know I still have a bit of a name in the scene and guys know what I can do. So his manager said to him, "It's OK, he's just going to move around with you."

'After that, Noble knew if he didn't take the piss, I'd let him take it. And he was very respectful, to be fair, so fair play to him. That's the way it is in the boxing world and that's the way I make my money now. For me, that's why I can only do this for a year. At the moment I still have respect in the boxing community and respect for myself. If I carry on longer, boxing in the way I do now, I'll lose that.

'When I boxed Rod Smith, [7 February 2014 in Sheffield] he came out like a steam train and tried it on. Some of them try to get cheeky. They're told what the score is but they think they can take the mick. He had a bit of a go, so I thought, "OK!" and I gave him a proper one. Dropped him in the first round! That's the way it is. That's my way of saying, "You learn your manners." After that he knew the score, was boxing nice and easy and I let him take it.'

Max encountered a similar scenario two months later, in April 2014. He accepted a fight on four hours' notice against a novice called Ryan Vaughan in Liverpool and was shocked when Vaughan came out swinging for the fences in round one.

'Look,' Max said, afterwards, 'I'm quite happy to go in there, put on a good show, help develop the future of the sport and teach them a few things, but that kid tried to take advantage, he cut my lip, gave me a small cut by one eye, all in the first minute, so I was like, OK then! And I switched it up and decked him with a right hand. He pissed me off, so after that it was always going to be my fight.'

Jon Pegg explained, 'For his last few fights Max has been boxing a bit easier, but the lad riled him a bit and you know, Vaughan will have learned a valuable lesson there. He tried to chin someone who'd done him a favour by turning up at the last minute and he paid the price for it. He's just learned something about the game and how it works.'

Maxwell was given a 38-37 decision by referee Mark Lyson, destroying Vaughan's unbeaten record and giving Max his first win for 36 fights, only three months before he was due to quit the sport.

In June Max won again, against Liam Conroy (6-2). It was his penultimate fight before retirement. 'I've been in training for the big finale,' Max said. 'I'm in the best shape I've been in for ages, so because I'm retiring in two weeks anyway, I thought why not? They can't stop giving me work now!'

His final fight, on 12 July, also resulted in an eight-round points victory over Damian Taggart for the British Masters Bronze title, meaning Max finished with two consecutive wins and another belt as a memento.

'You know, I'll be glad when the year is out,' he told me. 'Those dedicated journeymen, like Kris Laight, I can't do what they do. To do it year in, year out, it's so hard in its own way and I have massive respect for those guys. Making weight, week after week after week and showing these young prospects around, it's very tough.'

Max now intends to go into coaching and maybe even return to teaching. 'I enjoyed it and got respect from the kids, but I don't know if I could spend my life doing it.' He has already entered the lucrative personal training market, which is working well for him. He certainly seems to have the sense and charisma to make it work.

Max's eight children, all of whom live with their mothers, make it essential that he continues to earn a good living. 'All my kids know who their father is,' he said with a wide smile, gesturing at photos of them around his living room. 'I see them regularly and they never want for anything. Taking care of my kids is very important to me. I suppose it's like a lot of parents, I want them to have the things that I didn't, growing up in Jamaica.'

I left Maxwell's company feeling happier about the game and its twists and turns. At 33, in perfect health and about to walk away from the sport, he seemed genuinely at peace with himself, contented, someone who had ridden life's peaks and troughs with a sense of serendipity and strength. I admired his positive energy and felt that finally, here was someone who had made it all work for him, who had not just survived his journey through the boxing business, but managed to turn it to his own advantage.

He may not have cabinets full of belts or legions of fans, but in that way, a real way, he is perhaps the best role model a young boxer could find – a genuine boxing success story. When he called it quits in July, well-earned cash in the bank, he walked away from the ring in one piece, physically and emotionally. Very few fighters can say that.

13

Putting up with all the bullshit

Jason Nesbitt

Welterweight
Born: Birmingham, 15 December 1973
Active: 2000–present
Record: 10-173-4

I F Johnny Greaves is the nation's most famous journeyman, Kristian Laight is the busiest and Jody Meikle is the funniest, this chapter will introduce the book's unsung hero. A 40-year-old grandfather with almost 200 fights under his belt, cagey, with a right hand that could knock holes in a few contenders if used freely, Birmingham's Jason Nesbitt has appeared in venues up and down the length of the UK for the last decade and a half.

For many hardcore fight fans, he would be one of the first-mentioned of the fighters featured here. Jason has swapped punches with some stellar names and is more than capable of providing the odd upset. The weekend before I met him, he had picked up his first win for four years, by knocking out the big ticket selling debutant and former kickboxing champion Ryan Nandha in Walsall. He was matter-of-fact about the victory, his seventh by KO.

'It was just one of those things,' he said, a little smile twitching the corners of his mouth. 'The kid was a bit naive. He walked on to my right hand.' Later on he would tell me more about the circumstances surrounding the fight, making what happened all the more intriguing.

He met me in Eastside City Park in central Birmingham with Samantha, his girlfriend of 16 years, by his side. She attends fights with him and is often present in the dressing room before he walks out. During the course of our conversation she sometimes chipped in with comments or observations, seeming slightly defensive of her man, as if she is used to hearing him criticised.

Although we had never met before, I had spotted him from half a mile away when he was little more than a silhouette against the sky, appearing through a line of trees over the crest of a hill. Something about his gait and physical shape marked him out as a boxer from a distance. As he neared, the bald head and squinting, almost Chinese-looking eyes I had seen before from ringside became visible. He smiled warmly and shook my hand with a fighter's grip.

'What sort of an interview do you want?' he asked. 'How do you want this to go?' I told him what I told all the fighters. I would like him to be as honest as he felt comfortable with. What he said or didn't say was up to him.

'Because there's things they don't want the fans to know,' he replied. 'People in boxing know, but not the fans.' Jason knows the score.

I asked why he had never done an interview before. 'I've just never been interested,' he said, shrugging and smiling widely. 'I've had a few offers but never responded. What's the point? What would it do for me?'

Mystery surrounds Jason Nesbitt's earliest years. He doesn't remember them or life with his natural parents. His childhood was spent as a ward of the state in his home city and is not something he looks back on with fondness. He was taken into care at the age of two.

Prospects for children growing up in the UK care structure are proportionally bleak. Even today, a third of the UK's homeless and over a quarter of the prison population grew up in care. Childhood stories of those who went through the system, particularly in the 1970s and 80s, before attempts at reform were made, are frequently harrowing, involving bullying, physical and sexual abuse and neglect. Nesbitt visibly tenses when the subject arises, sitting up straighter. He had been staring at a point on the horizon but turned his head to look me straight in the eye.

'There were three of us that got put into the home at the same time,' he says. 'Me, my little brother and another lad, into a house with eight boys and ten girls, I lived there until I was 18 or 19. To be honest, it was one of the worst things that could have happened to me.'

He inhales deeply and slowly through his nose. He looks down.

'People talk about the things that happen in care homes and a lot of people don't get believed. But I believe in that kind of shit because I've seen it and lived it for myself. It's all true. Everything you've heard about it, it's all true. But for me personally, I can't talk about that stuff. There's things I've never told anyone. My childhood wasn't a happy time at all.'

Following a familiar pattern, his troubled home life led to complications at school and in his neighbourhood. He had major difficulties interacting successfully with other children and adults. Repeated and persistent problems plagued his time in the education system. He was violent, resistant to authority and easily angered. From a very young age he suffered the stigma of exclusion.

'I was a rough lad. Obviously I grew up in a house full of boys, a lot of them older than me and that made me tough. Believe me, I had to be. As I grew up I was in and out of units and boarding schools and key centres. I was always getting expelled from school. I was confronting the teachers, stealing things from other kids and fighting. I even got expelled from infant school.

'What a lot of people don't understand is, if you're brought up in a bad environment and you see bad things at home, you can go to nursery or school or wherever but you're going to bring it out. It's easy to blame a youngster who's acting out in certain ways, but sometimes you have to understand why it's happening. I didn't feel that teachers and people like that tried to understand that side of it, really. They just identified me as a problem and treated me like one. That's all it was. As I've got older, I've put it behind me and learned to deal with it. I suppose I'll always have my issues, but as a kid I couldn't cope with them. I took them out on other people.'

By the time he was 16, with 11 years of educational problems behind him, Nesbitt passed on to the next stage of the standard sociological sequence and began having issues with the police. His crimes were typical ones for an inner-city youth: vandalism, an occasional burglary, joyriding. He managed to stay clear of gang situations or drug offences. 'It was going on in the area,' he says. 'But it just weren't my thing.' His arrests never led to anything more serious than cautions, which he attributes to luck.

There is an old saying among fighters that they didn't choose boxing, but boxing chose them. Jason's initiation into the sweet science certainly seems to fit that pattern. 'It's funny, because if you speak to people who knew me as a kid they all say they knew I'd end up as a boxer because I was always fighting, always aggressive, but boxing isn't something I ever wanted to do, maybe it's destiny or something like that.

'I finally gave it a go when I was 18, through a friend of mine. I'd never been to a gym, hit a bag, nothing. I had no interest in it really. This mate of mine asked me to go training with him and I said OK. I went along to the Muirfield gym and I liked what I did. I enjoyed it. At that time I still didn't really intend to box seriously, but I liked the training so I kept going. I used to see the lads sparring and I liked what I saw. I think what attracted me to it was that I saw it as a fair fight. You know, it's not someone treading on someone's head or hitting them with a bottle, it's a straight-up battle between two guys. That's what drew me to it. And you know what? I still love it. The one thing I love is my boxing.'

Jason soon got over his reticence to compete and began boxing as an amateur, channelling the inner rage stored up from his rough start in life. His fiery approach and powerful right hand soon marked him out as a difficult challenge for anyone. He won 38 of 40 amateur contests.

'At the time I was hoping to go in for the ABAs,' he recalls. 'You know, certain shows I would turn up for and they'd say, "Oh, no, we don't want to box him." I'd be there, getting changed and then be told that I didn't have a fight. It got to the stage where I was finding it difficult to get fights anywhere. No one wanted me as an opponent. I was getting frustrated and it was then that I started thinking about the possibility of turning pro.

'Anyway, one thing led to another and I ended up going up to Nobby Nobbs's gym in Aston and that was that, really. Good old Nobby Nobbs. This was back in 1999 and Nobby was just getting going. He hadn't really established all that "Losers Unlimited" stuff yet. Anyway, I met Nobby, teamed up with him and away we went.

'I just wanted to turn pro, do a bit of training and see where it went. I didn't have any particular ambition. I just wanted to fight. I wasn't aiming for British title or world title or anything really. It was just something I liked doing and I wanted to do it. I knew I could get paid to fight and for me, that was perfect. So I took it up. I guess in that way me and Nobby suited each other well.

'So before my first fight, Nobby explained a little bit to me about the game. He took me to one side and said, "He's got two arms, he's got two legs, jump in the ring, do your thing, get your pay and go home." That was his explanation, his philosophy. It was as far as it went with Nobby! He just wanted the money really.

'At the time I didn't understand the business. As I've gone along I've heard the odd trainer, the odd promoter, the odd boxer, the odd official say the odd thing and you piece it all together. So then you know what you're up against. At the beginning I was clueless though, like a lot of lads.'

During this part of his life Jason also fathered his first child. But it's something he speaks of with regret. He has three children altogether but hasn't always had very much contact with them.

'The first one I can hold my hands up and say I did wrong, but with the other two, it's different. One of them, the mother didn't even tell me the kid was mine and disappeared for many years. They're all back in my life now and I've got a grandson as well, but it's not been easy, all that stuff.'

His pro career started on 6 November 2000 against Steve Chinnock in Wolverhampton. Predictably, boxing for Nobby in the away corner, he lost on points. He fought again in December and the following January, losing both, before picking up his first win against fellow journeyman Billy Smith in March 2001. At the time, Smith was 0-12.

'The thing was with Billy, we'd already fought in the amateurs and I beat him then. I remember turning up in the venue for that fight and he came over with a big grin and said, "Do you remember me? You beat me in the amateurs!" He was trying to be intimidating. I just laughed and told him I was going to beat him again.'

In his next fight, in May, he fought Sid Razak, who at the time was a prospect with a record of 2-0. Razak would also later become a well-known journeyman.

'I beat Sid!' Jason insists. 'Beat him clearly. He knows I beat him. But they didn't give it to me. It was a home decision, that one. I started to learn from then, I think. You know, now I never expect to get given one. You get used to it after a while. It just becomes like a little hobby.'

By Nesbitt's 20th professional contest, the pattern had been firmly established. He stood at 2-17, had been stopped four times but lost the rest on points. He fought Grimsby's Matt Teague in Hull over six two-minute rounds. Teague recalls that Jason had hit him harder than anyone else he fought.

'I was winning on points, I knew that,' Teague said, 'but in the last round he clocked me with a right hand that really buzzed me. It was a terrific shot. A couple of days later I was walking around and my face was in a mess, big black eye and all sorts. I bumped into Jason on the street and he asked me, "What happened to you?" I didn't want to tell him it was his punches that did it!'

'They all say that,' Jason smiles. 'All the managers know what I can do. Why do you think the lads get told to keep away from my right hand?'

Nesbitt has demonstrated the need for opponents to respect his power repeatedly. Seven of his ten wins have come by KO or stoppage. In November 2010 he broke Trowbridge welterweight Aaron Fox's jaw in two places with a punch in the first round. Countless times he has decked, wobbled or hurt opponents, only for them to seemingly regroup and nick a win on points. The reasons for this soon became clear.

Jason had given the impression from the beginning of our conversation that he had things he wanted to say and the night before we met he had fought a debutant called Ryan Martin in Swindon.

'Listen, this is how it works,' he said. 'I ain't mentioning no names, but look, the fight was set for 148lbs. At least that's what they told me. The lad came in at 143lbs. I came in at 150lbs, so obviously I'm half a stone heavier, although it's not really my fault. Anyway, behind closed doors, before we go out there, I get a quiet word in my ear. "Jase, you've got to take it easy. This lad's sold six grand's worth of tickets so we can't have him losing. If you go out there and knock him out or stop him then I promise you, you're not getting any fights. You're not going to hear anything for at least a couple of months."

'I had a very similar situation weight-wise, when I boxed Josh Leather [February 2014 at York Hall]. I was approached beforehand and told the same thing. To tell the truth, the taking it easy bit happens with most of my fights. I'm not actually trying to win because I'm told not to.

'They know at the end of the day that I'm experienced and I'll ride these kids around the ring. I'll take them the distance, whatever they want and that's what I'm being asked to do constantly now. It's not my fault if a person can't hit as hard as what they might think they can, or they've been told they can. It's not my fault if the promoter puts them in with someone like me, but then people worry that they can't take my right hand. I'm not supposed to be there to tickle them, I'm there to hurt them. That's what boxing is. It's two guys hurting each other.

'Now for my last couple that's what my intentions were. I was going in there to hurt them. But then someone has a word with me and I'm not allowed to. You know, this isn't a one-off type situation we're talking about. It's very regular, like most of the time. I will walk into a show and as soon as I go in I get a manager or a trainer coming up to me going, "Oh you're boxing my lad tonight, he's only young, just take him the distance, take him around, show him the ropes." I'll be like, "Fair play mate, I don't mind." And that's basically what I do to earn my money in boxing.

'To be honest it's been working like that with me since the early days with Nobby. I think that's how Nobby got going with all that. This is how my career has been. Like I said, I enjoy it, I love to box, so if the only way I can get work is to move someone around, I'm going to do it.'

After 80 fights, Jason moved from Nobby to the managership of Errol Johnson, as did most of Nobby's stable after he retired.

'With Errol, it's just a standard thing, you know. It's like a part of the deal when they sign Jason Nesbitt for a fight that I'm there to provide a particular service. Until last week I hadn't won for four years and people wonder why. That's why!

'The reality is in an honest boxing world, where I was free to fight how I want and the officials weren't biased I would easily have won more than half of my fights. I can win a lot of these fights and there's people in the game that know that. Maybe the fans don't but half of them don't know what they're on about. At the end of the day it's my weekly wage so I'm going to do what I need to do to keep it coming. If I put a few wins together I'll be out for a month or two.

'Even last week when I knocked out that boy, Nandha, I was told beforehand to take it easy with him and take him through the rounds, which is what my intentions were, but I think what it is, I've started doing some different training, training with heavier fighters than me, working to the body and all that, doing a few weights and to be honest I've been practising letting my shots go more. Maybe as I'm coming towards the end of my career anyway I'm thinking I might as well beat a few of them. Sometimes these things just happen instinctively.

'So yeah, I'm probably having more of a go now. With Nandha, I went in, just messing about to start with and he was catching me with these little tip-tap-tap punches but that's because I had to go out and play with him. If I was off the lead from the beginning I would have tagged him early on to give him something to worry about. The problem was, he wasn't up to much and I had to pick the pace up because otherwise it would have looked like I was play-acting.

'It's a fine balancing act that, to let the other guy win without making it obvious. There's a lot of skill in it. With Nandha, I was basically having to follow him around and let him hit me. So I upped my pace and as I upped my pace, I threw the right and he walked straight into it. Goodnight!'

While Jason told me about the Nandha fight, he looked over at Samantha and smiled. 'Why don't you tell him about it babe?' he said. Samantha shook her head and sighed, as if the memory annoyed her.

'After that, he didn't even get spoken to,' she alleges. 'That boy was Errol's lad [Errol Johnson, Jason's manager, also promoted Nandha]. I was in the front row and during the third round Errol came over and he sat next to me. He was telling me, "Shut up, shut up! Don't shout for him, don't cheer for him. If he wins this, that's it, he's finished, I'm finished with him. This boy's my ticket seller. He's my money maker. I'm not having it." That's the thing, he could see it coming, he could see Jason was having a bit of a go and the second it happened, when Jason landed and knocked him out, he got up and walked away. He didn't speak to him or me after that.'

'I had the same thing with Nobby,' Jason contends, cackling with laughter. He obviously enjoyed upsetting his managers. 'I boxed a lad called Greg Edwards [at the Marriott Hotel, Mayfair, London, March 2002] and I was only supposed to take it easy, which is what I was doing, moving around. To be honest it was more or less the same thing again. He walked right on to a right hand in the fifth round, got KO'd and Nobby just upped and left the building. He was meant to be giving me a lift back as well. I had to travel home on my own!

'So that shows how it is. I'm not there to win am I? I'm there to make the fight and to give the lad a workout. Any more than that and people get upset. So what can I do?

'You have to remember I've been restricted by the Board as well. Right now I'm only allowed to fight over six twos, so I'm only getting £800 a fight. That's the way it is. That's why I have to try and go with the flow.

'With all that, I don't really know what's gone on. It happened after I boxed [Commonwealth Games medallist] Bradley Saunders [at York Hall, February 2012]. They stopped the fight in the third round. I boxed a couple of times after that and no one said anything, then when I turned up to fight [current Southern Area light-welter champ] Ricky Boylan [in April at Elephant and Castle] they suddenly told me I was restricted to six twos.

'I went into the Board to discuss it and it's not the first time, believe me. They asked about the losses and I told them what they need to know. They don't really call me in too often now. You know I've discussed my record with them, like I'm stood up in front of them and say, "Hold on, half of you lot are there at the fights, you can see that I'm putting an effort in, you can see that sometimes I should have won the fight, or even been given a draw but there's nothing coming." And they know this. They don't argue.

'I do love my boxing, but the whole home and away thing can get you down a bit. I've always fought in the away corner and you see the home fighters getting favoured all the time. Do you see them coming out with their nappies on first? They look after them like fucking babies. It's all about tickets isn't it? Look fair play, the ref's there to do his job, which is to manage the fight and decide who he thinks has won. But if you get someone like me that goes in the ring and fights against a local boy like Ryan Martin, I'm not going to get the decision, I haven't sold no tickets. I just think the ref is under the wing of the promoter.

'If we've put a good effort in and we know how the fight's gone then it can be annoying, you know, give us a draw at least. It is a job but there's times when I think I should have got a win and it pisses me off, of course it does. When the time comes to hang up my gloves I'd like to look back at my record and see 20 or 30 wins on there, instead of just ten or whatever. I've got a maximum of three years left I reckon so lets see if I can pick a few more up and still get fights!'

Nesbitt has never quite managed to make a sole living from boxing. Outside the ropes he has done forklift work, warehouse work, he's worked at Land Rover and on the bins. Many a morning he can be seen around Birmingham, putting a shift in, in a high-vis vest.

'Look, you can't box forever. I want to reach 200 fights and I know when I reach 200 fights, if the Board says, "We're not going to let you carry on" then I've got something to fall back on. Of course, if I'm given the chance I'll carry on beyond the 200, I will, but it's not necessarily my decision to make. The thing is with boxing, and I keep saying it, but I do love it. I love getting in there and doing it.'

Jason would probably have passed the double century before we met with slightly better luck. Unfortunately he injured his shoulder against the current (at the time of writing) Southern Area lightweight champion Adam Dingsdale on 1 June 2013. After two minutes of round two, Jason pulled away from his opponent, turned his back and signalled to the referee that he had a problem in the shoulder. The young referee, Kieran McCann, looked confused and waved both fighters to continue boxing. Dingsdale promptly waded in and landed four or five unanswered shots with Jason helpless and half turned away, on the ropes.

Sensibly, Nesbitt went down to avoid further punishment, at which point McCann ended the contest. The official decision was therefore a TKO rather than a retirement, which angered Jason. Still, he was out for 28 days because of the stoppage, then had to wait for the shoulder to heal.

'Altogether I was out from 13 June until 14 February with the shoulder injury. I was cleared by the hospital after 28 days but the Board said they'd lost my scans and I ended up being out for eight months. What a piss-take! If I was Carl Froch do you think they'd treat me like that? If that hadn't happened, I'd be on about 220 by now.

'Apparently there's a little bit of a race on between me and Kristian Laight to see who gets to 200 first. Errol was talking about it yesterday. I know Kris really wants to go on even further than that but for me 200 is enough. If I get there, it's job done, I'll feel like I've achieved something and I can think about retiring.'

There are those who might suggest that as he enters his fifth decade of life and with nigh-on a double century of pro bouts behind him, Nesbitt should consider hanging them up sooner rather than later. He recognises this himself and there is a trace of sadness in his voice as he speaks.

'At 40 I know there's going to come a day when I have to stop. I've always had a clean bill of health, boxing-wise, touch wood. One year I had a shadow over my brain, they let me carry on but I had to go back a couple of months later to be checked again. When I went back they said it was fine. Personally I think it's because I went sparring the day before the scan.

'But I'm determined to get to the 200 and then we can see. I think if I make it to 200 fights, it sends a message to people, young people. If I can come from nothing and the terrible start that I had in life, then end up having 200 professional fights, it shows kids in similar situations that you can achieve something.

'It would have been nice if I'd managed to pick a belt up during my career. I had an International Masters title fight against Tony Owen [in Brighton, June 2011] but he'd been training for it for a couple of months and they only gave me a few days' notice. And I had to get to ten stone!

'I had a week of going running wearing three bin bags and three T-shirts to cut weight. I was hardly eating. Shedding weight like that gets much harder as you get older, so I went into that fight feeling really weak, but again the fans don't see that. To be honest even for six twos, a week or five days or something is probably the least I'd accept now. I'm not always a fan of the very short notice fights anymore and I tend to turn them down. At my age you need to let your body rest sometimes.

'And you know it's funny but now I'm probably training harder than ever before. Maybe I need to at 40. I'm in the gym twice a day sometimes and I get up and run three or four times a week. I take my training very seriously. I love it, so it's not a problem. I try to focus on different things. Lately it's been my speed. A lot of these lads that I'm boxing, they're 20 years younger than me and they're like little flies, moving around with fast hands and I like to try to match that.

'As I get closer to the 200 I'm aiming to pick up a few more wins. And at the very least I want to hurt them. Give them something to remember me by. You know maybe they can buzz around and take it on points, but I'm going to hurt them.'

After retirement Jason is keen to stay involved in the sport, possibly as a cornerman. He has already been offered work as a trainer but is unenthusiastic.

'I get it all the time. These young lads think they want to have a go and bug me and say, "Take me to the gym and teach me." So I take them down there and show them a few things, then they don't want to know anymore. It's hard work and a lot of lads don't get that at first and when they do get it, they don't want it.

They think it's just about having a row, but this is boxing, not a street fight.

'It's the same thing with a lot of the unlicensed stuff, white collar and all that. Those guys just want to go in there and have it. I've been asked many times to box unlicensed but you'll never get me on one of those shows. That's for mad people! It's the kind of sport you go in when you've got nothing else to live for. I've been to a few of those kind of shows, and you know, fair play, it may be a good night out but you're just watching brawlers. There's nothing technical about what they're doing. You can see that any night you want outside a rough pub.'

Jason is only too aware that many people will read his comments about skill and technique and find them ironic. This is a man, after all, who at the time of writing had failed to win 180 of his professional fights. He shrugs off the perceptions of the public with a grin.

'When I hear people talking about how many losses I've got and saying how crap I am, I love it. It gees me up. Even when I get into the ring and they announce my name and they're all booing and swearing at me, I love that too, it gives me a little buzz. Some of the remarks these fans come out with do bother me a little bit, but the fans don't understand what's going on.

'They're just seeing their mate come out and put on a show, not realising the man in the other corner is being paid to take it easy. The truth is you get these lads that have got to 7-0 or something and they've only really fought journeymen, they build up the record for them, then they put them in a proper fight and they get pasted because they don't have any real fight experience.

'But look, there's a lot of problems in the boxing world, but the honest truth is I don't regret my career. Not a bit. I'm happy as I am. Maybe that says something about me, I don't know. For any young boxer thinking of going on the road to earn a few quid, I'd say as long as you're ready for calls at late notice, turning up, doing your job, getting paid, going home, then getting another phone call a week later, you'll be alright. And having to take the losses, of course. That sounds straightforward, but it can be tough, mentally. You have to be able to cope with defeat after defeat.

'The one thing I would love before I retire is a journeyman prizefighter. I've spoken to some of the other boys and we would love it to happen. It would have been nice to do it when Billy Smith was still alive, but even now it would still be great to do. They say there's no market for it but I can't agree with that. If you go to any part of the country I reckon boxing fans would be interested.

'And you know, we're going in there to provide a service to boxing, so it would be a way to give us something back. We already give them so much, by going in with their lads who want to try and take the piss with us. We're putting up with all the bullshit, so why not?'

As the deadline loomed for sending this book to press, Jason once again found himself with something to put up with. Since the knockout win over Nandha he had suffered eight consecutive losses, with two of the last three coming by stoppage. The Board suspended him in July 2014 and arranged a meeting to discuss his record.

'I only need seven more,' Jason said. 'I hope they don't stop me getting to 200. I'm so close now. I deserve that, don't I?'

After everything he had been through, I thought, it would be desperately cruel if they didn't allow him that.

14

The Final Bell

'A boxing match is like a cowboy movie. There's got
to be good guys and there's got to be bad guys.
And that's what people pay for.
To see the bad guys get beat.' – *Sonny Liston*

WRITING a book like this about the current boxing
scene has posed some difficulties. It is much easier
to tell the story of boxers long retired. In the months it
took me to put everything together, updated results and events
constantly changed the landscape. Robin Deakin had several
shifts in direction, managing in his own inimitable way to keep
people talking about him. Acrimonious banter with Mickey
Helliet and various other characters popped up on social media
almost daily.

Nobody saw Jody Meikle's retirement coming in May, except
perhaps Jody himself and a few members of the Crown Prosecution
Service. I had anticipated that the book might introduce him to
a wider audience and he would go on to build a 100–150 fight
record, becoming a real face on the British sporting scene due to
his irrepressible character and the sheer entertainment value he
brings to the ring. Instead, he has exited the stage, just as his fame
was starting to snowball.

Added to this was the fact that journeymen in general, including some of the fighters featured here, had pretty successful starts to 2014. As already noted, Jason Nesbitt picked up his first win for four years in March by knocking out debutant Ryan Nandha in the fourth round in Walsall. William Warburton (12-61) won in April to add to another victory a month earlier. Before that he had won only once since November 2012.

Kristian Laight picked up a brace of wins in the spring. Prior to this golden spell he tallied one solitary 'W' since December 2008, that's in five years and 113 contests. Jody Meikle's victory at York Hall in April was also his second of this year. By comparison, he only won once in the whole of 2013.

Max Maxwell took decisions over Liam Conroy in June, Ryan Vaughan in April and Damian Taggart in July, to close a run of 36 straight defeats going back to September 2012. Big Moses Matovu (5-40-4) outpointed a debutant in March, winning 39-37 in Glasgow. It was his first win for two years. And so on.

What could this glut of journeyman victories mean? Some, like Max Maxwell, nearing retirement and having a go again, had obvious explanations. Possible reasons for the others varied. One theory suggested that journeymen were trying harder in order to keep the Board off their backs. Fighters like Deakin and Thorpe losing their licences in recent years had made others wary. Another school of thought held that the Board had become self-conscious about the home/away issue, referees had discussed it and now were consciously giving more away verdicts to avoid negative publicity. Whether it was just a passing phase or a long-term shift remains to be seen. By early July, the journeymen wins seemed to have dried up again.

In starting all this, I had wanted to know what motivated journeymen and to understand how their role worked. Through grappling with that it became clear that the one thing they had in common, with the exception of Bheki Moyo, was that they expressed a deep love for the sport of boxing, the training, the discipline, the thrill of physical confrontation – in their hearts, like all boxers, perhaps even more so than other boxers, journeymen are fighting men.

What really fascinated me was that for the majority, their love of the sport remained undiminished while they expressed dissatisfaction or even anger at the business and politics of the fight game. All of them felt they had been cheated, that promoters and officials had colluded to rob them of deserved victories, yet still their participation inside the ropes was like a euphoric drug which they struggled to live without.

Their life stories had much in common. Broken homes and childhood hardships were repeated, though not universal themes. Father figures were either absent or dubious role models. These would seem to be the elements in a youngster's early development that foster a need for violent expression, a need that is given scant attention in the modern world. For all of these characters, boxing gave them an identity and a legitimate way to express what they had inside. Without this outlet, aggression was dangerously repressed, in most cases leading to problems with the law.

A mercenary element is undeniable. Money permeates so much of what we do and while, for most, their participation in the sport was not solely financially motivated, it was a factor for all. For some, like Kris Laight and Max Maxwell it seemed perhaps their main motivation.

For others, like Johnny Greaves or Robin Deakin, there was a definite masochistic implication. Like those who self-harm, they craved the pain, relished the reputation as men who could absorb it and seemed almost to need it, as if the jolt of a wrapped fist served as a shoring-up of their being.

Others, like Jason Nesbitt, Jody Meikle and Matt Seawright, mainly retained a simple, earnest pleasure from boxing. In that way, the result was a side-issue. What mattered most was just being able to get in there and do it.

The final category were those such as Daniel Thorpe and James Child, who had not quite made peace with the order of things, who felt that perhaps fulfilment lay down another road, that they could do or have done more. For them, the tag of 'journeyman' may be a barrier to cross, something else to overcome in another battle, fought outside of the ring.

Bheki Moyo stood alone, with quiet dignity, a man at odds with what he once had been, a living paradox, a non-fighting fighter, critiquing the sport from within.

All of them deserve absolute respect.

In my own journey, delving into this side of the game, I uncovered things I had not necessarily intended to. I set out to tell an untold story, not to try to right the wrongs of the boxing business. Yet because the boxers spoke of them repeatedly, there are certain issues I have to confront.

Firstly, the manufacturing and massaging of records is nearly as old as boxing itself. From the start I understood that there would be more to journeymen's accumulated losses than meets the eye, but I had no idea the practice of 'moving about' and guaranteeing a result was as common as described. Of the fighters featured in this book, all but three openly admitted to having participated in it.

Manager/promoter Steve Goodwin accepted that paying journeymen extra to 'move about' frequently goes on although he is adamant it does not occur on his shows. 'I wouldn't do it because it's pointless,' he told me. 'If you've got a young fighter and the only way he can progress is to do that, then obviously he's in the wrong profession. He's never going to go anywhere and you're not doing him any favours by stringing him along. The only person who would benefit from it is a greedy promoter.'

The last Goodwin show I attended before finishing the book, at York Hall on 19 April 2014, featured two victories for journeymen (Jody Meikle and Mitch Mitchell) against Goodwin-managed debutants. Not only that, but both wins were by points, a fact which strongly supports Steve's claims to honesty.

Carl Greaves, proprietor of Carl Greaves Promotions and manager of both Johnny Greaves and Jody Meikle, was more taciturn. 'I've never directly come across that sort of thing. I've heard it goes on but I don't think it's that frequent. The only thing I could say might happen is when you've got an opponent who's come in much heavier than the home fighter. Then perhaps someone might have a word with him and tell him not to go too hard. But other than that, I don't think it's common at all.'

Jon Pegg took a similar view. 'It happens, but the bottom line, if you've got a lad who sells a lot of tickets and the only way you can keep him winning is by getting guys to move him about, it's just not worth it. The idea is to build him up into a title fight so you can make a few quid off him but it's self-defeating. Ultimately he'll just get clobbered when he moves up in class. People do it, but I wouldn't personally. It's difficult to do that sort of thing and keep any sort of credibility. You could maybe get away with it once, but then once the lad's been exposed you'll struggle to build him up again.'

Even Robert Smith, the general secretary of the British Boxing Board of Control, acknowledged the practice, but was unable to offer a solution. 'Look, it goes on. And it's crooked, isn't it? There's no two ways about it. A manager might have a lad who he thinks needs protecting, so he'll pay someone to do it. But we at the Board cannot read what is going on in a fighter's head.

'It can be very difficult, watching a fight from ringside, knowing whether an opponent is just being defensive, or whether they are moving someone about and giving them the rounds, especially if they're good at it. Of course if our officials at the venue deem what they have seen to be a cause for concern then we would investigate. That's all we can do.'

The managers and promoters who spoke to me denied that 'move-abouts' happen on their shows, as might be expected. This contradicts what the journeymen said, who in several cases told me specific stories about such shows, but I am not interested in pointing fingers and apportioning blame to the promoters for this.

Sections of the boxing community do direct anger in that direction, however. Alec Waller, an amateur trainer and coach from south London, expressed the views of many, who see fighters as victims of a greedy business. 'Once upon a time being a promoter was like being a gambler. You put your money down and took your chances. Boxers used to get a wage and it didn't depend on the gate. These days the promoters are not prepared to do anything for the boxers.

'The other week Danny Connor boxed [against journeyman Arek Malek, at York Hall] and by the time he paid out his expenses he boxed for nothing. What saddened me was that he still had to pay the promoter. I always thought the promoter paid the boxer! The boxer should have his eyes on belts and the manager and promoter should sort out the money for him. He's getting in there and getting hit, after all.'

A boxer taking all the physical risks, supposedly as a professional, yet in reality fighting for nothing is unpalatable to many people, but it must also be remembered it is the promoter who has costs to cover. If the choice for boxing fans is that this practice continues or such promoters go out of business, meaning fewer shows taking place, they would probably choose the former.

Carl Greaves confirmed that he has to swallow a loss on ten to 20 per cent of the shows that he promotes.

'It can be difficult,' he said, 'when you've got lads that are upset because you're not paying them as much as they were expecting, but I get boxers kicking off about money and if they haven't sold enough tickets, it just means I've got to take the hit. As much sympathy as I have for the fighters and I used to be one, so I know what it's like, I can't afford to do that every show, it's as simple as that. I say to lads, if you can sell three grand's worth of tickets, then there's a grand for you, £1,100 for your opponent and the rest for the promotion.

'On a typical show I need to make six grand to break even. That's my reality, otherwise I'm losing money. I know it's not easy. Even selling 50 tickets is hard graft, but that's the way it is. What other way is there these days? I tell you what, if I didn't rely on boxers selling tickets and just put an advert in *Boxing News* or whatever and left it at that, I wouldn't sell a ticket. Not one. The shows I put on are local shows, they're not big-name fighters and people just don't go to those kinds of shows any more unless they're connected to the boxer.'

Greaves is clearly right to point at wider circumstances. Just as local cinemas, theatres and music venues have closed down en masse in recent decades while advances in home entertainment left their former, regular customers slobbing on the sofa at home, the market for local boxing has been doubly decimated. Sky may make wealthy men of those at the top of the sporting hierarchy, but it doesn't do many favours for those down at the bottom.

Given a Saturday-night choice of world title fights in your lounge or novices at the town hall, few would opt for the latter, especially when it costs more. Tie that in with a society that has become increasingly anti-violent with each generation and small-hall boxing becomes an almost impossible sell. It may simply be that boxers hawking tickets to friends and family is the only way it can function and survive.

This is the real issue. After all 'move-abouts' are a development of the wider problem, the emphasis placed on ticket sales and the need to keep ticket-sellers winning. By occasionally calling journeymen in and removing their licences, the Board are only attacking the symptom because the disease is one they have no power to cure.

The real challenge for the boxing fan who wants all fights to be genuine and fairly scored, and boxers to be properly paid for what they do, is to think of a workable system for the sport which doesn't revolve around home fighters selling tickets.

One plausible suggestion is to introduce on-site betting into boxing venues. It works in the Far East, where it is well established. Casual fans may then be tempted to attend a show for the simple enjoyment of having a flutter, much like punters at racetracks or greyhound events. The fact that the audience have wagered on the fights would be guaranteed to create an atmosphere and the revenue from gambling could be offset on the gate, making ticket prices cheaper.

Without that, perhaps the sanest course of action is just to accept that 'moving about' goes on. That way fans attending the early career fights of a young prospect have no illusions about what they're seeing and journeymen won't be scapegoated because of their losing records.

The real task for a young prospect fighting a journeyman is not to beat him, because that outcome can almost be taken as read, but to look good in doing so. What can they show in the fight that all the other prospects who beat that journeyman couldn't?

The negative press journeymen often receive, and the attempts of the Board to clamp down on those with heavy losing records, has led to a recent trend within the small-hall scene of importing away-corner fighters from abroad, particularly Eastern Europe. While the former Communist Bloc is established as a leading region at world level, with the Klitschko brothers, Golovkin, Kovalev and the rest well entrenched among the game's elite, it has helped to lend credibility to the process. At least one promoter indulges in this while promising on their advertising materials 'superb, evenly matched fights' and 'boxers with winning records'.

Often sporting records that look decent on paper, these fighters are beneficiaries of boxing scenes which, below the upper levels, are far weaker than those of the UK. Johnny Greaves remarked, 'Half these boys from Latvia or wherever come over and look like they've never boxed before in their life.'

Steve Goodwin observed, 'Although I don't go in for move-abouts, the one thing I might do if I've got a lad who needs looking after is bring in a foreigner with a false record. A lot of these boys from Eastern Europe fit that category. I'd rather not do it, because it works out more expensive.

'If I use a UK journeyman on one of my shows I'll pay him £1,100, but when I bring in a foreigner, you're looking at £1,450 all in. Obviously the fighter himself only gets about £600, because there's lots of people taking a cut – his agent, a UK agent, a manager, then you've got to cover travel and accommodation and all the rest of it. But most of these lads, they're not up to the level of UK fighters so you know you're likely to get the W.'

Jon Pegg was able to explain a little more about how using foreign opponents works. 'A lot of these foreigners are awful, truth be told. These Eastern Europeans, half the fights on their record aren't real fights as we would see it here. More often than not it's two lads getting in the ring at the gym with a gym-mate, or another boxer, as the referee. It would barely qualify as any sort of contest in this country, nothing more than a hard spar.

'Even worse are the guys from some African countries, like Togo or Benin, they don't have boxing commissions in some of these places so often the records are just made up! You can bring a guy over who's meant to be 20-0 and he'll turn up and be absolutely useless. You don't learn anything off those kind of fighters and to be honest if you build a record of 15-0 knocking people like that over, the Board won't take any notice of you anyway, you won't get any nearer to real title fights because they know what's going on.'

To illustrate the point, early in 2014 I attended a small-hall show in London for BoxRec News. The card featured a strong Eastern European contingent, with the away corner showcasing fighters from Poland, Hungary and Georgia. Altogether six British or British-based fighters met Eastern European opposition, who all came with winning records. Of those six bouts, only one went the distance. At least three were so uncompetitive as to be uncomfortable to watch, with fish-out-of-water performances, leading to multiple knockdowns and early-round stoppages. By contrast, the one bout that featured a British journeyman went to points.

The worst display that night came from a Hungarian who took on a former English title holder. The Englishman is a capable fighter with a 30-11-3 record but had only stopped six opponents prior to the contest and is not regarded as a big hitter, yet the Hungarian literally ran away from him for two and a half rounds while going down virtually every time a meaningful blow was landed.

The ref eventually called a halt after a minute of the third and in my ringside report I wrote that the away boxer, 'circled and pedalled away, eyes wide with fear, throughout the three rounds the fight lasted…The impression was that if there had been a cupboard in the ring, he would have got inside it and closed the door.'

Assuming therefore, that in the real world and despite what their posters and websites say, promoters are not going to put young prospects in genuinely competitive fights, would the home-corner boys not have been given sterner examinations by British journeymen? Would they not at least have been stretched a little, forced to break down a stubborn defence or to use a bit of guile? And would the fans have benefitted from seeing them against more resolute opposition? The answer is almost certainly yes.

The nature of the relationship between promoters and officials is also a problematic area and not just on small-hall shows. Judging controversies dog the sport at all levels and this came up in virtually every conversation I had with the fighters.

Although the fees paid to referees and judges are determined by the Board, the promoter does indeed pay them from his earnings on the night. More often than not, for officials attending a show far from home, their accommodation and travel expenses are taken care of by the promoter too. I have personally sat at ringside and watched the promoter walk over to the Board table and hand small brown envelopes of money to the officials one-by-one.

That is not to suggest that anything underhand was occurring, but there are surely question marks over whether a referee who awards decisions to the promoter's fighters, before being handed an envelope full of notes by the promoter and going back to his hotel room, paid for by the promoter, is not demonstrating a conflict of interest.

This book is not a study of home advantage in professional boxing, but just to illustrate the point, I gathered some statistics from April this year using the records held on BoxRec.com. I chose April, in the spirit of fairness, as I knew that there had been a few journeyman victories that month. I suspect other months may give a more imbalanced picture.

There were 18 professional boxing shows in the UK in that month, in which a total of 124 contests took place.[6] Of those 124 contests, 108 resulted in home wins. In other words 87 per cent of all professional bouts in the UK in April saw victory for the blue corner.

This, in itself does not necessarily point to biased refereeing and judging, it also reflects matchmaking, but it demonstrates clearly the disparity between home and away victories. There were, in fact, three shows in April 2014 in which every contest on the card resulted in the home fighter's hand being raised. No show had more than two away wins.

In the face of this, Robert Smith gave the views of the British Boxing Board of Control. 'This has always been an issue in boxing. For as long as I can remember and I've been involved in the game a long time, people who lose fights always complain about the officials. Always have done, probably always will. What you have to remember is that judging a contest is a subjective business. We only want honest people being referees and judges, but obviously differences of opinion can occur. If we receive complaints about refereeing or judging, we look at them, of course we do, but I believe, hand on heart, that all our officials are honest.

'It's one of those things that sometimes people will say there's corruption and they have anecdotes about this fight and that show and this promoter and what have you, but when there's an investigation, no one wants to say anything to the authorities, so we are never shown any proof. Personally I think most of it is people who've lost looking for excuses and obviously journeymen, although I hate the word journeymen, but that's what people call them, tend to lose a lot.

---

6   This excludes 'Prizefighter' contests where the home/away situation is less easily defined.

'You have to bear in mind as well that a lot of people don't fully understand the rules of how a contest is scored. When I first started working for the Board, I was at a real barnstormer of a fight, Shea Neary against Darryl Tyson [in Liverpool, 1996]. Every round was action packed and it was very tight, but Neary edged nearly all of the rounds. It was close, but he did. But because it was a real battle, at the end when it was announced as a wide unanimous decision [Neary won by eight rounds on two judges' cards and nine rounds on the other] everyone was screaming "fix" and Tyson's people were very upset.

'But the bottom line is, if he lost the round, he lost the round. The fight is scored round-by-round. You don't go back at the end and say, "Well it was quite close actually so let's give half the rounds to that guy."

'You score it as you go, based on what you see. Another popular misconception is that if there's a knockdown it has to be a 10-8 round. That's not true. If one fighter is dominating the round but suffers a flash knockdown, the round could still be called even. There's lots of little things like that and if more people understood the rules it would help with some of the controversies.

'We get it a lot when TV commentators don't agree with what they've seen. Television is a great medium and we have to be grateful for the way it brings our sport to so many people who perhaps wouldn't go to watch it live, but the commentators are so influential. If they make a fuss about a particular decision then people tend to cotton on and do the same, but the TV commentators aren't necessarily right either. As I say, it's a subjective business. And I do feel, very strongly, that in the vast majority of cases, the fighter who wins the contest is the one who should win the contest.'

Pegg doesn't agree with the Board's analysis. 'I would say in my time in the sport the balance of close fights is about 90-10 in favour of the home fighter, when in a fair world it should be more like 50-50. That's the way it is. Once it goes to points, it nearly always goes to the home fighter. I'm not sure what's driving that, but there's something going on.'

Steve Goodwin also differed with the Board's view, 'I would challenge anyone to find incidences of unfairness on my nights. I work with certain referees a lot, Bob Williams for example. I've had some quite long chats with him as well, but I have never asked him or any other ref to do anything dodgy.

'I'm not saying that's true for all shows and I do think we see things on some shows that could and should be seriously questioned. It depends which part of the country you're in and who is promoting it. To be honest I see it a lot on some of the bigger shows. Often I've seen things that do concern me, but all I can say with regard to the fighters I manage is that if I think that sort of thing is likely to happen, I wouldn't allow them to be booked. I will not subject my fighter to a show where I believe he will be treated unfairly.'

Carl Greaves echoed Steve Goodwin's words to some extent, while also agreeing partly with the Board. 'I deal with both sides of it, as I manage some journeymen and some prospects and the truth is I've seen bad decisions go both ways. I would say, without naming any names, there are a couple of refs who are home corner refs, but the majority are pretty fair, I think. Even the couple that aren't, I really don't think anyone is telling them who to give decisions to or bribing them. I just think they are aware of how the promotions work and the game works and that's in the back of their mind. It's probably not even a deliberate thing.

'The only shows where I'm not always convinced that's true are the bigger, TV shows, when the officials have their travel expenses and other bills paid by the promoter as well. Often they all stay in the same hotel, the officials and promoters. They eat dinner and have a few drinks together and all this sort of thing. It's like they're sweetening them up and I don't think that's right.'

In 2005, N.J. Balmer of The Research Institute for Sport and Exercise Sciences of Liverpool John Moores University, published an article in the *Journal of Sports Sciences*. The piece discusses the home advantage that seems to be apparent in all sports that rely on judges to deliver verdicts and focuses on boxing as an example.

Balmer compared bouts that end by stoppage and those that end on points and concluded that 'points decisions significantly increased the likelihood of a home win', providing 'strong support for research demonstrating increased officiating bias, of various types'.

Balmer suggests that crowd noise is a major stress factor for officials, putting them under increased pressure and making them prone to home-biased decisions. 'In boxing,' he wrote, 'it could be argued that…the home boxer tends to be awarded closely fought rounds more often than the away boxer.' Balmer suggested that officials should be trained to cope with the stress of high-pressure, noisy environments to prevent this from happening.

Mickey Helliet agrees with Balmer's findings. 'The crowd are important. In this country, boxing crowds tend to be very noisy and if you are officiating a fight it's hard not to be influenced by that. If the home fighter has sold a few hundred tickets, when he throws a punch a huge cheer goes up and you're more likely to score that than a punch that comes the other way that's met by silence. It's human nature. We see it in most sports don't we? Home advantage is also an issue in football, so it's not as if it's a problem unique to boxing.'

Unfortunately the Board would not give me permission to question any currently active referees on this, which was disappointing. I had hoped to gain an insight from the officials and am aware that some people will regard the Board's cautiousness as an indication that they have something to hide, which I am not sure is necessarily true. Nonetheless, home advantage is clearly a massive issue, highlighted by journeymen's records and should be tackled for the sport to move forwards.

Professional boxing, for most of the people who work in it, is a tough way to make a living. If you're not Floyd Mayweather or Manny Pacquiao, or even Carl Froch, if you're not Oscar De La Hoya, Bob Arum or Eddie Hearn, then to some degree you are struggling. You are working in an industry that below the top levels has withered badly in the last 60 years. The likelihood is you are involved in the game more because you love it than because it makes you wealthy.

It may be an ugly truth that many small-hall, undercard fights are not real fights in the way most fans would hope. Home fighters are given every advantage and in some cases have a particular result paid for. Even this, however, does not ensure anything. Johnny Greaves told of how his 'move about' with Floyd Moore didn't work. Jody Meikle had a similar experience fighting the debutant, Aston Mount. Jason Nesbitt knocked out Ryan Nandha while under instruction to 'take it easy'. Whenever two men climb into a ring, there is always an element of uncertainty.

We can all wish that chicanery was not a part of the sport, that every fight was judged on its merits and that every fighter fought to the best of his ability every time, but at the lower levels this could signal the death knell for pro boxing in Britain. As long as there is no casual audience for small-hall shows and the whole business revolves around fighters selling tickets to their friends and family, then the financial imperative will remain to keep a profitable fighter winning.

Uncle Bob's mates from the pub are much more likely to buy tickets to see young Jack fight if he has an impressive-looking record and can claim to be the XYZ-intergalactic-iron-pyrite-champion than if he has lost as many as he has won and is clearly just a dime-a-dozen scrapper.

Knowing how boxing works involves developing the ability to look beyond numbers. Wins and losses only tell a small part of the story and there are spectators who regularly attend shows who appreciate what journeymen do. For most of the boxers featured here, this is enough. They aren't necessarily looking for fame and adulation, or even acceptance from the wider world. Nonetheless, I hope this book will help to raise awareness and support for those who fulfil one of the toughest, most demanding and misunderstood roles in professional sport.

In the final analysis, the stories contained here have not been about heroes. They have been about reality. Losing on purpose, for money, is not what sport is meant to be about. People may find it distasteful, but so are many things people do for cash. It must be remembered that journeymen didn't create the system, they just operate within it.

Journeymen get a tough time from the media and the general public for the simple reason that many people don't like reality, probably because they are forced to live in it every day. They prefer escapism, fantasy and glamour. In a celebrity and wealth obsessed world, a boxer quietly fighting for a grand a week, with a pragmatic attitude, is at odds with what people want from their sportsmen.

Through this perspective, Floyd Mayweather Jr, with his 46-0 record, holding wads of notes and buying Bentleys every week, is the pugilistic poster boy of our era. As the righteous anger of Ali represented the 1960s and 70s and Tyson's ferociousness and ghettofabulous entourage the 80s and 90s, for the boxing fraternity, Mayweather represents our collective aspirations, as they are now. It is worth thinking about. Journeymen are just the tails to Floyd's heads. Without Jason Nesbitt, there is no Money May.

Boxing, it is often said, needs a saviour, one with deep pockets who could sweep away all the pre-existing organisations and perfidies and start again, restructuring the sport with long-term goals in the interests of fans and fighters. Perhaps then, there would be no need for journeymen and the men in this book would simply be known as fighters.

Until such a messiah arrives, a journeymen prizefighter tournament would be the perfect way for boxing to show a bit of respect to itself. For one night only, use the hoopla for something genuine. Held at welter or light-welter, it could feature many of the names in this book, giving some of them one last shot at redemption, an evening in the limelight and for at least one, a bonanza payday. Every true fan should insist that it happens.

Epilogue

The Smiths, remembered

MATT **Teague**, former featherweight professional from Grimsby, remembers Ernie Smith. 'He looked like a real hard bastard. He just had that look about him. But he was really a very nice bloke. He told me he just did the boxing for extra money. He said he earned about £900 a time for fighting and went home every time and gave it to his missus. He was very cheerful, very friendly.'

Matt's brother **Luke Teague**, who retired at 5-0-1, campaigned at light-middleweight and went in with Ernie at the Winter Gardens in Cleethorpes in 2004. 'I was about half a stone heavier and a few inches taller than him. I was right up for the fight and when they brought us in to the middle of the ring before the first round, I was doing my mean face, you know taking it all really seriously. He just kept going up on his tiptoes and laughing.

'I hit him early on with a right hand that would have knocked out most guys. It was a perfect shot and I put everything into it. He just smiled at me and said, "Come on Teague!" I don't know where that comes from, that toughness. He could really hold a shot. Obviously we were boxing in front of my home crowd and the fans kept shouting "Teaguey, Teaguey!"

'But then Ernie started taking the piss. Whenever we went into a clinch, he was doing it too, leaning into my ear, going "Teaguey, Teaguey!" But my main memory of fighting him is just how hard his head was. It was like punching concrete. My fight with him ended up being my last because I broke both my hands on him! My left went in the first round and my right in the second. They never healed well enough for me to fight again. He must have had some special genetics or something.'

Current (at the time of writing) Southern Area light-middleweight champion **Freddie Turner** fought Billy Smith in his third professional contest in 2011. A picture taken during their bout accompanied *The Ring* magazine article about Billy's death. 'Billy was really a nice guy, very tough, steely I would call it, but really nice and friendly. He could really take punches, a very, very hard man. It was like hitting granite. He wasn't overly fit I wouldn't have said, but just so tough. He was game as well, he kept coming for me, there was nothing I could do to push him back.

'He was so friendly before the fight. Part of it's the psychology though, isn't it? All journeymen play it. They try and pal you up beforehand so you don't go too hard on them when you get in there, but Billy seemed like a genuinely nice guy to me. It's tragic what happened to both of them, but what a lot of people who've never done it don't understand is that boxing's a tremendously emotional thing. All the build-up and anticipation and then when you get in there… There's nothing else like it, really. And if it's taken away from you, like it was with Ernie when he had his licence withdrawn, it leaves a huge void and there's not much you can fill it with.

'I don't think it was boxing that made the Smith brothers do what they did. My take on it would be that they had demons elsewhere and boxing probably kept them in there and gave them a focus. After Ernie went, I reckon Billy's death was to do with that. They were identical twins, after all. Billy waited until he'd had the same number of fights as Ernie and then followed his brother.'

John Latham, a professional referee from Bury in Lancashire, recalled refereeing Billy five times before his death. 'I'd arrive at the venue and look at the bouts I'd been allocated. If I got Billy, I always knew my job would be easy. He was always in great shape, very tough and had a good defence. I never had a single problem with him, really, he was a joy to work with. It was such sad news when Billy passed away and I'm sure everyone in boxing remembers and misses Billy around the circuit.'

Former light-middleweight pro **Shaun Farmer**, from Liverpool, maintained a friendship with Billy Smith up until his death and Farmer's good friend, the middleweight banger **Graham Delehedy**, once fought Ernie, stopping him in the third round. 'Both Billy and Ernie fought like winners,' Farmer said. 'They didn't seem to go in there with a typical journeyman survival attitude. With Billy I was chatting to him online a week or so before he died. There was no indication that he was feeling down. We were chatting away about our kids. He seemed like such a doting father. I don't understand what happened, really. Both of them were sound guys and it was a real shock for me when Billy died. I didn't see it coming at all.'

Andy 'Spud' Woollat, a busy figure in various roles around the UK boxing scene for the last 15 years, recalls Billy Smith being 'a right character. I whipped a number of shows he boxed on. He was a proper nice lad, but he had that look not to be messed with. I called him ugly once for a joke and he gave me a right look. Then when he saw I was shitting myself, he laughed and took the piss.

'Another time he arrived at the venue late and I was in a flap because we had him on second fight. I told him I'd try and get the running order changed and he replied, "What the fuck's wrong with you Spud? I'm here now" and he basically went out and fought about five minutes after he turned up, got it over with, collected his money and left.

'When the tragic news came out about his death, like a lot of people I was genuinely gutted, life is so complex. Personally

I don't think we will ever understand why people want to take their lives, but boxing is definitely poorer without the likes of Billy around.'

Kristian Laight knew both Smith brothers from around the circuit. 'The Smiths were good friends of mine. Both of them were absolute legends. Billy had more skill whereas Ernie was more raw and was probably slightly tougher. But the end? I think Billy had planned it. After Ernie died, you could look into his eyes and see that something had gone.

'One time before a fight he even said to me, "I can't go on, I miss Ernie too much." I didn't really know how to take it, to be honest. I didn't know what to say. I boxed on the same show as him for his last fight and there was definitely something different about him that night. He was usually such a lively character, cracking jokes, walking around, shaking hands, but that night he just didn't seem interested. I think it's because he knew in his mind what he was going to do and what that last fight meant.'

Johnny Greaves admired the Smiths before he even turned pro. 'They were an inspiration for me before I started. They were both exactly what they looked. Hard bastards. Me and Billy boxed on the same shows regularly and became good mates. We always shared info, tales and a few snouts before we went out to fight. We spoke regularly on the phone. He was an out and out hard bastard.

'There were never any signs of what was about to happen, but I've thought about this a lot and I think, personally, he knew what he was going to do. He had it planned for a while. I spoke to him about a week before he did it and he was fine, laughing and joking. I don't think it was a bout of depression. Their deaths, Billy's in particular, hit me quite hard and made me look at my own life. I often think of them when I'm struggling a bit myself. I'll always remember the Smiths, always.'

Jason Nesbitt remembered Billy's sense of humour. 'He always lit the place up, a real lively character. You couldn't help but like him. Such a funny man. He was one of my favourite people in boxing.'

Daniel Thorpe agrees. 'Ernie and Billy were just jokers. They were loud and brash and didn't seem to care what people thought of them. They were always having a laugh. I used to go and have a fag with them after we'd had our hands wrapped. I don't think being a journeyman makes you feel that way [suicidal]. All sorts of people get depression, don't they? In fact, for us lads, I think it's the opposite. No matter how many fights you've lost, we all loved going out and boxing. It's a buzz like no other. It gives you a real lift.'

Carl Greaves boxed Ernie Smith at the Doncaster Dome in 1999. 'When we boxed he still had a winning record [Ernie was 3-2-1 at the time] and he was coming to win. He was very tough but I managed to put him down with a left hook in the second round, which was pleasing because not many people put Ernie over. I cornered for Billy a few times later on as well. He was a really nice kid to work with, never any bother, a great character.

'I'm not too sure what triggered it all. Obviously Ernie lost his licence and I heard he was having some problems at home as well, so that must have put him on a downer. I think with Billy, he just couldn't live without Ernie and he planned it. It was horrible, I still think about them sometimes. Boxing can be a lonely sport. You're living like a monk and training, you lose touch with your old mates. You just live in a little boxing world and when you have to leave that and go back into normal life it can be really hard. You feel like you've lost your touch.'

One of **Jon Pegg**'s first jobs in pro boxing was as cornerman to Billy Smith in 2006. 'I was a bit nervous because I was new at it, but Billy was great. I looked after him like a baby. He was always joking about. We used to travel around a lot with Baz Carey when they were on the same shows and stuff. It was interesting because you could see Billy's face change. If Baz was fighting and getting a bit of a beating, he'd stop messing about and suddenly get all serious. He was a very compassionate guy, as well as a hard-case.

'To be honest though, towards the end I had a feeling something wasn't right. I saw him at a show at the Paragon hotel in Birmingham a couple of weeks before he died and he seemed a little bit off. His record was obviously getting close to Ernie's and I think he knew he was going to do something. Ernie was always the dominant twin out of the two of them and I think Billy found it hard to cope without him.

'I was really, really upset about Billy's death. He was such a great guy, so funny, such a top character. Whether he was a boxer or not I would have liked him. If you were in a boxing dressing room, down the pub at work or wherever, he was the sort of guy you'd want by your side. I'll always miss him.'

As with any deaths of this nature there is always an element of mystery. No one can be sure exactly what was happening in Ernie Smith's life that was so awful he had to end it. Any of us can offer opinions, but it reaches a point where it is almost disrespectful to do so. Whatever he was dealing with, internally or externally is probably a private matter and not one that should be discovered and repeated, for public discussion.

But the fact remains that the judgements of those who knew and worked with him are not that it was his many hard nights in the ring, the punches he took or all his losses that caused his suicide. To some degree, it was the opposite. It was losing his licence to box that tipped him over the edge. Distraught at his identical twin's death, Billy then chose to follow him, waiting until his record matched.

Perhaps it could be said that if whatever medical issue caused the Board to revoke Ernie's licence had not arisen, this tragic sequence of events would never have unfolded. This is and can only be speculation. But it appears a far more valid conclusion than suggesting, as *The Ring* magazine did, that it was life as journeymen that killed them.

From here, all anyone can ask is that they be remembered as they lived, as genuine, honest, tough, fighting men. They had that in common with all the other boxers featured here. It may not be fashionable in the modern world, but that's what they were.